NFL Football

THIS IS A CARLTON BOOK

This edition published by Carlton Books Limited 1997

© NFL Properties, Inc., 1996 & 1997

Printed and bound in Italy

ISBN 1 85868 365 3

**The publishers would like to thank NFL Photos for their kind
permission to reproduce many of the pictures in this book.
Photographer credits are as follows:** John E. Biever: 87, 89, 93, 120 right
middle; Vernon Biever: 19, 50 left; Jeff Blake: 22; David Boss: 16-17 top, 106-7,
109, 120 bottom middle, 122; Mark Brettingen: 42; Peter Brouillet: 55, 59, 61, 103;
Dale Carter: 26; Michael Conroy: 35; Jimmy Cribb: 43; Bill Cummings: 96; Scott
Cunningham: 101, 107 right; Gioc Del Pallone: 9 left; David Drapkin: 117; Brian
Drake: 57; Mike Eliason: 69; Gin Ellis: 58; Malcolm W. Emmons: 13, 16 left, 79,
85; Nate Fine: 80, 86; James F. Flores: 74, 120 top left; Tracy Frankel: 29; Gerald
Gallegos: 67; Hall Of Fame: 10 top, 11 top and right mid, 119; Glen James: 20, 113
top; Paul Jasienski: 3, 63, 73 left, 94, 100; Allen Kee: 32, 37, 44; Heinz Kluetmeier:
83; LC Lambrecht: 65, 112; Ross Lewis: 14 left; Long Photography: 95; Richard
Mackson: 97; Tak Makita: 81; John McDonough: 53, 90, 92; Al Messerschmidt: 28,
33, 110, 114 top right; Peter Read Miller: 54, 70; Herman Moore: 40; Steven
Murphy: 60, 113 bottom; Patrick Murphy-Racey: 114 bottom left; NFL Photos: 8, 9
top right, 10 bottom right, 11 bottom, 73 right, 75, 82; Darryl Norenberg: 72, 76;
Bernie Nunez: 45; Joe Poellot: 23; Richard Raphael: 78; John H. Reid: 115; Frank
Rippon: 12; Joe Robbins: 38; Bob Rosato: 27, 46, 62, 66; Todd Rosenberg: 41;
Manny Rubio: 88; Mark Sherengo: 47; Carl Skalak Jr: 50 right, 123; Bruce Smith:
21; James D. Smith: 31, 52; Paul Spinelli: 24, 48, 99, 109, 118-9; Brian Spurlock:
39; Allan Dean Steele: 71; David Stluka: 25, 34; Tony Tomsic: 14-15 top, 51, 77, 82,
84, 91, 121; Corky Trewin: 108; Greg Trott: 30, 35, 49, 64; Jim Turner: 102; Ron
Vesely: 4–5, 6, 56, 68; Michael Zagaris: 71, 98.

**No kidding:
Linebacker Junior Seau
overcame a bad shoulder
injury to lead the
San Diego Chargers into
Super Bowl XXIX.**

NFL Football

THE OFFICIAL FANS' GUIDE

CARLTON

Ron Smith

Contents

In the Grasp: Drew Bledsoe is sacked by Reggie White during the Packers' 35–21 victory over New England in Super Bowl XXXI.

A Sign of the Times: Brett Favre threw 77 touchdown passes in 1995 and 1996 as the Green Bay quarterback earned back-to-back MVP awards.

Introduction

The images remain firmly implanted in the mind: Johnny Unitas leading his Baltimore Colts on a desperation drive. Steve Myhra kicking the game-tying field goal with seven seconds remaining. Alan Ameche slamming over the middle for a touchdown, ending the first sudden-death overtime in National Football League Championship Game history.

December 28, 1958. A monumental forward step in league history, viewed by 64,185 fans at New York's Yankee Stadium and millions more across the country on television. The game that lifted the national consciousness of professional football and blazed the trail that would lead to unfathomable popularity, international awareness and untold riches, both in athletic accomplishments and monetary rewards.

Every long journey requires a first step, and this was more like a giant leap for the sport that had not been able to find its way out of the shadows for almost forty years.

Now, nearly four decades later, the NFL's showcase event, the Super Bowl, is viewed from Afghanistan to Zimbabwe and preseason games are being played before sellout crowds on foreign soil. Fall and winter Sunday afternoons and nights and Monday nights belong to the NFL, which beams its highlights into more than 171 countries and territories around the world. The NFL's players have become international personalities and even its April draft, the sometimes-plodding selection process to restock rosters with fresh college talent, is analyzed and dissected for the better part of two days by television cameras and hungry audiences.

Professional football's meteoric rise has been fueled by its own ever-advancing marketing abilities. From the dawning of the television era and the arrival of marketing genius Pete Rozelle in 1960 as its sixth commissioner/president, the NFL has steadily moved to the head of the team sports class. All the polls hail football as America's new National Pastime and such talk is supported by unprecedented attendance figures and the sport's impact on the American public, both at the professional and collegiate levels.

But no amount of marketing will change one basic fact: a sport is only as strong as the product it puts on the field. And professional football has been blessed by a steady stream of gifted athletes whose ever-advancing skills mirror the evolution of its ever-advancing offensive and defensive philosophies.

In the great tradition of modern trend setters Unitas and Jim Brown, such talents as Bart Starr, Larry Csonka, Terry Bradshaw, Walter Payton, Roger Staubach, Lawrence Taylor, Mike Singletary and Joe Montana helped carry the game to new heights of popularity. Coaches like Vince Lombardi, Tom Landry, Chuck Noll, Don Shula, Bill Walsh, Joe Gibbs and Mike Ditka molded sophisticated game plans that created such championship teams as the Packers, Cowboys, Steelers, Dolphins, 49ers, Redskins and Bears.

And the beat goes on. As the NFL barrels toward a new century, such veteran stars as Dan Marino, John Elway, Steve Young, Jerry Rice, and Reggie White are passing the baton to such young lions as Barry Sanders, Junior Seau, Drew Bledsoe, Brett Favre, Emmitt Smith, Marshall Faulk, and Mark Brunell.

The journey continues.

In the beginning

THE HISTORY OF THE NFL

I t started inauspiciously at a Canton, Ohio, Hupmobile car dealership when a handful of men, representing ten teams, sowed the seeds that would germinate into a multi-billion dollar bonanza known today as the National Football League.

That September 17, 1920, gathering poured the foundation for a professional game that would evolve over the next three-quarters of a century from the single-wing, cloud-of-dust mentality of yesteryear into the sophisticated, one-back, aerial wizardry of the 1990s.

For a mere $100 entry fee that was never collected, ten owners were granted charter franchises in the American Professional Football Association, a union that was cemented with the election of aging all-sports star Jim Thorpe as the league's first president—not because of his administrative acumen, but because of his ability to play football and garner publicity. The APFA would need all of that it could get.

And it would need visionary officials, tough-minded owners and star-quality players who could bring skeptical fans through the turnstiles.

One such visionary was George Halas, a former University of Illinois end who was present at the September meeting as a representative of the Decatur (Ill) Staleys. What brought Halas and his fellow organizers to Ralph Hay's Canton Hupmobile dealership was the fly-by-night status of their professional sport, which was operating primarily in the Midwest in chaotic obscurity.

Professional football was not a new phenomenon. Players had been paid for their abilities as early as the 1890s and athletic clubs had fielded teams on a regional basis for the first two decades of the century. But teams were without structure, player raids were common, collegians were being enticed to play under assumed names and salaries were rising to unmanageable levels. Teams operated independently, without the common-interest restrictions of a league unit. The APFA was an attempt to address those problems.

Papa Bear: George Halas was a long-time player, coach and owner of a Chicago Bears franchise that started as the Decatur Staleys.

GROWING PAINS

The 14 teams (four were added during the season) that concluded the 1920 campaign under the APFA umbrella didn't act much differently than those that had competed in 1919. Schedules were self-generated and uneven, owners ignored pledges not to raid opposing rosters and salaries continued to rise. The league, with teams representing five states, did not even keep standings and selected the unbeaten Akron Pros as its first champion by consensus vote.

In 1921, the APFA elected a new president, Joe Carr, and operated under a constitution that restricted player movement and provided needed structure. In 1922, the league played its first season as the NFL and Halas' now Chicago-based team played its first as the Bears. But stability would not come easily. The NFL ranged from ten to 22 teams during the 1920s, as poorly-financed owners battled for fan support as well as victories. Professional football lagged well behind baseball, college football and boxing as the choice of sports-viewing America.

The league's first breakthrough occurred in 1925, when Halas signed Harold (Red) Grange, the "Galloping Ghost" who had drawn national acclaim for his ball-carrying feats at the University of Illinois. The flamboyant Grange, equal in stature to baseball player Babe Ruth and boxer Jack Dempsey, joined the Bears late in the season and a league-record crowd of 36,000 turned out for his Thanksgiving Day debut—a scoreless tie against the cross-town Cardinals.

But that turnout was dwarfed by the 73,000 fans who paid to see Grange and the Bears meet the Giants in a postseason exhibition game at New York's Polo Grounds and the 75,000 who watched the Bears defeat the semi-pro Los Angeles Tigers a few weeks later at the LA Coliseum. The NFL had its first superstar, and plenty more would

Indian runner: Jim Thorpe, who was voted America's top athlete of the first half of the twentieth century, was the first president of the fledgling NFL.

Galloping Ghost: When Harold (Red) Grange joined the Chicago Bears team, coach George Halas arranged a barnstorming tour to show off his latest signing.

follow. Fullback Ernie Nevers arrived a year after Grange and halfback Johnny (Blood) McNally led a 1929 Green Bay Packers charge that resulted in their first of three consecutive championships. The Bears' 1930 signing of bruising fullback/tackle Bronko Nagurski signaled a new era of power football in Chicago.

A MODERN LOOK

Not even the drawing power of Grange, Nevers, Blood and Nagurski could get the NFL through the Great Depression unscathed. But the economic turmoil that gripped America during the early 1930s had several positive side-effects.

Small-market owners, already strapped to pay the bills, found they could not compete and folded their franchises. By 1931, the NFL was a more manageable ten-team circuit. By 1932, the number was eight—the lowest membership in league history. But all the teams, with the exception of Green Bay and Portsmouth, were located in major cities and supported by a solid fan base.

The trimmed-down NFL took several giant steps toward prosperity in 1933. Recognizing the need to establish its own personality and break from the mold of the more-conservative college game, officials pushed through innovative measures that would change the course of professional football.

Several were the result of a season-ending 1932 playoff game,

Pioneer: Ernie Nevers was an early NFL fullback. He only played five seasons for the Duluth Eskimos and Cardinals when they were still in Chicago.

Unstoppable force: Bronko Nagurski was a powerful runner and blocker with the Chicago Bears. He helped the Bears win three NFL titles in 1932, 1933 and 1943.

necessitated by a regular-season tie between the Bears and Portsmouth Spartans. The game was scheduled for Chicago's Wrigley Field. But a monster snowstorm buried the city and Halas, in desperation, moved the game to Chicago Stadium—an indoor arena that allowed room for an 80-yard field only. To compensate, the goal posts were moved from the end lines to the goal lines and hashmarks were drawn for ball placement ten yards from the side walls that butted the field. The Bears won the bizarre game 9-0.

But the significance of that game lives on. The hashmarks and re-positioned goal posts became permanent changes for 1933, as did a rule allowing quarterbacks to pass from any point behind the line of scrimmage (previously, they had to be more than five yards behind the line.). The eventual result was a wide-open game utilizing the full field. The NFL also was divided into two divisions, with winners to meet in an annual championship game.

But the 1933 epiphany did not end there. The NFL beefed up its membership to ten teams and introduced three forceful personalities who would play major roles in the game's sometimes painful, always colorful evolution. Art Rooney (Pittsburgh Pirates) and Bert Bell (Philadelphia Eagles) entered the league with new teams. Charles Bidwill purchased the Chicago Cardinals. That trio locked arms with holdovers Halas, Curly Lambeau (Packers), Tim Mara (Giants), George Preston Marshall (Redskins) and Carr to form a leadership block that would rule the game for decades.

Ringing the changes: Bert Bell, founder of the Philadelphia Eagles, was the NFL Commissioner from 1946 until his death while watching a game in 1959.

Record breaker: Sid Luckman holds the Bears' records for touchdown passes in a game, season and career. The seven he threw in a 1943 game have been matched only four times.

But the immediate future belonged to Halas, who never deviated from his quest for football perfection. The Bears had prevailed in 1932 using a T-formation offense altered by coach Ralph Jones, who split the ends and halfbacks wider and added a man in motion. When Jones resigned after winning the 1932 title, Halas took over and led the 1933 Bears to a 23-21 victory over the Giants in the NFL's first scheduled championship game.

Halas' Bears would use the innovative offense to procure six Western Division titles and three more NFL championships over the next decade. The centerpiece for his so-called Monsters of the Midway was Nagurski, but a steady stream of talent flowed into Chicago. Elusive Beattie Feathers became the NFL's first 1,000-yard rusher in 1934. Lineman George Musso was fearsome on both sides of the ball. Quarterback Sid Luckman arrived in 1939 to take the ever-evolving "Split-T" to a new level of sophistication.

In 1940, Luckman and the Bears lifted the NFL to new heights of awareness. Avenging an earlier loss to Washington, the Bears posted a stunning 73-0 championship game victory over the Redskins, a still-standing NFL record for domination. It was the first championship game broadcast nationally on radio.

But Halas did not have the corner on talent. (Slingin') Sammy Baugh arrived in Washington in 1937 and set the standards by which future passers would be judged. Don Hutson, generally considered one of the greatest pass-catchers of all time, joined the Packers in 1935 to team with passers Arnie Herber and Cecil Isbell and fullback Clarke Hinkle. Byron (Whizzer) White, who would go on to greater fame as a U.S. Supreme

Court justice, won the 1938 rushing title playing for Pittsburgh. And Mel Hein dominated both sides of the line as a center and linebacker with the New York Giants.

DRAFTING A FUTURE

As the modernized NFL escaped the clutches of economic catastrophe in the mid-1930s, it became clear that the balance of power rested in four cities. The Bears, Packers, Redskins and Giants would combine to win all but one championship from 1933-44.

The have-nots, unable to outbid their powerful opponents for talent, needed a competitive boost. They got it when the NFL voted in 1935 to adopt Bell's proposal for a draft of college players, with teams making selections in inverse order of finish from the previous season. Appropriately, Bell's Eagles were awarded the first pick of the inaugural 1936 draft and grabbed the rights to University of Chicago halfback Jay Berwanger, who had just won college football's first Heisman Trophy. (The Eagles traded the rights to Berwanger to the Bears, however, and he never played pro football.)

Touchdown man: In his 11-year career Don Hutson averaged nine touchdown catches per season. His 99 touchdown receptions stood as a record for 44 years.

The draft, which would become an NFL institution and force teams to build and expand coaching and scouting staffs, was not the only innovation of the period. The first of 42 College All-Star Games, which pitted a team of collegiate all-stars against the defending NFL champion at Chicago's Soldier Field, was played in 1934. The league adopted a standard 12-game schedule in 1936, and it played its first postseason Pro Bowl game in 1939.

Prosperity was becoming more than a George Halas pipedream. By the end of the decade, every team had its own radio outlet, and television had experimented with its first NFL telecast. More than a million spectators passed

Two-way star: Washington's Sammy Baugh was the NFL's passing leader in 1943, but he also set an NFL record that season, making four interceptions in a game.

through turnstiles in 1939—an NFL first.

The NFL also completed the decade without Carr, who died in 1939. The league launched a search that eventually led to its first commissioner—Elmer Layden of "Four Horsemen" fame.

WAR AND PEACE

Success wouldn't be that easy. The NFL's fast-paced rise to national awareness was halted on December 7, 1941, when Japanese planes launched their surprise attack on Pearl Harbor and thrust the U.S. into World War II. By 1943, professional football had been stripped of its best athletes and those who remained were Sunday performers who spent the rest of the week in war-related activities.

That the NFL was able to continue play was because of President Franklin D. Roosevelt's belief that American sports provided a necessary recreational outlet for a war-weary society. He told baseball and football officials to carry on in whatever manner possible.

The NFL did so—creatively. The Rams suspended operations in 1943, while Pittsburgh and Philadelphia merged into one team called the "Steagles." The Rams returned in 1944, the "Steagles" disbanded and the Boston Yanks joined the NFL. But membership remained at ten, as the Steelers and Cardinals merged into "Card-Pitt."

When the fighting ended in 1945 and athletes returned from Europe and the South Pacific, the NFL found itself embroiled in a different kind of war. Three times in its history the NFL had survived challenges from short-lived rival circuits calling themselves the American Football League. But suddenly there was a new kid on the block—with deep pockets and far-reaching ideas.

Not only was the All-America Football Conference ready and willing to outbid the NFL for new talent, it was willing to take players who wanted to jump from existing rosters. And the AAFC took great pride in the "All-America" portion of its title. Indeed, the eight-team AAFC fielded West Coast franchises in San Francisco (49ers) and Los Angeles (Dons) in 1946, its inaugural season.

The AAFC threat presented serious problems, but its overall impact was positive. When the war ended, former college players, collegians with eligibility remaining and returning veterans formed a talent pool big enough to stock several leagues. And all were eager to play because the AAFC was forcing the NFL to revise its conservative salary structure.

The AAFC also forced the NFL to think bigger. After Dan Reeves watched rookie quarterback Bob Waterfield lead his Cleveland Rams to a 15-14 championship game victory over the Redskins in 1945, he packed up his team and moved to Los Angeles. With air travel and radio advances linking the country from coast to coast, marketing and major population centers suddenly became priority considerations. And the NFL, with Bell now running the show as the commissioner, became aware of image as well as bottom lines.

Ottomatic: Cleveland quarterback Otto Graham's physical and leadership skills carried through his ten seasons in the All-America Football Conference and National Football League.

The AAFC, stocked with quality players, provided entertaining football for four seasons. But it couldn't get past one unfortunate flaw in its game plan—the Cleveland Browns were too good. The star-studded Browns, who outdrew the Rams, compiled a 47-4-3 record and won all four league championships. Their success was a legacy that would not die with the AAFC.

When a peace treaty finally was signed after the 1949 season, the AAFC folded and the NFL absorbed three of its teams: the Browns, 49ers and Baltimore Colts. The bigger and stronger NFL, featuring 13 teams and a myriad of new stars, was ready for a new decade and another period of prosperity.

A MASTER BUILDER

When Paul Brown was asked to build and coach the new AAFC franchise in Cleveland, he was assured there would be plenty of money and no front-office interference. The AAFC, and the rest of the pro football world, was in deep trouble.

Brown, a former Ohio State and Great Lakes Naval Station coach, began building a football machine that would become the toast of the new league and a city that had refused to embrace the NFL's Rams. His greatest gift was talent assessment and he quickly loaded his roster with future Hall of Famers.

Quarterback Otto Graham, whom Brown had watched play at Northwestern, became the heart and soul of a team that included tackle/kicker Lou Groza, fullback Marion Motley, guard Bill Willis, receivers Dante Lavelli, Mac Speedie and Dub Jones and center Frank Gatski. The Browns were solid offensively and defensively, superbly coached by the innovative and detail-minded Brown and confident they could continue their winning ways as members of the NFL.

Few NFL proponents believed they could, including Bell, who scheduled the Browns to play a 1950 season-opening game at Philadelphia. The powerful Eagles were preparing to defend consecutive NFL championships.

It wasn't pretty. The Eagles, playing without injured 1,000-yard rusher Steve Van Buren, were helpless to stop the Browns' sophisticated passing attack and fell meekly, 35-10. The game was viewed by 70,000 stunned fans.

"We really bristled that night," Brown recalled years later. "We had been storing up steam for four years, waiting for a crack at the

 The best? Johnny Unitas threw 290 touchdown passes, passed for 40,239 yards, and tossed at least one scoring pass in 47 consecutive games.

CROSSING THE COLOR LINE

Jackie Robinson has become an American hero for breaking baseball's color barrier in 1947 with the Brooklyn Dodgers. But lost in Robinson's shadow was the desegregation of professional football, which had quietly begun a year earlier when Cleveland Coach Paul Brown signed fullback Marion Motley and guard Bill Willis to play for his All-America Football Conference team and Rams Owner Dan Reeves signed halfback Kenny Washington and end Woody Strode for his team's first season in Los Angeles.

Reeves' action ended a 12-season period without black players and other teams quickly followed suit. Whereas baseball had not permitted blacks in its game since the 1880s, the NFL had employed a few black performers as late as 1933.

The most celebrated early NFL blacks were halfback Fritz Pollard, who played and coached for a number of teams in the 1920s, and end Paul Robeson, who played three seasons (1920-22) and later pursued a successful acting career. Tackle Duke Slater played for a decade (1922-31) and halfback Joe Lillard was the last black to play (1932-33) before 1946.

National League. When we exploded, there was no stopping us. The Cleveland team that day was the best I ever saw on a given day—anywhere, in any kind of competition."

The AAFC upstarts, competing in the American Conference of the realigned NFL, went on to post a 10-2 record, losing twice to the Giants. But the Browns avenged those losses by defeating the New Yorkers, 8-3, in a conference playoff battle and completed their first-season title run with a 30-28 victory over the Rams. The Browns were undisputed kings of professional football—and they were just getting started.

They captured the next five conference crowns and two more NFL championships. The Browns closed their incredible run (ten consecutive championship game appearances in two leagues) with victories over Detroit and Los Angeles in 1954 and 1955 and then said farewell to Graham, who retired with the greatest success record in pro football history.

As Graham bowed out, a worthy successor to his legacy arrived. Johnny Unitas, who would go on to shatter virtually every NFL passing record over an outstanding 18-year career, joined such talented signal-callers as Bob Waterfield, Norm Van Brocklin, Bobby Layne and Y.A. Tittle.

Unitas wasn't the only arrival of note. The Browns reloaded their backfield with the selection of Syracuse star Jim Brown in the 1957 draft and the second-year star rewarded them a year later by rushing for an NFL-record 1,527 yards. The Packers changed their sagging fortunes in the late 1950s when they drafted a quarterback named Bart Starr and hired Vince Lombardi as their coach.

But the defining event of the decade was played out before a national television audience in 1958 when Unitas' Colts met the Giants for the NFL championship at New York's Yankee Stadium. What the game lacked in artistry it made up for with drama and nail-biting emotion—in the media hub of North America.

The game was made to order for publicity-minded NFL officials.

Unitas, who passed for 361 yards and a touchdown, led the Colts on a desperation 73-yard fourth-quarter drive that resulted in Steve Myhra's game-tying 20-yard field goal that forced the first sudden-death overtime in NFL history. The Colts recorded a 23-17 victory when Alan Ameche ran one yard for a touchdown ending "the greatest game of all time" 8:15 into the extra period.

But the NFL's fourth decade would not end on such a positive note. The league, which had survived the challenges of three American Football Leagues and the All-American Football Conference in its first 30 years, was jolted by the 1959 announcement that Dallas businessman Lamar Hunt was forming a new rival circuit that would begin play in 1960. The eight-team league would be called the American Football League.

SURVIVAL OF THE FITTEST

The NFL received another jolt late in the 1959 season when Commissioner Bell died of a heart attack while watching an Eagles-Steelers game. A new, creative mind would be needed to guide professional football through a turbulent and costly era.

It took 23 ballots before Rams General Manager Pete Rozelle was offered the job as a compromise candidate in 1960. Rozelle accepted

the challenge, moved his office to New York and began drawing the blueprint for a prosperous future. But Rozelle's early road to success would be bumpy and difficult.

The AFL, with Hunt as its president and Joe Foss as its first commissioner, quickly made it clear the NFL was facing a long, expensive battle. The new league held its first player draft in November 1959, touching off a bidding war for college talent, and then signed a five-year television contract with ABC. The NFL, in an effort to claim virgin territory, quickly placed new franchises in Dallas and Minneapolis and moved the Cardinals from Chicago to St Louis. The AFL butted heads with the NFL in New York, Los Angeles and Dallas while claiming new markets in Boston, Denver, Houston, Oakland and Buffalo.

But the real war was fought in the trenches after each year's college draft. The AFL made painful inroads and the price of football talent shot up. Its first big prize was former Louisiana State halfback

Long-time leader: Pete Rozelle was the NFL Commissioner from 1960 to 1989, a period of unprecedented growth in the league.

had produced long-term benefits.

"Looking back, the timing was very right for there to be a second league," Hunt recalled. "The AFL helped popularize the game on a national basis. The game had been centered in the northern and eastern part of the country. We took football to a lot of new areas. The AFL made it a national game and nurtured the rivalry that ultimately created the Super Bowl."

It also more than doubled the NFL's size, produced innovative changes that helped attract fans, improved player salaries and benefits, brought about a whopping increase in television revenue and turned the sport into a big, profitable business.

While the young AFL was attracting fans with its pass-first, no-defense philosophy, the NFL was trying to cope with another kind of monster. After losing to the Eagles, 17-13, in the 1960 championship game, Vince Lombardi's Packers defeated the Giants in 1961 and 1962, the Browns in 1965 and the Cowboys in 1966 and 1967. It was the most dominating run in NFL history.

But of more importance, the Starr-led Packers upheld the NFL's honor in the first two AFL-NFL championship games, battles that later would be called Super Bowls. The Packers overpowered the AFC-champion Kansas City Chiefs in Super Bowl I, 35-10, and blew away the Raiders in Super Bowl II, 33-14.

Smug NFL patrons smiled broadly in anticipation of what the powerful Colts, 34-0 NFL Championship Game winners over the Browns in 1968, would do to the upstart Jets in Super Bowl III. And they laughed out loud when the brash Namath announced, "The Jets will win on Sunday, I guarantee it." But AFL fans were the ones laughing when Namath and the Jets delivered a stunning 16-7 victory, earning the league some much-needed respect. When the AFL Chiefs followed with a 23-7 victory over the NFL Vikings in Super Bowl IV, the AFL began the merger with heads held high.

By the end of the 1960s, the NFL's tentacles had expanded into the Deep South (Atlanta, New Orleans and Miami) and the Super Bowl was being hailed as the greatest show on Earth. The new decade would begin with the 26-team NFL locked into a four-year, $150-million television contract that included $8 million from ABC for a 13-game Monday Night Football package. The NFL was on a roll.

ONWARD AND UPWARD

The NFL, buoyed by record-setting attendance in 1969, prepared for its first 26-team season with a sense of relief and optimism. The new-look league would begin in 1970 with two 13-team conferences: The AFL newcomers would join the Browns, Colts and Steelers in the American Football Conference; the other NFL holdovers would compete in the National Football Conference.

But before the first pass could be thrown, a new problem surfaced. NFL players, aware of the big money suddenly flowing into coffers around the league, threatened to sit out the season unless management allocated money for their pension fund and other benefits. The surprisingly strong union maneuver resulted in a major boost to the pension fund and a contract agreement that would insure peace until at least 1974. But the player-management bickering was a portent of things to come.

That became obvious when renegotiations started in 1974 amid renewed strike threats and legal hassles. At issue was the so-called "Rozelle Rule," which gave the commissioner the right to decide compensation for free agents and thus discouraged teams from pursuing opposing players. When a federal court struck down the "Rozelle Rule" as illegal, the owners and players finally reached a contract agreement in 1977, creating a new free-agent system that proved equally as restrictive. The players were locked in for another five years.

Despite the labor unrest, the game prospered on the field and in the eyes of a growing fan base. The early part of the decade belonged to

Above average: Cleveland's Jim Brown was the NFL's rushing leader eight times in nine seasons. His 5.22 yards per carry average is another NFL record.

and Heisman Trophy winner Billy Cannon. And a Who's Who list of big-name stars followed: safety Johnny Robinson, tackle Ron Mix, center Jim Otto, wide receiver Lance Alworth, defensive tackle Buck Buchanan, running back Mike Garrett, linebacker Bobby Bell, wide receiver Fred Biletnikoff and many more.

But the AFL's biggest coup occurred in 1965 when New York Jets Owner Sonny Werblin, badly in need of a star attraction to steady his wobbling franchise, landed quarterback Joe Namath. Broadway Joe, charismatic and unpredictable, was enthusiastically embraced by the New York City media and fans.

The war raged for seven years before a truce was called in 1966. On June 8, Rozelle announced a merger agreement that called for a championship game between the rival leagues after the 1966 season, a combined draft and interleague preseason play in 1967, and a common schedule beginning in 1970. All existing franchises would be retained.

As with the AAFC merger 17 years earlier, the bitterly fought war

The 2,003-YARD MAN

As the 1973 season progressed, the football world watched intently to see if Buffalo's OJ Simpson could top the greatest one-season rushing performance in NFL history—Jim Brown's 1963 mark of 1,863 yards.

And with two games remaining, it appeared Simpson had a pretty fair shot at history. He needed to total 280 yards against the New England Patriots and New York Jets to pass Brown and he had rushed for 250 against the Patriots in the Bills' season opener.

But Simpson took his challenge a step further. He exploded for 219 yards against New England on December 9 and closed with a 200-yard outburst against the Jets. Not only had he topped Brown, he had crossed the previously unthinkable barrier of 2,000 yards. Here are Simpson's game-by-game totals:

	ATT.	YARDS
NEW ENGLAND	29	250
SAN DIEGO	22	103
NY JETS	24	123
PHILADELPHIA	27	171
BALTIMORE	22	166
MIAMI	14	55
KANSAS CITY	39	157
NEW ORLEANS	20	79
CINCINNATI	20	99
MIAMI	20	120
BALTIMORE	15	124
ATLANTA	24	137
NEW ENGLAND	22	219
NEW YORK JETS	34	200
TOTAL	332	2,003

Perfect season: Miami Dolphins (left to right) Larry Csonka, Jim Kiick and Coach Don Shula look on as the defense keeps the perfect season intact.

Coach Don Shula and his Miami Dolphins; the later years to Coach Chuck Noll's Pittsburgh Steelers.

The Dolphins, featuring the power running of Larry Csonka, Jim Kiick and Mercury Morris, the crafty quarterbacking of Bob Griese and a "No-Name Defense" that swarmed and stuffed opposing offenses, reached national prominence in 1971, when they captured their first AFC crown before losing to Dallas in the Super Bowl. But the 1972 Dolphins would not be denied—by anybody.

They crafted a 14-0 regular season, beat Cleveland and Pittsburgh in the playoffs and completed the NFL's first perfect season (17-0) with a 14-7 victory over Washington in Super Bowl VII. The Dolphins were not perfect in 1973, but they were good enough to defeat Minnesota, 24-7, in Super Bowl VIII. The closest thing to 1973 perfection was the performance of Buffalo running back O J Simpson, who became the NFL's first 2,000-yard rusher.

The Dolphins' grip was released the next season when a "Steel Curtain" dropped menacingly over the NFL. The Steelers, a long-dormant franchise, rode the strong arm of Terry Bradshaw, the running of Franco Harris and a stifling defense, featuring tackle (Mean) Joe Greene and linebackers Jack Ham and Jack Lambert, to four Super Bowl titles in the next six years.

The Miami and Pittsburgh influences, plus the threat of another rival league in 1974, resulted in changes that would make the game more entertaining and exciting. By mid-decade, the high-scoring, pass-happy days of the 1960s were but a distant memory as coaches gravitated toward power offenses and a safer, more conservative defensive philosophy. When the World Football League formed, however, the NFL adopted rule changes that would force excitement back into its stodgy product.

The most far-reaching rule was sudden-death overtime to eliminate ties. But the NFL also moved the goal posts back ten yards to the end lines to cut back on field goals, limited defensive backs to

Labor took center stage in 1982 when negotiations for a new basic agreement broke down and the players staged a successful 57-day in-season strike. But owners were prepared five years later when the players walked out again after Week 2 of the 1987 season. After a week without games, the owners continued their schedule for three weeks using replacement players. The union, stung by players crossing the picket lines, gave in after 24 days.

Such distractions did not seem to faze the league's newest bully. The San Francisco 49ers, with coach Bill Walsh handing the keys to his new West Coast offense over to Montana, won their first Super Bowl after the 1981 season and began a record-setting journey that would culminate with four Super Bowl victories in the decade and a fifth after the 1994 season under coach George Seifert and quarterback Steve Young. The 1980s also witnessed the return of three long-dormant franchises to the championship throne. The 1982 and 1987 Redskins won Super Bowls, as did the 1985 Bears and 1986 Giants. Different kinds of championships were claimed by Chicago running back Payton, who became football's all-time career rushing leader with 16,726 yards, and San Francisco's Rice, who claimed virtually every career receiving record.

The 1980s ended with the 49ers riding the crest of their fourth Super Bowl and the Dallas Cowboys, another proud franchise now under the direction of new owner Jerry Jones and new coach Jimmy Johnson, sinking under the strain of a 1–15 record. That would change.

BACK TO THE FUTURE

By the mid-1990s, the NFL was displaying resilience amid prosperity and confusion. It had survived yet another rival league (the three-season United States Football League) and expanded to 30 teams with new franchises in Charlotte, NC, and Jacksonville, Fla. Rozelle, the commissioner who had led the league to great prosperity, retired and was replaced by Paul Tagliabue, who turned his sights to foreign markets while establishing international credibility with the proliferation of the American Bowl and the creation of the World League. But nothing regenerated the enthusiasm of frustrated fans more than a 1993 labor contract that ended years of bickering and put the game back on the field at least through 1999. The owners got a salary cap and the players got unrestricted free agency after four years and the promise of higher salaries. Everybody reveled in a 1993 TV contract that brought $4.35 billion into the coffers.

The salary cap ushered in a new era of quick player movement and forced franchise-rebuilding that made long-term domination difficult. The Cowboys, revived under the direction of Johnson, won consecutive Super Bowls after the 1992 and 1993 seasons behind the passing of Troy Aikman and the running of Emmitt Smith and added a third championship after the 1995 campaign under coach Barry Switzer. But free-agency player defections and salary cap restrictions eventually took their toll and opened the door for other teams to jump into the title picture. The 1996 Packers, featuring the passing of Brett Favre and the defensive work of Reggie White, returned to the championship throne after a 29-year drought. The expansion Panthers and Jaguars made incredibly quick runs to respectability. The Panthers, constructed cleverly through free agency and the draft, finished 7–9 in their first season and 12–4 in a second that featured an exciting run to the NFC Championship Game. The Jaguars enjoyed a 9–7 second season and reached the AFC title game.

It was amid such revolution and evolution that football fans bid farewell to one of the game's great legends. Dolphins coach Don Shula, who had posted an all-time record of 347 victories over seven seasons with the Baltimore Colts and 26 with Miami, retired. He was replaced after the 1995 season by Jimmy Johnson, the man who had led the Cowboys to their 1992 and 1993 Super Bowl wins.

one bump of eligible pass receivers and reduced the penalty for offensive holding.

The WFL threat was short and expensive. The new league did lure a number of stars with big-money inducements, but midway through its second season, facing huge debts and no promise of future success, the WFL folded.

FORWARD VISION

The NFL, bolstered by expansion to Tampa and Seattle in 1976 and an increase to a 16-game regular-season format in 1978, played to rave reviews as the 1980s dawned. Record attendance figures were posted and the old guard was passing its mantle to a new wave of rising stars. Such former crowd-pleasers as Namath, Simpson, Harris and Roger Staubach were either gone or fading fast. Players like running backs Walter Payton, Tony Dorsett, Marcus Allen and Barry Sanders, tight end Kellen Winslow, wide receiver Jerry Rice and quarterbacks Joe Montana, John Elway and Dan Marino were rising to prominence.

But the game was not without problems. First the issue of franchise stability crept into the spotlight, frustrating and bewildering the fans. Then labor scuffling turned into a war that tested the very fabric of the game.

Little did Raiders Owner Al Davis realize the can of worms he would open when, upset because the league turned down his request to move from Oakland to Los Angeles, he took his case to court in 1980 and two years later won the long, bitter battle that weakened the NFL's stranglehold over its franchises. Davis' victory had a trickling effect. In 1984, the Colts moved from Baltimore to Indianapolis and four years later the Cardinals left St. Louis for Phoenix. The dam broke in 1995, 1996 and 1997 when the Los Angeles Rams relocated to St. Louis, the Raiders returned to Oakland, the Cleveland Browns made a gut-wrenching shift to Baltimore (as the Ravens) and the Oilers finalized plans to leave Houston for Nashville. The promise of new stadiums and increased income was too good to ignore and owners could not resist the overtures from football-hungry cities.

Everybody wants to play

★★★★★★★★★★★★★★★★★★★★★★

In the long history of the National Football League, not one individual has ever won an NFL championship or a Super Bowl. Teams win championships; individuals win accolades and honors. Scoring and passing titles are showy and nice, but they don't fit the ego quite like a Super Bowl ring.

Just ask Detroit's Barry Sanders if he would trade one of his three rushing titles for a championship. Green Bay quarterback Brett Favre shrugs when asked about his consecutive MVP awards, but his eyes light up when he recalls his team's victory in Super Bowl XXXI.

Team success is the backbone of all sports competition, but it's also the most difficult level to attain. Finding talented players to fill roster spots is one thing; blending them into cohesive, working units is another. Once an organization does taste success, sustaining it over an extended period is the ultimate test of its leadership and coaching.

That's an especially difficult task in professional football, where a "team" consists of 45 players divided into three distinct units—offense, defense and special teams. Basketball coaches have to coordinate the efforts of 12 players, all of whom play both offense and defense; baseball managers have 25. The sheer numbers, combined with the physical toll football takes on its players, explains why the 1960s-era Green Bay Packers, perhaps the NFL's greatest dynasty, lasted only seven years.

Vince Lombardi was the architect of that glorious run and he did it with old-fashioned principles—discipline, commitment to winning and a demanding work schedule. He sought out players who would embrace his philosophy, molded his offense and defense into smooth-running machines that valued efficiency over individual glory and instilled his hatred for losing. Lombardi, a demanding, forceful and sometimes-abrasive personality, translated his intensity into five NFL championships in seven seasons.

Lombardi's methods were not all that much different from those used by George Halas, Chicago's Papa Bear, who built the "Monsters of the Midway" powerhouse that won five NFL titles and appeared in three more championship games from 1932-43. But they were light years removed from the coaching innovations of Paul Brown, who directed the Cleveland Browns to four consecutive All-America Football Conference championships and three titles in the team's first six NFL seasons.

Brown, considered one of the greatest talent judges in football history, was analytical, precise and innovative. He was a teacher as much as a coach. And he was always the gentleman, although his calm, stately exterior was only a cover for the competitive fire that burned inside. His methods might have been different from Lombardi's, but his philosophies were strikingly similar.

All coaches must be astute judges of talent, but successful coaches take their assessment abilities beyond the field. Like Halas, Lombardi and Brown, they must be able to spot character players and overachievers who often bring more to the team concept than their more athletically gifted competitors. Coaches like Don Shula, Chuck Noll, Bill Walsh and Jimmy Johnson parlayed their special abilities into more recent successful runs that are especially impressive in the context of rising player salaries.

Shula led the Miami Dolphins to three consecutive Super Bowl appearances from 1971-73 and back-to-back championships (1972-73). Noll's Pittsburgh Steelers came close to matching the Packers with four Super Bowl championships in six years from 1974-79. Walsh was the architect of the San Francisco 49ers express that rolled to four Super Bowl titles in the 1980s (three under his coaching), and Johnson brought the Dallas Cowboys back from the dead to win consecutive Super Bowls after the 1992 and 1993 seasons. Super

or a winner

Division rivals: Minnesota's rivalry with Green Bay is one of the most intense in the NFL. Here Cris Carter is tackled by a Packer defender.

Bowl-winning coaches like Tom Landry, Joe Gibbs and Bill Parcells also have brought winning attitudes to organizations that previously lacked direction.

Several common threads run through the fabric of football's greatest teams. Foremost is the presence of a quarterback more gifted as a leader than athletically. Chicago's Sid Luckman, Cleveland's Otto Graham and Green Bay's Bart Starr were not the most talented passers or runners—but they knew how to win. So did Miami's Bob Griese, Pittsburgh's Terry Bradshaw, San Francisco's Joe Montana

and Dallas' Troy Aikman. Montana was a third-round draft pick; Starr came on the 17th round. Griese's statistics have been dwarfed by current Dolphins quarterback Dan Marino, but Marino has never won a championship.

The great teams also have big-play running backs and, of course, defenses that operate with machine-like efficiency—a characteristic common to every winning team in every sport.

In football, like in basketball, baseball and hockey, such efficiency is called teamwork. It produces championships, not just gaudy statistics.

Baltimore Ravens

REBUILDING IN CLEVELAND

In the beginning: Baltimore's football roots trace back to 1947, when the Baltimore Colts played their first game as a second-year member of the All-America Football Conference. After three AAFC seasons, the Colts were one of four franchises that made the merger jump into the NFL. But after a 1–11 1950 debut, the team folded under financial strain. Football returned to Baltimore two years later when an ownership group headed by Carroll Rosenbloom was awarded a Dallas Texan franchise besieged by financial problems. The new Colts would become one of football's most revered teams over the next three decades, until owner Robert Irsay spirited the franchise away to Indianapolis in 1984. Baltimore remained on the perimeter of professional football from 1984 until 1996, when the Ravens arrived to fill a long, frustrating void.

The glory years: Johnny Unitas, Lenny Moore, Raymond Berry, Alan Ameche, Gino Marchetti, Tom Matte, Bubba Smith… the names roll off the tongue of any Baltimore football fan. All were instrumental in a Colts winning legacy that included three NFL championships and one Super Bowl title. Any hopes the Ravens have of adding to that tradition will require patience, a financial commitment to rebuilding a roster that has produced only one winning record in the last seven seasons and an accelerated maturing process for a lot of young players. The Ravens, boasting a nice blend of veteran and youthful talent, are not without hope, despite a dismal first-year record in Baltimore.

Down and out: The 1996 Ravens struggled through a 4–12 debut, but they lost second-half leads in 10 of their final 11 games and were 0–4 in games decided by 3 or fewer points. They blew one 15-point second half lead and two other 11-pointers.

That championship feeling: This will be the true test of the Art Modell legacy: can the Ravens owner put together the Super Bowl winner for Baltimore that he was unable to create for Cleveland?

Back to the future: Coach Ted Marchibroda has an offense that will create problems for any team. Now can he build his defense to title-contending status? The offensive trigger is pulled by quarterback Vinny Testaverde, who passed for 4,177 yards and 33 touchdowns in his first Baltimore season. Testaverde has some dangerous targets in Michael Jackson, Derrick Alexander and Jermaine Lewis, and running back Bam Morris has a big and talented offensive line. The arrival of defensive linemen Tony Siragusa and Michael McCrary bolsters a front wall that also includes James Jones and provides a foundation for a young linebacking corps with two rookie starters. The defensive secondary problem will have to be addressed before the team can contend for anything.

FACTS AND FIGURES

CONFERENCE/DIVISION	AFC Central		
FIRST YEAR IN NFL	1966		
STADIUM/CAPACITY/SURFACE	Memorial Stadium (65,000) /Grass		
FORMER CITIES/NICKNAMES	Cleveland Browns (1950-95); AAFC (1946-49)		
NFL CHAMPIONSHIPS	1950, 1954, 1955, 1964		
SUPER BOWL CHAMPIONSHIPS	None		

PLAYING RECORD	W	L	T	PCT
Regular Season	378	278	10	.575
Playoffs (23 Appearances)	11	19	0	.367

Coming into his own: Baltimore quarterback Vinny Testaverde has enjoyed a career revival behind center for the Ravens.

Buffalo Bills

FOUR'S NOT A CHARM

★★★★★★★★★★★★★★

In the beginning: Their early life in the American Football League was nothing to brag about and their final AFL years were downright embarrassing. But, oh, those middle years were just fine. After making their first playoff appearance in 1963—their fourth season—the Bills and Coach Lou Saban rode the strong passing of quarterback Jack Kemp to consecutive AFL championships in 1964 and 1965 and a title-game loss to Kansas City in 1966. But just as quickly as the Bills had risen to prominence, they dropped back into oblivion. They spent their final three years of AFL life compiling an unsightly 9–32–1 record.

The glory years: The AFL championships were memorable, but most Buffalo fans point to 1986 as the beginning of football life. That's when new Coach Marv Levy began molding an AFC winning machine. Quarterback Jim Kelly was lured from the United States Football League in 1986 to run Levy's no-huddle offense. Players like running back Thurman Thomas, receiver Andre Reed and tackle Howard Ballard arrived via the draft. Levy built his attacking defense around end Bruce Smith and linebackers Cornelius Bennett and Darryl Talley. After the 1988 season, the Bills advanced to the AFC title game and lost to Cincinnati. Two years later, they began a run that produced three AFC East Division titles in four years, a 9–0 AFC playoff run and a record four straight Super Bowl appearances. The catch: they lost all four by a combined 139–73 score—and all that success was masked by a haze of futility.

Down and out: From 1970—the Bills' first NFL season—until 1987, they made three brief playoff appearances. But the 1970s were not a total loss. Buffalo fans were treated to the rushing feats of OJ Simpson, who ran for an incredible 2,003 yards in a record-setting 1973 season and never failed to enchant his fans. But for all of his accomplishments, Simpson led the Bills to only three winning records and one playoff appearance.

That championship feeling: Until the Bills win their first NFL title, they will be remembered as the team that compiled an incredible 49–15 regular-season record from 1990–93—and failed to win a Super Bowl. Buffalo is one of three NFL teams with 0–4 records in football's biggest game.

Back to the future: After failing to qualify for the postseason in 1994 for the first time in seven years, the aging Bills revived behind Kelly, Thomas and Smith for consecutive playoff appearances. But after a 10–6 1996 season, Kelly retired and turned the quarterback reins over to young Todd Collins. Any hopes for Buffalo duplicating its early 1990s success in the latter years of the decade will depend on Levy's ability to rebuild on the run.

FACTS AND FIGURES

CONFERENCE/DIVISION	AFC East
FIRST YEAR IN NFL	1970 (AFL—1960-69)
STADIUM/CAPACITY/SURFACE	Rich Stadium (80,091) /Artificial
FORMER CITIES/NICKNAMES	None
AFL CHAMPIONSHIPS	1964, 1965
SUPER BOWL CHAMPIONSHIPS	None

PLAYING RECORD	W	L	T	PCT
AFL Regular Season	65	69	6	.486
NFL Regular Season	196	210	2	.483
AFL Playoffs (4 Appearances)	2	2	0	.500
NFL Playoffs (11 Appearances)	12	11	0	.522

Double teamed: Bruce Smith was the first overall pick of the 1985 NFL Draft and he has lived up to expectations for a decade.

Cincinnati Bengals

BACK TO THE FUTURE

In the beginning: A creation of former Cleveland founder Paul Brown, the Bengals took the field in 1968 as an expansion member of the American Football League. It didn't take long for Brown's new team to make an impact. In 1970, Cincinnati's third season and football's first year under the AFL-NFL merger agreement, the Bengals compiled an 8–6 record, won the AFC Central Division title and lost a first-round playoff game. Such success would be erratic, but it only enhanced Brown's reputation as a master football architect.

The glory years: Brown's Bengals produced four winning records and two AFC Central titles from 1970 to 1975, and Bill Johnson coached them to winning marks in 1976 and 1977. Those were prosperous years under the direction of quarterback Ken Anderson, a 1971 draft pick who deployed such offensive weapons as running backs Boobie Clark and Essex Johnson and wide receiver Isaac Curtis. Clark and Johnson were gone by 1981 when the Bengals, coming off three losing seasons, unexpectedly soared to a 12–4 record, another division title and a Cinderella run to Super Bowl XVI, where they lost a tight 26–21 battle to San Francisco. That team featured Anderson throwing to Curtis and Cris Collinsworth, while fullback Pete Johnson carried the running load behind outstanding tackle Anthony Muñoz. Linebacker Jim LeClair and end Ross Browner anchored an opportunistic defense.

Down and out: A five-year rebuilding stretch from 1983 to 1987 preceded Cincinnati's 1988 run to a second Super Bowl appearance, this one under Sam Wyche. The current Bengals are mired in a six-year drought that cost Wyche and David Shula, the son of former Miami coaching great Don Shula, their jobs. Shula was replaced midway through the 1996 campaign by Bruce Coslet.

That championship feeling: The Bengals' two Super Bowl excursions were both unexpected and exciting. After their narrow loss to San Francisco following the 1981 season, they made a similar run after the 1988 campaign, losing again to the 49ers (20–16) on Joe Montana's final-minute touchdown pass to John Taylor. The 1988 AFC champions featured Boomer Esiason at quarterback, James Brooks and Ickey Woods at running back, Muñoz at tackle and Eddie Brown at wide receiver.

Back to the future: The challenge facing Coslet is to turn around the futility of the 1990s. He got off to a good start when he stepped in for Shula and guided the 1996 Bengals to a season-closing 7–2 run and a final 8–8 mark. The skill-position pieces are in place—quarterback Jeff Blake throwing to Carl Pickens, Ki-Jana Carter running the ball—and the defense is anchored by tackle Dan Wilkinson, a No. 1 overall pick in 1994, and cornerback Ashley Ambrose.

 **One to watch: Cincinnati's future is in the safe hands of quarterback Jeff Blake, who led the Bengals to an 8–8 record in 1996.**

FACTS AND FIGURES

CONFERENCE/DIVISION	AFC Central
FIRST YEAR IN NFL	1970 (AFL 1968-69)
STADIUM/CAPACITY/SURFACE	Cinergy Field (60,389) /Artificial
FORMER CITIES/NICKNAMES	None
AFL CHAMPIONSHIPS	None
SUPER BOWL CHAMPIONSHIPS	None

PLAYING RECORD	W	L	T	PCT
AFL Regular Season	7	20	1	.268
NFL Regular Season	193	215	0	.473
AFL Playoffs	0	0	0	.000
NFL Playoffs (7 Appearances)	5	7	0	.417

Denver Broncos

A ROCKY MOUNTAIN HIGH

In the beginning: Life as one of the original eight American Football League pioneers was not easy for the Broncos. In the league's 10-year existence, they never finished above .500 or qualified for the playoffs. The lack of direction was illustrated by a coaching succession that included Frank Filchock, Jack Faulkner, Mac Speedie, Ray Malavasi and Lou Saban and an unimpressive quarterback line that included Frank Tripucka, Mickey Slaughter, Jacky Lee, John McCormick, Steve Tensi and Marlin Briscoe.

The glory years: The storybook 1977 season was choreographed by Coach Red Miller and executed to near perfection by quarterback Craig Morton, running back Otis Armstrong and the renowned "Orange Crush" defense featuring end Lyle Alzado, linebackers Randy Gradishar and Tom Jackson and tackle Rubin Carter. A 12–2 regular season marked Denver's first serious brush with success and it was followed by a fantastic playoff voyage that culminated in Super Bowl XII. Despite a 27–10 loss to the Cowboys, the fever pitch of that 1977 Rocky Mountain high continued into 1978 and 1979, seasons that produced 10–6 records, a second AFC West Division title and a pair of quick playoff losses. But it wasn't until John Elway, a No. 1 overall draft pick by the Colts, acquired in a 1983 trade, that the Broncos became a consistent playoff threat. Coach Dan Reeves, manipulating a lineup that included Elway, running back Sammy Winder, receiver Steve Watson, linebacker Karl Mecklenburg and safety Dennis Smith, led the Broncos to five AFC West titles, six playoff appearances and three Super Bowls between 1983 and 1991. They also lost once in the AFC championship game.

Down and out: The early years were the only long period of futility. The Broncos managed only three winning records and did not qualify for the playoffs in their first 17 seasons.

That championship feeling: Denver reached the Super Bowl four times and lost all of them—by a combined score of 163–50. Three of those losses came with Elway at the controls.

FACTS AND FIGURES

CONFERENCE/DIVISION	AFC West
FIRST YEAR IN NFL	1970 (AFL 1960-69)
STADIUM/CAPACITY/SURFACE	Mile High Stadium (76,273) /Grass
FORMER CITIES/NICKNAMES	None
AFL CHAMPIONSHIPS	None
SUPER BOWL CHAMPIONSHIPS	None

PLAYING RECORD	W	L	T	PCT
AFL Regular Season	39	97	4	.293
NFL Regular Season	230	172	6	.594
AFL Playoffs	0	0	0	.000
NFL Playoffs (10 Appearances)	9	11	0	.450

Back to the future: Reeves departed after the 1992 season and the next three years produced one brief playoff appearance and two postseason misses. The 1996 season under Coach Mike Shanahan had all the makings of another Super Bowl challenge, but the 13–3 Broncos, AFC West champions for an eighth time, self-destructed in an early playoff loss to Jacksonville. The Broncos entered the late-1990s with Elway still directing an offense that now featured such weapons as running back Terrell Davis and tight end Shannon Sharpe, and a nice blend of young and veteran defensive talent that included tackle Michael Dean Perry, end Neil Smith and safety Steve Atwater.

Success is catching: Denver tight end Shannon Sharpe has followed his brother Sterling as an outstanding NFL receiver.

Indianapolis Colts

THE END OF AN ENIGMA

In the beginning: The Colts joined the NFL in 1953 when a Baltimore group was awarded the holdings of a Dallas team that had died midway through its first NFL season in 1952. The Baltimore Colts stumbled through their first four seasons before rising to prominence behind the strong right arm of young quarterback Johnny Unitas.

The glory years: Under the astute direction of Coach Weeb Ewbank, the Colts rode the passing of Unitas to Lenny Moore and Raymond Berry, the running of Alan Ameche and the defensive work of Gino Marchetti into the championship spotlight. The Colts claimed their first and second Western Conference titles in 1958 and 1959 and followed both seasons with championships. The Colts, who would add such stars as John Mackey, Bubba Smith, Tom Matte and quarterbacks Earl Morrall and Bert Jones to the mix in the ensuing years, remained an NFL power through 1977, winning once and losing once in two Super Bowl appearances and falling in one NFL championship game and one AFC title game. In the 20 seasons between 1958 and 1977, the Colts recorded 15 winning records and won eight division titles under Ewbank, Don Shula, Don McCafferty and Ted Marchibroda.

Down and out: From 1978 through 1983, the Colts failed to record a winning record and owner Robert Irsay spirited his franchise away to Indianapolis. But this didn't help much. Despite the coming and going of such talented stars as running back Eric Dickerson, linebacker Cornelius Bennett, wide receiver Andre Rison and quarterback Jeff George, the Colts continued to lose, recording three winning records and making one brief playoff appearance through the 1994 season.

That championship feeling: The 1958 championship was delivered by one of the most memorable games in football history—a nationally televised victory over the New York Giants in the NFL's first-ever overtime game. The first Super Bowl loss was equally memorable—the New York Jets and Joe Namath shocking the powerful Colts in one of the great upsets in football history. The Colts' only Super Bowl victory was fashioned when Jim O'Brien kicked a 32-yard field goal to beat Dallas with five seconds remaining.

Back to the future: Under the guidance of Marchibroda, the Colts

pulled a 1995 surprise by qualifying for the playoffs and advancing all the way to the AFC title game. The 1996 Colts, under new Coach Lindy Infante, also qualified for the postseason, but lost their wild-card opener. The Colts' future looks bright, thanks to a solid defense and an offense that features Jim Harbaugh handing off to Marshall Faulk and passing to Marvin Harrison.

Looking to bounce back: Marshall Faulk was slowed by injuries in 1995 and 1996, but he remains a threat every time he gets the ball.

FACTS AND FIGURES

CONFERENCE/DIVISION	AFC East
FIRST YEAR IN NFL	1953
STADIUM/CAPACITY/SURFACE	RCA Dome (60,127) /Artificial
FORMER CITIES/NICKNAMES	Baltimore Colts (1953-83)
NFL CHAMPIONSHIPS	1958, 1959, 1968
SUPER BOWL CHAMPIONSHIPS	1970

PLAYING RECORD	W	L	T	PCT
Regular Season	307	316	7	.493
Playoffs (13 Appearances)	10	10	0	.500

Jacksonville Jaguars

FIRST IMPRESSIONS ★★★★★★★★★★★★★★★★

In the beginning: The Jaguars are the AFC half of the 1995 two-team expansion that also brought Carolina into the NFL fold. The Jaguars were constructed from the 1995 expansion draft, the NFL's annual draft of college players and a free-agent system that benefits new teams without an existing salary base. Jacksonville struggled to a 4–12 first-year record that provided only subtle hints of the success that would follow.

The glory years: Based on the Jaguars' 1996 performance, there are going to be many. Jacksonville's second season opened with a victory over defending AFC champion Pittsburgh and concluded in the AFC championship game after two stirring playoff victories. The 9–7 regular-season record was good for second place in the AFC Central Division, one game behind the Steelers, and it matched the second-best record ever compiled by a second-year expansion team, topped only by Carolina's equally surprising 12–4 mark in 1996. The Jaguars qualified for the postseason with a season-closing five-game winning streak that included a wild card-clinching final-day victory over Atlanta. When the Jaguars took the field for their AFC championship game against New England after playoff upsets of Buffalo and Denver, their starting lineup included 12 free-agent signees, 4 players selected in the 1995 and 1996 drafts, 3 players acquired on waivers, 2 players from the 1995 expansion draft and 1 player obtained in a trade. Five of the 31 players selected in the expansion draft remained on the second-year roster.

Down and out: Not even the 1995 first-year struggle could be considered a down season. It included a victory over the Steelers and plenty of reason for optimism.

That championship feeling: Nobody will underestimate the Jaguars again. The 1996 team ranked second in the league in total offense (360 yards per game) and first in passing (256.9). Much of that can be attributed to the dangerous left arm of quarterback Mark Brunell, who turned both Keenan McCardell and Jimmy Smith into 1,000-yard receivers. The Jaguars also got a big late-season boost from bruising running back Natrone Means, the former San Diego star, who posted big numbers running behind tackles Tony Boselli and Leon Searcy.

Back to the future: Coach Tom Coughlin's 1996 team caught everybody by surprise. That won't happen again. The offense should be a force for years to come, but Coughlin will have to fill holes on a defense that ranked a respectable 16th in its second season. Players like end Tony Brackens, safety Dana Hall and veteran linebacker Clyde Simmons provide a nice foundation.

★★★★★★★★★★★

Look left: Southpaw quarterback Mark Brunell had a brilliant 1996 season, leading the second-year Jacksonville Jaguars to the conference championship game.

FACTS AND FIGURES

CONFERENCE/DIVISION	AFC Central			
FIRST YEAR IN NFL	1995			
STADIUM/CAPACITY/SURFACE	ALLTELL Stadium (73,000)/Grass			
PLAYING RECORD	**W**	**L**	**T**	**PCT**
Regular Season	13	19	0	.406
Playoffs (1 Appearance)	2	1	0	.666

Kansas City Chiefs

RECLAIMING PAST GLORY

In the beginning: Lamar Hunt brought them to life as the Dallas Texans, shifted operations to Kansas City in 1963 and watched his team rise to prominence as a heavyweight contender in the American Football League. Hunt, the founding father and brains behind the AFL, created a monster that would terrorize the new league while waging a fierce battle against the Oakland Raiders for AFL supremacy. The early roster featured such outstanding players as quarterback Len Dawson, running back Mike Garrett, wide receiver Otis Taylor, tackle Jim Tyrer, defensive end Buck Buchanan, linebackers Willie Lanier and Bobby Bell and safety Johnny Robinson.

The glory years: The Chiefs, coached by Hank Stram, captured three division titles, three AFL championships and a Super Bowl in their first 12 seasons. Their 23–7 victory over Minnesota in Super Bowl IV was the crowning achievement, but it also brought down the curtain on their first era of prosperity. The second didn't begin until

FACTS AND FIGURES

CONFERENCE/DIVISION	AFC West
FIRST YEAR IN NFL	1970 (AFL 1960-69)
STADIUM/CAPACITY/SURFACE	Arrowhead Stadium (79,101) /Grass
FORMER CITIES/NICKNAMES	Dallas Texans (1960-62)
AFL CHAMPIONSHIPS	1962, 1966, 1969
SUPER BOWL CHAMPIONSHIPS	1969

PLAYING RECORD	W	L	T	PCT
AFL Regular Season	87	48	5	.639
NFL Regular Season	199	202	7	.496
AFL Playoffs (4 Appearances)	5	2	0	.714
NFL Playoffs (8 Appearances)	3	8	0	.273

Hard hitter: Kansas City defensive back Dale Carter is a ball-hawking cornerback who delivers punishing hits on any receiver who ventures into his part of the field.

1989, when new coach Marty Schottenheimer started building a machine that would capture two AFC West Division titles and qualify for the playoffs from 1990 through 1995. The new-breed Chiefs were anchored by running backs Marcus Allen and Greg Hill, offensive tackle Jon Alt, defensive end Neil Smith, pass-rushing linebacker Derrick Thomas and cornerback Dale Carter. Schottenheimer's Chiefs also were blessed with cameo appearances by quarterback Joe Montana and 1,000-yard rushers Christian Okoye and Barry Word.

Down and out: From 1971, when they captured a West Division championship, to 1989, the Chiefs disappeared into a haze of futility. Over 18 long seasons, they produced only five winning records and made one quick playoff appearance. Five coaches were hired and fired during that span.

That championship feeling: The Chiefs lost to Vince Lombardi's Green Bay Packers in the inaugural Super Bowl, but gained revenge three years later with their dramatic upset victory over the powerful Vikings. That championship was choreographed by Stram and Dawson in the final Super Bowl before the AFL-NFL merger became official. It was a major step for the AFL in its quest for recognition and respect.

Back to the future: Under Schottenheimer, the Chiefs have regained status as an NFL power. But so far they have been unable to step back into the Super Bowl spotlight. They tried the power approach in the early 1990s with Okoye and Word. When the Chiefs couldn't get past the second playoff round, they did an about-face and hired the aging Montana, who guided them to the 1993 AFC title game—a loss to Buffalo. A 13–3 regular season in 1995 was followed by a shocking first-round playoff loss to Indianapolis and the 9–7 Chiefs failed to qualify for the 1996 playoffs. That disappointment led to the signing of former 49ers quarterback Elvis Grbac, who will be asked to return the Chiefs to playoff form. He should get plenty of help from free-agent wide receivers Brett Perriman and Andre Rison, and rookie tight end Tony Gonzalez.

Miami Dolphins

THEY, TOO, WILL PASS

★ ★ ★ ★ ★ ★ ★ ★ ★ ★ ★ ★

In the beginning: The Dolphins began their football life in 1966 as an expansion team in the American Football League. And under Coach George Wilson, they played like an expansion team for four predictable seasons. But the unpredictable happened in 1970, the first year under the AFL-NFL merger, when a roster full of young, talented players was handed to a new coach. Don Shula led the 1970 Dolphins to a 10–4 record, a second-place finish in the AFC East Division and their first playoff appearance. The best was yet to come.

The glory years: The 1971, 1972 and 1973 Dolphins became the first team to appear in three straight Super Bowls. The first resulted in a loss to Dallas. The second concluded with a victory over Washington, completing the first—and, to date, only—perfect season (17–0) in NFL history. The third resulted in a victory over Minnesota. The 1974 (11–3) and 1975 (10–4) seasons weren't too shabby either, but both came up short in the playoffs. Shula choreographed that success around a solid cast that included quarterback Bob Griese, running backs Larry Csonka, Jim Kiick and Mercury Morris, wide receiver Paul Warfield and such defensive stars as Nick Buoniconti, Dick Anderson and Jake Scott. Shula returned his Dolphins to the Super Bowl after the strike-shortened 1982 season with a quarterback named David Woodley. But there would be nothing suspect about the quarterback position from that point on. With the 1983 arrival of first-round draft pick Dan Marino, Shula instituted a passing offense and his team responded. The Marino-led Dolphins lost in Super Bowl XIX to San Francisco and returned to the AFC title game after claiming its third consecutive division title in 1985.

Down and out: From Shula's arrival in 1970 until his 1995 retirement as the winningest coach in NFL history, the Dolphins suffered only two losing seasons and won 11 AFC East titles. Marino, who has thrown to such receivers as Mark Clayton, Mark Duper, Irving Fryar, Keith Jackson and OJ McDuffie during his record-setting career, has experienced one losing campaign. There was a four-year playoff lull from 1986–89, but the Dolphins finished .500 or better in three of those seasons.

That championship feeling: Since 1973, there have been no championships. However, two Super Bowls and two other title-game appearances have kept Miami fans on the edge of their seats. There could be more excitement under the guidance of Shula's replacement, Jimmy Johnson—the architect of two Super Bowl winners at Dallas.

Back to the future: The Dolphins finished 8–8 in Johnson's first season. But most observers are expecting a bright future. With Johnson reconstructing a suspect defense and Marino, McDuffie, young receiver Yatil Green, and young running back Karim Abdul-Jabbar carrying the offensive load, success could be right around the corner.

FACTS AND FIGURES

CONFERENCE/DIVISION	AFC East
FIRST YEAR IN NFL	1970 (AFL 1966-69)
STADIUM/CAPACITY/SURFACE	Pro Player Stadium (74,916) /Grass
FORMER CITIES/NICKNAMES	None
AFL CHAMPIONSHIPS	None
SUPER BOWL CHAMPIONSHIPS	1972, 1973

PLAYING RECORD	W	L	T	PCT
AFL Regular Season	15	39	2	.286
NFL Regular Season	265	141	2	.652
AFL Playoffs	0	0	0	.000
NFL Playoffs (16 Appearances)	17	14	0	.548

A long time coming: In 1996, rookie tailback Karim Abdul-Jabbar became the Miami Dolphins' first 1,000-yard rusher in 16 seasons.

New England Patriots

BEST-LAID PLANS GO AWRY ★★★★★★★★★★★★★★

In the beginning: The Boston Patriots began operation in 1960 as a charter member of the American Football League and coasted through a nondescript 10-year existence in the new circuit. The Patriots did win an Eastern Division title in 1963 behind quarterback Babe Parilli, wide receiver/kicker Gino Cappelletti and linebacker Nick Buoniconti, but they lost in the championship game to San Diego. The Patriots traded their "Boston" affiliation for "New England" after the 1970 season, their first in the NFL.

The glory years: In the 13-year period from 1976 through 1988, the Patriots compiled 11 winning records, captured their first two AFC East Division titles and advanced to the first of two Super Bowls. The team's first sustained success came under the guidance of four coaches—Chuck Fairbanks, Ron Erhardt, Ron Meyer and Raymond Berry—and was executed by such players as quarterback Tony Eason, wide receivers Stanley Morgan and Irving Fryar, running backs Tony Collins and Craig James, offensive guard John Hannah, linebacker Andre Tippett and defensive back Raymond Clayborn.

Down and out: The early years were the most difficult. For 16 seasons, the Patriots ranked among football's most frustrated franchises. They managed only the one division title in their AFL existence and they failed to even post a winning record in their first six NFL campaigns. The Patriots also experienced a difficult rebuilding period from 1987 to 1993, when they failed to qualify for postseason play. But that changed with the 1993 arrival of Coach Bill Parcells.

That championship feeling: The Patriots have reached the Super Bowl twice—in a Cinderella run after the 1985 season when they were overmatched by the powerful Chicago Bears and after an 11–5 1996 campaign when they lost to the Packers. The 1996 Patriots, featuring quarterback Drew Bledsoe, wide receiver Terry Glenn, big-play tight end Ben Coates and running back Curtis Martin, did win their third AFC East title.

Back to the future: The Patriots won the hearts of New England fans with their 1996 Super Bowl run, but they lost their coach. Bill Parcells left the comfort of New England for New York and was replaced by San Francisco assistant Pete Carroll. The foundation is in place for a team that could contend for league honors through the rest of the decade if Carroll can add defensive help to a unit that already includes end Willie McGinest, safety Lawyer Milloy and cornerback Ricky Reynolds.

Master of all he surveys: Patriots quarterback Drew Bledsoe took New England all the way to Super Bowl XXXI.

FACTS AND FIGURES

CONFERENCE/DIVISION	AFC East
FIRST YEAR IN NFL	1970 (AFL 1960-69)
STADIUM/CAPACITY/SURFACE	Foxboro Stadium (60,292) /Grass
FORMER CITIES/NICKNAMES	Boston Patriots (1960-70)
AFL CHAMPIONSHIPS	None
SUPER BOWL CHAMPIONSHIPS	None

PLAYING RECORD	W	L	T	PCT
AFL Regular Season	63	68	9	.482
NFL Regular Season	185	223	0	.453
AFL Playoffs (1 Appearance)	1	1	0	.500
NFL Playoffs (7 Appearances)	5	7	0	.417

New York Jets

BREAKING WITH TRADITION

★★★★★★★★★★★

In the beginning: The New York Titans began operation as an "original eight" member of the American Football League in 1960. Three years later, the team changed its name to "Jets" and went into its first rebuilding mode under Weeb Ewbank—the man who would guide the franchise to its greatest glory. By any name, the early Jets were weak, failing to get above .500 in their first seven seasons.

The glory years: The 1968 and 1969 seasons were all too brief. But they weren't lacking for drama. The 1968 Jets, led by colorful quarterback Joe Namath, posted an 11–3 record, won their first division title and made their first playoff appearance. That magical season concluded with one of the most memorable games in football history: the Jets' 16–7 Super Bowl III upset of the powerful Baltimore Colts—a victory predicted and choreographed by Namath. The Jets, who had entered the game as 18-point underdogs, also got big performances from running backs Matt Snell and Emerson Boozer, wide receivers Don Maynard and George Sauer, and a defense that included end Gerry Philbin, linebacker Al Atkinson and cornerbacks Johnny Sample and Randy Beverly. Not only did the victory lift the Jets to football's championship throne, it also provided the fledgling AFL some much-needed respect. The 1969 Jets followed with a 10–4 record and a second Eastern Division title. But the 1970 AFL-NFL merger signaled a long, frustrating dry spell for unsuspecting New York fans.

Shaft of light: The New York Jets have suffered trying times in recent seasons, but running back Adrian Murrell is a big-game player.

FACTS AND FIGURES

CONFERENCE/DIVISION	AFC East			
FIRST YEAR IN NFL	1970 (AFL 1960-69)			
STADIUM/CAPACITY/SURFACE	Giants Stadium (77,803) /Artificial			
FORMER CITIES/NICKNAMES	New York Titans (1960-62)			
AFL CHAMPIONSHIPS	1968			
SUPER BOWL CHAMPIONSHIPS	1968			

PLAYING RECORD	W	L	T	PCT
AFL Regular Season	69	65	6	.514
NFL Regular Season	162	244	2	.400
AFL Playoffs (2 Appearances)	2	1	0	.666
NFL Playoffs (5 Appearances)	3	5	0	.375

Down and out: In the eight seasons before 1968, the Jets posted one winning record. In the 11 seasons after 1969, they did not break .500 and failed to qualify for the playoffs. The Jets have posted only one winning record and made one brief playoff appearance since 1986.

That championship feeling: The Jets have been under the direction of 10 different coaches since Ewbank departed after the 1973 season. But they did come within one step of a second Super Bowl after the strike-shortened 1982 campaign. With quarterback Richard Todd throwing to Wesley Walker and handing off to Freeman McNeil, the Jets advanced to the AFC championship game where they lost 14–0 to Miami. The 1985 and 1986 seasons were followed by playoff appearances, thanks to McNeil and the Ken O'Brien–Al Toon deep-passing combination.

Back to the future: The Jets' future looks promising, thanks to the arrival of Bill Parcells—a three-time Super Bowl coach. Parcells has his work cut out for him. The Jets completed the 1996 season with a 1–15 record and numerous holes—particularly on defense. But Parcells did have a strong offensive nucleus in quarterback Neil O'Donnell, 1,000-yard rusher Adrian Murrell, and receivers Keyshawn Johnson, Wayne Chrebet and Jeff Graham.

Oakland Raiders

SILVER AND BLACK AND BLUE

In the beginning: Born in 1960 as one of the American Football League's "original eight," the Raiders quickly became an on-field reflection of Al Davis, their long-time coach, general manager and owner. A football maverick who served briefly as AFL commissioner and helped negotiate the 1967 merger agreement with the NFL, Davis instituted his "vertical" passing philosophy, built his team with a keen eye for talent and promoted an aggressive style that constantly embroiled his team in controversy. Davis' Raiders, who seemed to relish their sinister Silver-and-Black reputation, won their first AFL championship in 1967, lost to Green Bay in Super Bowl II and lost in the AFL championship game in each of the AFL's final two seasons.

The glory years: There have been many. Since that 1967 Super Bowl appearance, the Raiders have

FACTS AND FIGURES

CONFERENCE/DIVISION	AFC West
FIRST YEAR IN NFL	1970 (AFL 1960-69)
STADIUM/CAPACITY/SURFACE	Oakland Coliseum (62,500) /Grass
FORMER CITIES/NICKNAMES	Oakland Raiders (1960-81); Los Angeles Raiders (1982-94)
AFL CHAMPIONSHIPS	1967
SUPER BOWL CHAMPIONSHIPS	1976, 1980, 1983

PLAYING RECORD	W	L	T	PCT
AFL Regular Season	77	58	5	.568
NFL Regular Season	251	151	6	.623
AFL Playoffs (3 Appearances)	3	3	0	.500
NFL Playoffs (15 Appearances)	18	12	0	.600

never had more than a four-year playoff drought. From 1972 to 1977, under Coach John Madden, they won five consecutive AFC West Division titles, reached the AFC championship game five times and won their first Super Bowl. They also won Super Bowls after the 1980 and 1983 seasons under Coach Tom Flores and made an AFC championship game appearance after a 12-4 1990 campaign under Coach Art Shell. Through the years, their roster of skill-position players reads like a who's who of football: quarterbacks Daryle Lamonica, Ken Stabler and Jim Plunkett; running backs Clem Daniels, Mark van Eeghen and Marcus Allen; wide receivers Cliff Branch, Fred Biletnikoff and Tim Brown; tight ends Dave Casper and Todd Christensen. The defensive roster also is impressive: ends Howie Long and John Matuszak, linebacker Ted Hendricks, cornerbacks Willie Brown and Mike Haynes, and safety Jack Tatum.

Down and out: In their first seven seasons, the Raiders failed to qualify for the playoffs. From 1986–89, there was a four-year lull under Flores and Mike Shanahan. That's it. The biggest inconsistency has been the constant battle of Davis against the NFL establishment and two franchise shifts: from Oakland to Los Angeles after the 1981 season and back to Oakland after the 1994 campaign. Davis' first move was delayed two years by a bitter court battle against the NFL.

That championship feeling: Only three teams—Pittsburgh, San Francisco and Dallas— have won more Super Bowls than the Raiders. Enough said.

Back to the future: The volatile Davis turned the coaching reins over to Mike White in 1995, and Joe Bugel in 1997 as he groped for answers to a three-year playoff drought. In 1997, he paid big money for strong-armed, controversial Jeff George to replace quarterback Jeff Hostetler and revive the discarded "vertical" passing attack. With such weapons as wideout Tim Brown, and running backs Harvey Williams and Napoleon Kaufman, the George–Davis relationship could succeed.

Catching on: Sure-handed Tim Brown is the big-play receiver for an Oakland passing game with rifle-armed Jeff George at quarterback.

Pittsburgh Steelers

ALMOST LIKE OLD TIMES

★ ★ ★ ★ ★ ★ ★ ★ ★

In the beginning: Art Rooney brought his "Pirates" into the NFL fold in 1933 with visions of victories and championships. But Rooney's plan was short-sighted. Most of the team's early existence was spent in the bottom rungs of the league's standings and not even a nickname switch to "Steelers" after the 1940 season could change its sagging fortunes.

The glory years: The 1970s provided a sweet reward for the man who

Handy receiver: Pittsburgh's wideout Yancey Thigpen is likely to be one of quarterback Kordell Stewart's favourite targets in 1997.

had shown unflinching patience through four losing decades. Rooney hired Chuck Noll to coach the floundering Steelers in 1969 and he began rebuilding through the draft. Noll fashioned his "Steel Curtain" defense around linemen "Mean" Joe Greene and LC Greenwood, linebackers Jack Lambert and Jack Ham, and cornerback Mel Blount. Quarterback Terry Bradshaw, running back Franco Harris, and wide receivers Lynn Swann and John Stallworth became the centerpieces for an efficient offense. The young Steelers won the franchise's first division title in 1972 but were banished in the AFC title game by powerful Miami. But from 1974 through 1979, the Steelers claimed six straight AFC Central titles, reached the AFC championship game five times and appeared in four Super Bowls—winning them all. Four Super Bowl winners in six years—the Steelers had almost magically transformed themselves from the NFL's most beleaguered franchise into its most glamorous.

Down and out: During the 39 seasons from 1933 through 1971, Pittsburgh posted eight winning records and made one unsuccessful playoff appearance. Since 1972, the team has struggled through only one difficult period—a four-year losing stretch from 1985 through 1988, near the end of Noll's long coaching reign.

That championship feeling: The Steelers became the first franchise to claim four Super Bowl victories when they won after the 1974, 1975, 1978 and 1979 seasons. But it took them another 16 years to return to the big game, even though they earned five division titles and advanced to the championship game three times during that period. They finally made it after the 1995 campaign and lost to the Cowboys—a defeat that allowed Dallas to join the San Francisco 49ers as five-time winners and kept the Steelers out of that exclusive club.

Back to the future: The Steelers claimed their 1996 AFC championship despite an inconsistent quarterback situation (Mike Tomczak and Kordell Stewart shared duties) and some key injuries. Now Stewart appears to be the quarterback of the future, and he has two nice targets in Yancey Thigpen and Charles Johnson, and a 1,000-yard runner in Jerome Bettis. Given Coach Bill Cowher's ability to mold attacking defenses, the Steelers should remain in title contention through the 1990s.

★ ★ ★ ★ ★ ★ ★ ★ ★ ★ ★ ★ ★ ★

FACTS AND FIGURES

CONFERENCE/DIVISION	AFC Central
FIRST YEAR IN NFL	1933
STADIUM/CAPACITY/SURFACE	Three Rivers Stadium(59,600) /Artificial
FORMER CITIES/NICKNAMES	Pittsburgh Pirates (1933-40)
NFL CHAMPIONSHIPS	None
SUPER BOWL CHAMPIONSHIPS	1974, 1975, 1978, 1979

PLAYING RECORD	W	L	T	PCT
Regular Season	402	415	19	.492
Playoffs (18 Appearances)	20	14	0	.588

San Diego Chargers

SEARCHING FOR CONSISTENCY

In the beginning: They were born in 1960 as the Los Angeles Chargers and moved to San Diego after one season. By any name, the Sid Gillman-coached Chargers were the bullies of the early American Football League, appearing in five of the AFL's first six championship games. But getting there and winning are two different things, and the Chargers captured their only AFL title in 1963 behind the passing of Tobin Rote and John Hadl, the running of Keith Lincoln and the pass catching of future Hall of Famer Lance Alworth.

The glory years: From 1979 to 1982, the Chargers were the most entertaining team in the NFL under the guidance of Don Coryell—known by both friends and foes as "Air Coryell." To say these Chargers were offensive is both an understatement and a compliment. With strong-armed quarterback Dan Fouts throwing to prolific receivers Charlie Joiner, John Jefferson and Kellen Winslow and Chuck Muncie delivering plenty of rushing and receiving yards out of the backfield, the Chargers could score points in bunches. Conversely, the San Diego defense usually allowed points in the same manner. Coryell's team was good enough to dominate the AFC West Division in 1979, 1980 and 1981 and it advanced to the AFC championship game in two of those seasons, but the defense wasn't good enough to take the next step. By 1986, Coryell would be gone

FACTS AND FIGURES

CONFERENCE/DIVISION	AFC West
FIRST YEAR IN NFL	1970 (AFL 1960-69)
STADIUM/CAPACITY/SURFACE	Qualcomm Stadium (60,794) /Grass
FORMER CITIES/NICKNAMES	Los Angeles Chargers (1960)
AFL CHAMPIONSHIPS	1963
SUPER BOWL CHAMPIONSHIPS	None

PLAYING RECORD	W	L	T	PCT
AFL Regular Season	86	48	6	.636
NFL Regular Season	187	216	5	.464
AFL Playoffs (5 Appearances)	1	4	0	.200
NFL Playoffs (7 Appearances)	6	7	0	.462

Putting a charge into the defense: Perennial All-Pro linebacker Junior Seau has been a shining star in San Diego and one of the NFL's hardest hitters.

and with him the chances for a San Diego championship.

Down and out: After their early AFL run, the Chargers went 13 years without a playoff appearance. After Coryell's 1982 team lost in the second round of the playoffs, the Chargers went nine more years without another postseason appearance. The 1992 arrival of Coach Bobby Ross finally got the San Diego express back on track.

That championship feeling: After their 1963 championship, the Chargers needed a painful 30 years to reach their first Super Bowl. After an 11–5 regular season and AFC West title, Ross' 1994 team made a surprising playoff run that ended with a 49–26 loss to San Francisco on Super Bowl Sunday. That near miss was choreographed by quarterback Stan Humphries, running back Natrone Means and the outstanding play of linebacker Junior Seau.

Back to the future: Ross departed after a disappointing 1996 season and was replaced by Kevin Gilbride. With Seau still anchoring the defense and Humphries throwing to big-play receivers Tony Martin and Eric Metcalf, Gilbride's Chargers are capable of returning to 1994 form if he can find a running game and fill a few defensive holes.

Seattle Seahawks

A MATTER OF RESPECT

In the beginning: The Seahawks were born in the 1976 NFL expansion that also included the Tampa Bay Buccaneers. They struggled to a 2–12 record in their inaugural season under Coach Jack Patera, but two years later they surprised the football world with a 9–7 record. With quarterback Jim Zorn firing to Steve Largent and handing off to Sherman Smith, the 1979 Seahawks proved that was no fluke by duplicating that 9–7 finish.

The glory years: The Seahawks played their most inspired football during the first six years of Coach Chuck Knox's nine-year coaching reign. Knox built his offense around the passing of Dave Krieg, the receiving of Largent, and the 1,000-yard running ability of Curt Warner. He constructed his defense around end Jacob Green and cornerback Kenny Easley. In 1983, the Seahawks posted a 9–7 record, qualified for the playoffs for the first time, and made a Cinderella run to the AFC championship game—beating Denver and Miami before losing to the Los Angeles Raiders. Knox's Seahawks finished 12–4 the next season, 10-6 in 1986 and 9-6 in 1987. But it wasn't until 1988 that Seattle was able to capture its first AFC West title—with a 9–7 mark. The Seahawks managed only a 1–3 record in three playoff appearances after almost qualifying for the Super Bowl after the 1983 season.

Down and out: Since 1988, the Seahawks have posted only one winning record and have not played in the postseason. Knox, Tom Flores and current Coach Dennis Erickson have not been able to lift the losing shroud. One of the highlights of the Knox era was the performance of Largent, who set all-time NFL receiving records for catches, yardage and touchdowns, all of which have since been broken.

That championship feeling: The only bright spots have been the AFC Championship Game in 1983 and the one division title in 1988. Fans can only hope that the best is yet to come.

Back to the future: Erickson has guided the Seahawks to 8–8 and 7–9 records and he does have some offensive weapons at his disposal. John Friesz wrestled the quarterback job away from young Rick Mirer in 1996 and is capable of posting big passing numbers. Joey Galloway is an exciting young receiver, and Chris Warren hopes to return to his 1,000-yard rushing form, although he is being pressed by Lamar Smith. Erickson's biggest challenge is a defense that features tackle Cortez Kennedy, end Michael Sinclair, linebacker Chad Brown and a lot of questions. The 1996 Seahawks surrendered more than 23 points per game.

Making them miss: Seattle Seahawks running back Chris Warren is an elusive runner and hard to bring down in the open field.

FACTS AND FIGURES

CONFERENCE/DIVISION	AFC West
FIRST YEAR IN NFL	1976
STADIUM/CAPACITY/SURFACE	Kingdome (66,400)/Artificial
FORMER CITIES/NICKNAMES	None
SUPER BOWL CHAMPIONSHIPS	None

PLAYING RECORD	W	L	T	PCT
Regular Season	148	176	0	.457
Playoffs (4 Appearances)	3	4	0	.429

Tennessee Oilers

BETTER LUCK NEXT TIME

In the beginning: The Oilers began play as an American Football League original in 1960 and posted a 31–10–1 record in their first three seasons. They also captured AFL championships in their debut and second campaigns and advanced to the AFL title game in 1962. That early power, unfortunately, would never be repeated in the team's 10-year AFL tenure or beyond.

The glory years: The Oilers made their first NFL noise in the late 1970s under colorful Coach Bum Phillips, a consummate Texan.

FACTS AND FIGURES

CONFERENCE/DIVISION	AFC Central
FIRST YEAR IN NFL	1970 (AFL 1960-69)
STADIUM/CAPACITY/SURFACE	Liberty Bowl (62,380)/Grass
FORMER CITIES/NICKNAMES	Houston Oilers (1960-96)
AFL CHAMPIONSHIPS	1960, 1961
SUPER BOWL CHAMPIONSHIPS	None

PLAYING RECORD	W	L	T	PCT
AFL Regular Season	70	66	4	.514
NFL Regular Season	181	225	2	.446
AFL Playoffs	0	0	0	.000
NFL Playoffs	5	7	0	.417

Phillips' offense, featuring strong-armed quarterback Dan Pastorini and five-time 1,000-yard rusher Earl Campbell, was good enough to challenge the powerful Steelers for AFC Central supremacy from 1978 to 1980, but two seasons ended with AFC championship game losses to Pittsburgh and a third concluded with a wild-card loss to Oakland. Both Steelers teams and the Raiders went on to win the Super Bowl. The franchise's next prosperous period began in 1987, when Jerry Glanville started the team on the road to seven straight playoff appearances. Glanville and successor Jack Pardee rode the passing of quarterback Warren Moon to speedy receivers Ernest Givins, Haywood Jeffires and Drew Hill to a pair of division titles, but the teams were not strong enough defensively to get past the second round of the playoffs. Pardee and his run-and-shoot offense were sent packing midway through the 1994 season and the coaching reins were turned over to Jeff Fisher.

Down and out: After their auspicious beginning, the Oilers struggled through a 15-year drought that produced two one-game playoff appearances. Another lull from 1981-86 preceded Glanville's arrival and set the stage for Moon's exciting run at the quarterback controls.

That championship feeling: It all happened too fast. The Oilers captured AFL championships in 1960 and 1961 behind the passing of George Blanda to Billy Cannon—and Houston fans would never see them win again. After 37 years in Southeast Texas, the Oilers packed up operations after the 1996 season and moved the franchise to Nashville. With games scheduled for two seasons at Memphis' Liberty Bowl while a Nashville facility was under construction, the team adopted the name "Tennessee" Oilers.

Back to the future: Fisher and his Oilers finished their final Houston season with an 8–8 record and hopes for a bright future. The optimism centers around young quarterback Steve McNair, running back Eddie George, big-play receiver Chris Sanders and an improving defense.

The future is now: Strong-armed quarterback Steve McNair has been given the starting job for the Oilers in their first season in Tennessee.

Arizona Cardinals

NOWHERE TO GO BUT UP

★ ★ ★ ★ ★ ★ ★ ★ ★ ★ ★ ★

In the beginning: The Cardinals are one of two current franchises that can trace their roots back to the NFL's 1920 inaugural season. The Cardinals began their existence in Chicago, one of three cities they would call home over the years, with a modest 6–2–2 record under coach Paddy Driscoll. They would play 40 seasons in Chicago and 28 in St. Louis before moving to Phoenix after the 1987 campaign. They changed their name from Phoenix Cardinals to Arizona Cardinals after the 1993 season.

The glory years: There haven't been many. The early Cardinals, featuring such players as running backs Driscoll and Ernie Nevers, and center Guy Chamberlin, won a league championship in 1925 and recorded four straight winning records. The 1946–48 Cardinals under Jimmy Conzelman used the running of Charley Trippi and Elmer Angsman to win a pair of Western Division titles and a championship. And the mid-1970s' offensive machine of Don Coryell rolled up points, victories and two more division titles. St. Louis fans enjoyed the Air Coryell production that featured quarterback Jim Hart throwing to such receivers as Mel Gray, Ike Harris and Jackie Smith and handing off to Terry Metcalf and Jim Otis. But Coryell's two division winners lost first-round playoff games and the 1982 team, coached by Jim Hanifan and fueled by five-time 1,000-yard rusher Ottis Anderson, reached the playoffs, only to lose a first-round battle to Green Bay. The team has not made a postseason appearance since.

Down and out: How bad has it been? Over their first 77 seasons, the Cardinals won only four division titles and qualified for postseason play five times. Four of those five playoff ventures ended with first-round losses. After moving to St. Louis in 1960, it took the Cardinals 15 seasons to qualify for the playoffs. Since moving to Phoenix in 1988, the Cardinals have not even posted a winning record.

That championship feeling: The Cardinals have experienced it twice: in the pre-playoff 1925 season and in 1947, when they defeated the Eagles in the first of consecutive championship game appearances. Since 1948, they have not even come close.

Back to the future: Vince Tobin took the coaching reins from fiery Buddy Ryan after the 1995 season and brought a sense of direction back to the team. It might take a few years for Tobin's patient approach to pay dividends, but he has some promising weapons in quarterback Kent Graham, fullback Larry Centers, wide receivers Rob Moore and Frank Sanders, and defensive line stalwarts Simeon Rice and Eric Swann.

FACTS AND FIGURES

CONFERENCE/DIVISION	NFC East
FIRST YEAR IN NFL	1920
STADIUM/CAPACITY/SURFACE	Sun Devil Stadium (73,521)/Grass
FORMER CITIES/NICKNAMES	Chicago Cardinals (1920-59); St. Louis Cardinals (1960-87); Phoenix Cardinals (1988-93)
NFL CHAMPIONSHIPS	1925, 1947
SUPER BOWL CHAMPIONSHIPS	None

PLAYING RECORD	W	L	T	PCT
Regular Season	402	543	39	.417
Playoffs (5 Appearances)	1	4	0	.200

Long look forward: Quarterback Kent Graham has been charged with bringing success to a Cardinals franchise which has not been to the playoffs since its days in St. Louis.

Atlanta Falcons

SEARCHING FOR THE MISSING LINK

In the beginning: The Falcons joined the NFL as an expansion team in 1966, the year the AFL-NFL merger was announced. The team lived up to expansion expectations under first-time Coach Norb Hecker, winning six times over three seasons. The Falcons posted their first winning record (7–6–1) under Norm Van Brocklin in their sixth campaign.

The glory years: The team's best success came from 1978–82 under the direction of Leeman Bennett. With Steve Bartkowski calling the signals and handing off to running backs Dave Hampton and William Andrews, and throwing to Wallace Francis and Alfred Jenkins, the Falcons qualified for the playoffs three times in five seasons, won the franchise's first postseason game and West Division title and made life difficult for the NFC powers. Bartkowski, who passed for 23,468 yards over his 11-year Atlanta career, was the only postseason-caliber quarterback in Falcons' history until Chris Miller directed Jerry Glanville's 1991 "Red Gun" offense to a 10–6 record and a first-round playoff victory and strong-armed Jeff George guided June Jones' 1995 run-and-shoot Falcons to a surprising playoff berth.

Down and out: To say that this franchise has lacked consistency is an understatement. The Falcons have posted only seven winning records in their three-plus decades,

FACTS AND FIGURES

CONFERENCE/DIVISION	NFC West
FIRST YEAR IN NFL	1966
STADIUM/CAPACITY/SURFACE	Georgia Dome (71,280) /Artificial
FORMER CITIES/NICKNAMES	None
NFL CHAMPIONSHIPS	None
SUPER BOWL CHAMPIONSHIPS	None

PLAYING RECORD	W	L	T	PCT
Regular Season	175	284	5	.383
Playoffs (5 Appearances)	2	5	0	.286

and they have never won in back-to-back seasons, despite such big-play performers as Bartkowski, Miller, George, Hampton, Andrews, running back Gerald Riggs and wide receivers Andre Rison, Michael Haynes, Terance Mathis and Eric Metcalf. They have won only one division title (1980) and five playoff appearances have produced only two postseason victories.

That championship feeling: The Falcons have never come close to reaching the Super Bowl. They won playoff games in 1978 and 1991, but that modest success was followed in each case by losing seasons.

Back to the future: New Coach Dan Reeves, who directed the Broncos to three Super Bowl appearances in the 1980s, was hired to perform surgery on a franchise that had stumbled to double-digit losses in nine of 13 seasons. Reeves, the team's third coach in four years, started his rebuilding project by dumping Jones' run-and-shoot offense and installing veteran Chris Chandler at quarterback. Chandler entered his first season with 1,000-yard running back Jamal Anderson and speedy receivers Mathis and Bert Emanuel at his disposal. Reeves' first defense was anchored by veteran linebackers Jessie Tuggle and Cornelius Bennett.

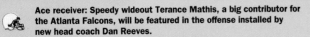
Ace receiver: Speedy wideout Terance Mathis, a big contributor for the Atlanta Falcons, will be featured in the offense installed by new head coach Dan Reeves.

Carolina Panthers

EXPANDING HORIZONS

In the beginning: If it seems like only yesterday that the Panthers made their debut as part of a two-team expansion, that's because in football history terms it was. Carolina unveiled its new product in 1995 and created a sensation by posting a 7–9 record—the best expansion mark in NFL history. Coach Dom Capers' overachievers came within three final-game points of a .500 debut and competed for a wild-card playoff berth into the final weekend. Both the Panthers and the 4–12 Jacksonville Jaguars toppled the previous expansion record of three victories.

FACTS AND FIGURES

CONFERENCE/DIVISION	NFC West
FIRST YEAR IN NFL	1995
STADIUM/CAPACITY/SURFACE	Ericsson Stadium (72,520) /grass
SUPER BOWL CHAMPIONSHIPS	None

PLAYING RECORD	W	L	T	PCT
Regular Season	19	13	0	.594
Playoffs (1 Appearance)	1	1	0	.500

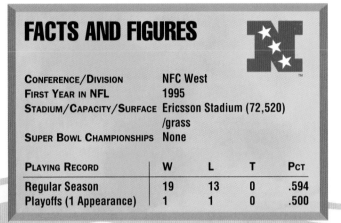

The glory years: There have been two—the team's only two. How do you follow a first-season act like the Panthers put together? You carve out a 12–4 record, claim a share of the NFC West Division title, defeat the vaunted Dallas Cowboys in your first playoff game, and advance to within one game of the Super Bowl. In only their second season, the Panthers matched the number of division titles won by Atlanta, Seattle and New Orleans in their history, they came closer to reaching the "Big Game" than some established franchises have ever come, and they served notice that the NFC power structure has a new player. Since losing the first five games in their 1995 debut season, Carolina has won 20 of its last 29 and appears capable of sustaining that success through the rest of the decade.

Down and out: The 1995 Panthers were down for their first five games. But that frustration was wiped away by a four-game winning streak that included a victory over defending Super Bowl-champion San Francisco and set the stage for their shocking 1996 playoff performance.

That championship feeling: It shouldn't be long in coming. After the Panthers earned a home-field advantage for their divisional playoff battle against Dallas, they treated the fans at new Ericsson Stadium to a 26–17 victory. The euphoria of that success could not be diminished by their 30–13 loss to eventual Super Bowl-champion Green Bay in the NFC title game.

Back to the future: Expectations will be brutal for Capers and company as they try to take that next giant step. But he has the offensive weapons and a veteran defense that ranks among the best in the league. Young quarterback Kerry Collins is a good starting point for an offense that also features running backs Tim Biakabutuka and Anthony Johnson, and receivers Muhsin Muhammad, Rae Carruth and Wesley Walls. Defensive strength can be found in a linebacking corps that features Lamar Lathon, sack-master Kevin Greene and Sam Mills. Kicker John Kasay provides instant points from long range.

On the prowl: Kerry Collins was drafted as the quarterback of the future by Carolina in 1995, but he exceeded almost all expectations by leading the second-year Panthers to the NFC West title in 1996.

Chicago Bears

A GLORIOUS PAST, BY GEORGE

In the beginning: The NFL's most venerable franchise was the creation of George Halas, the famed "Papa Bear" who provided the driving force for Chicago football as founder, player, coach and owner for 64 years before his death in 1983. Halas, one of the NFL's founding fathers in 1920, named his first team the Decatur Staleys, changed it to Chicago Staleys after one season and to Chicago Bears before the 1922 campaign. The Bears won the NFL's second championship in 1921, serving quick notice they would be a title factor for years to come.

Making tracks: The ground game has always been a major part of football in Chicago and the current standard-bearer is third-year back Rashaan Salaam.

FACTS AND FIGURES

CONFERENCE/DIVISION	NFC Central
FIRST YEAR IN NFL	1920
STADIUM/CAPACITY/SURFACE	Soldier Field (66,944)/Grass
FORMER CITIES/NICKNAMES	Decatur Staleys (1920); Chicago Staleys (1921)
NFL CHAMPIONSHIPS	1921, 1932, 1933, 1940, 1941, 1943, 1946, 1963
SUPER BOWL CHAMPIONSHIPS	1985

PLAYING RECORD	W	L	T	PCT
Regular Season	598	394	42	.599
Playoffs (21 Appearances)	13	15	0	.464

The glory years: From 1930 through 1944, the Monsters of the Midway strung together 15 straight winning seasons, won seven Western Division titles and captured five championships. After a 3–7 struggle in 1945, the Bears won another championship and extended their string of winning campaigns to 21 in 22 seasons. The roster of early players reads like a who's who of football: running backs Red Grange and Bronko Nagurski, end Bill Hewitt, quarterback Sid Luckman, guard George Musso, tackle Joe Stydahar and center George Trafton. Sustained success would become elusive until the 1984 Bears, coached by former Chicago star Mike Ditka, began a five-year run that would produce five straight NFC Central Division titles, three trips to the NFC championship game and the team's only Super Bowl victory. Ditka's defensive-minded Bears were powered by linemen Dan Hampton, Steve McMichael, Richard Dent and William (Refrigerator) Perry and linebacker Mike Singletary while free-spirit quarterback Jim McMahon called the offensive signals and handed off to Walter Payton, who would finish his career as the NFL's all-time leading rusher.

Down and out: There was a 25-year lull from 1952 to 1976, but the Bears made the most of their opportunities. Their only two playoff appearances resulted in a trip to the NFC title game and a championship. Even the team's bad times were not unbearable. Such future Hall of Famers as defensive end Doug Atkins, linebackers Bill George and Dick Butkus and running back Gale Sayers passed through town, leaving a memorable trail of blood, sweat and tearful excitement.

That championship feeling: Halas, who divided his 40 years as coach into four 10-year shifts, masterminded six championships. Halas-coached teams won in 1921, 1933, 1940, 1941, 1946 and 1963. The Bears also won in 1932, 1943 and 1985—Ditka's Super Bowl season.

Back to the future: Ditka was replaced after the 1992 season by Dave Wannstedt, who has kept the team competitive. But in order to take that next big step, Wannstedt will have to improve on an offense built around quarterback Rick Mirer, running backs Raymont Harris and Rashaan Salaam, and receiver Curtis Conway.

Dallas Cowboys

A MODEL OF CONSISTENCY

In the beginning: The birth of "America's Team" came inauspiciously in 1960 with an 0–11–1 expansion debut under first-time coach Tom Landry. And it took all the patience owner Clint Murchison Jr. and General Manager Tex Schramm could muster when the young Cowboys bumbled their way to four more losing records and residence among the dregs of the NFL's Eastern Conference. But that patience would pay off as the Cowboys gradually transformed into one of the most revered franchises in football history.

The glory years: The Cowboys, a model of consistency, have had two owners and three coaches over their first 37 years. They have experienced only 10 losing seasons, half of them coming in that 1960–64 beginning. From 1966 to 1985, they strung together an NFL-record 20 straight winning seasons, qualifying for the playoffs in 18 of them. They have appeared in a record eight Super Bowls, winning five.

Down and out: Following their five-year expansion struggle, the Cowboys did not experience another losing stretch until after the 1985 season, when they began rebuilding. During that five-year losing hiatus, Jerry Jones purchased the team and brought in Jimmy Johnson to replace Landry. The Cowboys also began bringing in such players as quarterback Troy Aikman, running back Emmitt Smith, wide receiver Michael Irvin and tight end Jay Novacek to complement a replenished defense. Not even a 1–15 debut by Johnson in 1989 could deter the Cowboys from the path that would lead them back to NFL prominence.

That championship feeling: Five of the team's Super Bowl appearances came under the leadership of quarterback Roger Staubach and resulted in championships after the 1971 and 1977 seasons. Staubach directed an attack that also featured running backs Duane Thomas, Robert Newhouse and Tony Dorsett and receivers Drew Pearson, Golden Richards and Tony Hill. The defense was loaded with tackles Bob Lilly and Randy White, ends Harvey Martin and Ed (Too Tall) Jones, linebacker Lee Roy Jordan and safeties Cliff Harris and Charlie Waters. Johnson's later-edition Cowboys, led by Aikman, Smith and Irvin, stormed to consecutive Eastern Division titles and Super Bowl victories after the 1992 and 1993 campaigns. When Johnson was replaced by Barry Switzer after the 1993 win, the Cowboys captured three consecutive division titles and made another successful Super Bowl run in 1995.

Back to the future: Switzer's Cowboys will continue to be an NFL force as long as Aikman and Smith hold up and management can replenish a defense that has been beset by numerous free-agent defections. The defections have taken their toll, but the 1996 Cowboys still were good enough to share a division title and win a first-round playoff game.

Sooner or later: Former Oklahoma and UCLA quarterback Troy Aikman, one of the NFL's brightest stars, has directed Dallas to three Super Bowl victories.

FACTS AND FIGURES

CONFERENCE/DIVISION	NFC East
FIRST YEAR IN NFL	1960
STADIUM/CAPACITY/SURFACE	Texas Stadium (65,812) /Artificial
FORMER CITIES/NICKNAMES	None
SUPER BOWL CHAMPIONSHIPS	1971, 1977, 1992, 1993, 1995

PLAYING RECORD	W	L	T	PCT
Regular Season	328	212	6	.599
Playoffs (24 Appearances)	32	19	0	.627

Detroit Lions

A BREATH OF FRESH AIR

In the beginning: The franchise was born in 1930 as the Portsmouth Spartans and moved four years later to Detroit. The Lions compiled a 10–3 first-year record and advanced all the way to the NFL championship game in 1935, where they beat the New York Giants. That would be the highlight of the franchise's Detroit existence until Buddy Parker's coaching reign in the 1950s.

The glory years: There have been only two successful stretches. Under Parker and successor George Wilson, the team compiled six winning records in seven seasons, won four conference titles and captured three NFL championships. That run was orchestrated by quarterbacks Bobby Layne and Tobin Rote, running back Doak Walker, end Leon Hart, and defenders Joe Schmidt and Yale Lary. The Lions made only sporadic playoff appearances after that until 1989, when running back Barry Sanders arrived to ignite a stagnant offense. With Sanders topping 1,000 yards in his first eight seasons while capturing three rushing titles, the Lions returned to prominence. They won the NFC Central Division in 1991 and advanced all the way to the NFC championship game. In a five-year stretch, they won another division title and qualified for the playoffs four times.

Down and out: From 1958 to 1990, the Lions made only three quick playoff appearances. During that 33-year stretch, they compiled only 10 winning records and won one division title. That frustration was endured under eight coaches before Wayne Fontes inserted Sanders into his lineup and beefed up his offensive line to open holes for him.

That championship feeling: The Lions have known that feeling only four times, in 1935 under Potsy Clark, in 1952 and 1953 behind Layne and in 1957 behind Rote. Only the 1991 Detroit team came close to qualifying for a Super Bowl and that failure cost Fontes his job after eight seasons. Former San Diego Coach Bobby Ross takes over the coaching reins with a mandate to get the high-scoring Lions into pro football's Big Game.

Back to the future: Ross inherits an offense that starts with Sanders and includes quarterback Scott Mitchell, premier wide receiver Herman Moore and a number of other skill-position weapons. Ross' biggest challenge will be a defense that Fontes could never build to the level of his offense. If he can find the formula for defensive success and strike an offensive balance between the pass and the run, Ross could bring plenty of Super Bowls into Detroit's future.

FACTS AND FIGURES

CONFERENCE/DIVISION	NFC Central
FIRST YEAR IN NFL	1930
STADIUM/CAPACITY/SURFACE	Pontiac Silverdome (80,365) /Artificial
FORMER CITIES/NICKNAMES	Portsmouth Spartans (1930-33)
NFL CHAMPIONSHIPS	1935, 1952, 1953, 1957
SUPER BOWL CHAMPIONSHIPS	None

PLAYING RECORD	W	L	T	PCT
Regular Season	426	439	32	.493
Playoffs (12 Appearances)	7	8	0	.467

Moore the merrier: Detroit Lions' wideout Herman Moore is one of the best possession receivers in the NFL today, and he will be a big part of new head coach Bobby Ross' game plan.

Green Bay Packers

THE LONG ROAD BACK

In the beginning: The Packers, who joined the 1-year-old NFL in 1921, were rescued two years later by a public non-profit corporation that kept the team in business under the direction of Curly Lambeau. More than three-quarters of a century later, the team exists as the only public-owned franchise in sports—and the most successful in NFL history.

The glory years: Green Bay's Vince Lombardi era is the Rembrandt of football success stories. Under the sometimes frightening, always intense direction of Lombardi from 1960 to 1967, the Packers mowed down rivals with methodical consistency en route to an 82–24 regular-season record, six Western Division titles, three

FACTS AND FIGURES

CONFERENCE/DIVISION	NFC Central
FIRST YEAR IN NFL	1921
STADIUM/CAPACITY/SURFACE	Lambeau Field (59,543)/Grass
FORMER CITIES/NICKNAMES	None
NFL CHAMPIONSHIPS	1929, 1930, 1931, 1936, 1939, 1944, 1961, 1962, 1965
SUPER BOWL CHAMPIONSHIPS	1966, 1967, 1996

PLAYING RECORD	W	L	T	PCT
Regular Season	527	437	36	.541
Playoffs (17 Appearances)	20	8	0	.714

NFL championships, and victories in the first two Super Bowls. Lombardi's Packers were molded offensively around quarterback Bart Starr, halfback Paul Hornung, fullback Jim Taylor, wide receivers Carroll Dale, Marv Fleming and Max McGee, tackle Forrest Gregg and center Jim Ringo. End Willie Davis and tackle Henry Jordan anchored a defense that also included linebacker Ray Nitschke, cornerback Herb Adderley, and safety Willie Wood. While that run was the highlight of the franchise's storied history, it wasn't the only one. Lambeau's Packers were a power from 1929–44, thanks to such players as halfback Johnny (Blood) McNally, tackle Cal Hubbard, guard Mike Michalske, quarterbacks Arnie Herber and Cecil Isbell and pass-catching wizard Don Hutson.

Down and out: From 1945 through 1959—Lombardi's first season—the Packers did not qualify for the playoffs. From Lombardi's departure in 1968 through 1992, they made only two cameo postseason appearances. The post-Lombardi frustration built until the 1992 arrival of Coach Mike Holmgren put the franchise back on the fast track.

That championship feeling: Lambeau's team produced championships in 1929, 1930, 1931, 1936, 1939 and 1944. Lombardi's team won in 1961, 1962, 1965, 1966 and 1967. But no Green Bay title team captured the hearts of its fans more thoroughly than the 1996 Packers, who swept to the franchise's first championship in 29 years. Holmgren's Super Bowl triumph was preceded by three consecutive playoff ventures and a loss to Dallas in the 1995 NFC championship game.

Back to the future: Holmgren's Packers appear capable of winning several more Super Bowls before the decade ends. Two-time MVP quarterback Brett Favre is the trigger man for an offense that includes running backs Dorsey Levens and Travis Jervey, and wideouts Antonio Freeman and Robert Brooks. The strength of the defense is up front with Reggie White, Gilbert Brown and Santana Dotson.

The Pack is back: Super Bowl XXXI champion Green Bay Packers is strong in every position and defensive back Craig Newsome (21) makes passing on the Packers as risky as running into Reggie White and Gilbert Brown.

Minnesota Vikings

IMAGES FROZEN IN TIME

★★★★★★★★★★

In the beginning: The Vikings began play in 1961 as the NFL and AFL dug in for what would be a long and costly war. A 3–11 debut and a 2–11–1 second-season disaster prepared hungry Minnesota football fans for the inevitable building process, a patience that would pay big dividends. After seven difficult seasons, the Vikings almost magically turned the frozen tundra of Metropolitan Stadium into the NFL's most dreaded home-field advantage.

The glory years: To say that the Vikings made up for lost time is an understatement. After seven years of frustration, the Vikes reached the Super Bowl in their ninth season. In their 16th, they played in a fourth Super Bowl—more than any team up to that point. Minnesota has been a model of consistency. Since winning the first of 14 NFC Central Division titles in 1968, the Vikings have qualified for postseason play 19 times and won multiple playoff games in eight of those years. Minnesota won four straight division titles from 1968 to 1971, six straight from 1973 to 1978 and 11 of 13 from 1968 to 1980. The downside, of course, is that Minnesota has never won a championship and is one of football's three 0–4 Super Bowl teams.

Down and out: Since their first seven years, the Vikings have struggled only once—a four-year stretch from 1983 to 1986 in which they failed to qualify for the playoffs.

That championship feeling: So close and yet so far. The first brush with success came under Coach Bud Grant in 1969, when quarterback Joe Kapp and a "Purple People Eater" defense featuring Carl Eller, Jim Marshall and Alan Page led a charge that produced a 12–2 regular-season record, two playoff wins and a berth in Super Bowl IV. But the heavily favored Vikings were upset by

AFL-champion Kansas City. Four years later, scrambling quarterback Fran Tarkenton and hard-running Chuck Foreman sparked another surge that resulted in three Super Bowl appearances in four years. But Minnesota lost to Miami, Pittsburgh and Oakland. The Vikings have not been to a Super Bowl in two decades now, but they have seldom been far away. Under current Coach Dennis Green, the Vikings can boast of four postseason appearances in five years.

Back to the future: While the Vikings have been making the playoffs under Green, they have failed to get out of the first round. Green, trying to get his team out of neutral, has turned the offense over to untested quarterback Brad Johnson, who can throw to one of the NFL's best receiving tandems—Cris Carter and Jake Reed. Tackle John Randle and linebacker Ed McDaniel are the centerpieces for a capable defense.

FACTS AND FIGURES

CONFERENCE/DIVISION	NFC Central
FIRST YEAR IN NFL	1961
STADIUM/CAPACITY/SURFACE	Metrodome (64,035)/Artificial
FORMER CITIES/NICKNAMES	None
NFL CHAMPIONSHIPS	1969
SUPER BOWL CHAMPIONSHIPS	None

PLAYING RECORD	W	L	T	PCT
Regular Season	289	236	9	.550
Playoffs (19 Appearances)	13	19	0	.406

Get it to Carter: Cris Carter has been the big receiver in the Minnesota offense for a number of years, but in 1997 he will be catching bombs from Brad Johnson instead of Warren Moon.

New Orleans Saints

DEFENSE AND FUNDAMENTALS

★★★★★★★★★★

In the beginning: The Saints were born in 1967 and experienced long-term growing pains. A 3–11 debut season under Tom Fears was just about as good as it would get for the team's first two decades.

The glory years: There have been no championships and the Saints have not even won a playoff game in their 30 NFL seasons. But all has not been bleak. New Orleans actually was an NFC force through most of the coaching reign of Jim Mora, who introduced his New Orleans team to the gospel of fundamentals and defense. Mora's teams were not exciting, but they were successful. Featuring an outstanding linebacking corps of Rickey Jackson, Sam Mills, Pat Swilling and Vaughan Johnson, the Saints compiled winning records in five of the six seasons from 1987 through 1992 and won the franchise's first division title in 1991. But they were consistently frustrated by NFC West Division rival San Francisco, which was winning Super Bowls and deflating hopes of other NFC contenders. When matched against the 49ers, the ball-control offense with Bobby Hebert and Jim Everett handing off to Dalton Hilliard and Rueben Mayes and passing to Eric Martin simply was not strong enough to be successful in the playoffs.

Down and out: The Saints' early history is a story of frustration. It took the franchise 20 seasons, eight coaches, 196 losses and 11 last-place division finishes to post its first winning record—a 12–3 mark in 1987. Things got so bad in 1980 that the fans, watching their team struggle to a 1–15 record, attended games wearing bags over their heads, not wishing to be identified. Before 1987, the Saints could boast of only one finish above third place while playing for most of their existence in four-team divisions.

That championship feeling: New Orleans fans have no choice but to remain optimistic. Their teams have made four playoff appearances—and lost first-round games each time. Any revival will have to come under new Coach Mike Ditka, who replaced Mora after the Saints struggled to a 3–13 record in 1996.

Back to the future: Ditka brings an old-style philosophy—and a new quarterback—to New Orleans. Ditka, who guided the 1985

Chicago Bears to a Super Bowl championship, had not coached since moving to the broadcast booth in 1992. But he quickly began shuffling the Saints' deck, signing free-agent quarterback Heath Shuler and handing incumbent Everett his walking papers. Shuler will operate with running back Mario Bates and wide receiver Randal Hill, but Ditka will have to do a lot more shuffling before he returns the Saints' defense to contending status.

Best defense: Hard-hitting defensive back Mario Bates is sure to become one of new head Coach Mike Ditka's favorite players.

FACTS AND FIGURES

CONFERENCE/DIVISION	NFC West
FIRST YEAR IN NFL	1967
STADIUM/CAPACITY/SURFACE	Louisiana Superdome (70,852) /Artificial
FORMER CITIES/NICKNAMES	None
NFL CHAMPIONSHIPS	None
SUPER BOWL CHAMPIONSHIPS	None

PLAYING RECORD	W	L	T	PCT
Regular Season	177	268	5	.399
Playoffs (4 Appearances)	0	4	0	.000

★★★★★★★★★★★★

New York Giants

SEVERAL GIANT STEPS FORWARD

In the beginning: Tim Mara's Giants began operation in 1925, the NFL's sixth season. They jumped into title contention quickly, carving out 8–4 and 8–4–1 records in their first two campaigns before an 11–1–1 third season that produced a championship. The early years, especially the 1930s and

FACTS AND FIGURES

CONFERENCE/DIVISION	NFC East
FIRST YEAR IN NFL	1925
STADIUM/CAPACITY/SURFACE	Giants Stadium (78,148) /Artificial
FORMER CITIES/NICKNAMES	None
NFL CHAMPIONSHIPS	1927, 1934, 1938, 1956
SUPER BOWL CHAMPIONSHIPS	1986, 1990

PLAYING RECORD	W	L	T	PCT
Regular Season	513	424	32	.546
Playoffs (23 Appearances)	14	18	0	.438

1940s under Coach Steve Owen, were filled with success, excitement and memorable moments supplied by Hall of Fame-caliber players.

The glory years: Owen guided the Giants to eight Eastern Division titles, eight NFL championship games and two championships in his impressive 24-year coaching reign. He coaxed such outstanding players as quarterbacks Eddie Danowski and Frank Filchock, running backs Tuffy Leemans and Ward Cuff, center Mel Hein and defensive back Emlen Tunnell to sustained success. After a brief lull, the Giants reloaded, with running backs Frank Gifford and Alex Webster, quarterbacks YA Tittle and Charley Conerly, offensive tackle Roosevelt Brown and linebacker Sam Huff leading another charge that produced another championship and six title-game appearances over an eight-year span from 1956–63. The Giants would not return to prominence until the arrival of Coach Bill Parcells in 1983, the beginning of another nice run that ended with his departure eight years later.

Down and out: Parcells' first-year record of 3–12–1 ended a 20-year blur in which the Giants managed only three winning records and one playoff appearance. The team's only other extended down period had occurred from 1947–55, when the Giants managed only one playoff appearance over nine seasons.

That championship feeling: The Giants hold the record for championship-game losses. They won titles in 1927, 1934, 1938 and 1956 but finished second 11 times through 1963. Parcells, who built a defensive monster around linebackers Lawrence Taylor, Carl Banks and Harry Carson and ends George Martin and Leonard Marshall, added Super Bowl championships after the 1986 and 1990 seasons. Quarterbacks Phil Simms and Jeff Hostetler and running backs Joe Morris and Ottis Anderson carried the offensive load for those two winners.

Back to the future: The Giants have made only one playoff appearance since winning Super Bowl XXV, and Jim Fassel was hired after the 1996 season to rekindle the fire. Fassel, who replaced Dan Reeves, is building around quarterback Dave Brown, running back Tyrone Wheatley, receivers Ike Hilliard and Chris Calloway and a pair of top-notch defensive backs—Phillippi Sparks and Jason Sehorn.

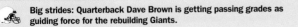

Big strides: Quarterback Dave Brown is getting passing grades as guiding force for the rebuilding Giants.

Philadelphia Eagles

A RAY OF HOPE

In the beginning: The Eagles were born in 1933, when Bert Bell purchased the old Frankford Yellow Jackets. Bell's Eagles broke out of the gate slowly, recording losing marks in each of their first 10 seasons and failing to generate anything resembling excitement until Greasy Neale led them around the corner in the mid-1940s.

The glory years: Neale's Eagles were a force for only three years, but that short run produced three Eastern Division titles and a pair of NFL championships. The next golden period started in 1978 under Coach Dick Vermeil, who kept the franchise in title contention for four seasons and took the Eagles to their only Super Bowl. Coach Buddy Ryan arrived in 1986 and fashioned an outstanding defense that carried the Eagles to an Eastern Division title and three consecutive playoff appearances, all of which ended with disappointing first-round losses that cost Ryan his job. Ryan's defense, featuring ends Reggie White and Clyde Simmons, tackle Jerome Brown, linebacker Seth Joyner and cornerback Eric Allen, broke up under new Coach Rich Kotite, who enjoyed only spotty success in his four seasons.

Down and out: After struggling through their first 14 seasons without so much as a playoff sniff, the Eagles enjoyed that three-year run under Neale before beginning a 28-year drought that produced only one postseason appearance—a 1960 NFL championship game victory. After Vermeil's modest run, the Eagles went another six years before Ryan could return them to title contention.

That championship feeling: The Eagles' 1948 and 1949 championships were keyed by the impressive quarterback/running back combination of Tommy Thompson and Steve Van Buren. The surprising 1960 championship was choreographed by Coach Buck Shaw and featured Norm Van Brocklin throwing to Tommy McDonald and handing off to rookie running back Ted Dean. The last of the great two-way players, center/linebacker Chuck Bednarik played on both the 1949 and 1960 teams. Vermeil's Super Bowl XV offense was built around quarterback Ron Jaworski, three-time 1,000-yard rusher Wilbert Montgomery and wide receiver Harold Carmichael. For a team that reached the playoffs only 14 times over its first 64 years, the Eagles have been productive—three championships and two title-game losses.

Back to the future: Kotite gave way after the 1994 season to Ray Rhodes, who guided the Eagles to consecutive playoff appearances. Rhodes is mapping out his plan for continued success around running back Ricky Watters, quarterback Ty Detmer and veteran receiver Irving Fryar. If Rhodes can rebuild a young defense around tackle Andy Harmon and corners Troy Vincent and Bobby Taylor, he could be in business.

Running Watters: Former 49ers star Ricky Watters has brought respect to the Eagles' running game.

FACTS AND FIGURES

CONFERENCE/DIVISION	NFC East
FIRST YEAR IN NFL	1933
STADIUM/CAPACITY/SURFACE	Veterans Stadium (64,889) /Artificial
FORMER CITIES/NICKNAMES	None
NFL CHAMPIONSHIPS	1948, 1949, 1960
SUPER BOWL CHAMPIONSHIPS	None

PLAYING RECORD	W	L	T	PCT
Regular Season	376	442	3	.461
Playoffs (13 Appearances)	9	11	0	.450

St. Louis Rams

ANOTHER NEW BEGINNING

★★★★★★★

In the beginning: The Cleveland Rams began play in 1937 under Dan Reeves, the man who would turn the NFL into a coast-to-coast operation nine years later with a move to Los Angeles. Before heading west after the 1945 season, Reeves and the Rams gave Cleveland fans a going-away present—the team's first winning record and the first of two NFL championships.

The glory years: From 1973 to 1989, Los Angeles was one of the most consistent teams in the NFL. Coaches Chuck Knox, Ray Malavasi and John Robinson guided the Rams to eight NFC West Division titles (seven in a row), 14 playoff appearances in 17 years and their only Super Bowl appearance. Seven times the Rams reached the NFC championship game but they won only one. The team went through a succession of quarterbacks (John Hadl, James Harris, Pat Haden, Vince Ferragamo) and some sensational running backs (Wendell Tyler, Cullen Bryant, Lawrence McCutcheon, Eric Dickerson). Defensive standouts included ends Fred Dryer and Jack Youngblood, linebackers Jim Youngblood and Jack (Hacksaw) Reynolds and safety Nolan Cromwell. The bottom finally fell out in 1990. It marked the first of seven straight losing campaigns, two of which came after a 1995 franchise move to St. Louis.

Down and out: The Rams' first seven seasons all resulted in losing records, but the longest stretch of frustration lasted from 1956 to 1972. Those 17 seasons produced only two playoff appearances and nothing resembling a title run. Despite the presence of such players as quarterback Roman Gabriel and the "Fearsome Foursome" defensive line of Merlin Olsen, Rosey Grier, Deacon Jones and Lamar Lundy, the Rams couldn't turn the corner until late 1972, when Baltimore Owner Carroll Rosenbloom traded his Colts to Los Angeles Owner Robert Irsay for his Rams. Rosembloom began a new era by replacing Coach Tommy Prothro with Knox.

That championship feeling: The team's only two titles came in 1945 and 1951. Quarterback Bob Waterfield orchestrated the first title run and Waterfield and fellow quarterback Norm Van Brocklin the second. The Rams' only other brush with destiny occurred after the 1979 season when they lost in Super Bowl XIV to Pittsburgh.

Back to the future: The Rams head toward the 21st century with a new coach and a young team that appears on the brink of resuscitation. Dick Vermeil, the former Eagles coach who was lured out of retirement, has a young quarterback in Tony Banks, and a pair of top-notch receivers in Eddie Kennison and Isaac Bruce. The key is what Vermeil can prod out of a defense that features linebacker Roman Phifer and young safeties Keith Lyle and Toby Wright.

Better to receive: Speedy, sure-handed, wide receiver Isaac Bruce is second-year quarterback Tony Banks' favorite target in St. Louis.

FACTS AND FIGURES

CONFERENCE/DIVISION	NFC West
FIRST YEAR IN NFL	1937
STADIUM/CAPACITY/SURFACE	Trans World Dome (66,000) /Artificial
FORMER CITIES/NICKNAMES	Cleveland Rams (1937-45); Los Angeles Rams (1946-94)
NFL CHAMPIONSHIPS	1945, 1951
SUPER BOWL CHAMPIONSHIPS	None

PLAYING RECORD	W	L	T	PCT
Regular Season	411	368	20	.538
Playoffs (22 Appearances)	13	20	0	.394

San Francisco 49ers

FIVE AND COUNTING

★ ★ ★ ★ ★ ★ ★ ★ ★ ★ ★ ★

In the beginning: The 49ers made their professional football debut as members of the All-America Football Conference in 1946 and were one of the three AAFC franchises absorbed by the NFL when the league folded after four seasons. Early life in the NFL was not kind as the 49ers struggled to a 3–9 debut in 1950 and failed to make their first playoff appearance until 1957.

The glory years: Consecutive NFC championship game appearances in 1970 and 1971 were simply warmups for the glorious 1980s and 1990s, when coaches Bill Walsh and George Seifert and quarterbacks Joe Montana and Steve Young directed the 49ers to 13 full or shared NFC West Division tites and five Super Bowl wins. The 1970, 1971 and 1972 49ers, guided by coach Dick Nolan and featuring the passing of John Brodie to Gene Washington, put together an impressive run that netted the first three division titles in the team's history and two NFC title game appearances. But they couldn't match the excellence that would follow. With Montana directing Walsh's West Coast offense and deploying such weapons as running backs Wendell Tyler, Roger Craig and Ricky Watters and receivers Dwight Clark, Freddie Solomon, Jerry Rice and John Taylor, the 49ers rose to prominence in the1980s and sustained success throughout the decade and well into the next. Walsh gave way to Seifert after the 1989 season, and Montana handed the reins to Young in 1991, but the 49ers continued winning division titles and captured their fifth Super Bowl after the 1994 season.

Down and out: San Francisco fans earned their 1980s reward the hard way. From 1950 through 1980, the team made only four playoff appearances (three in that 1970-72 run) and won only three division titles (all from 1970-72).

That championship feeling: Montana's outstanding leadership and ability to perform in the clutch was complemented by such outstanding defenders as linebacker Jack Reynolds, end Fred Dean, nose tackle Michael Carter, and cornerbacks Ronnie Lott and Eric Wright. The result was Super Bowl championships after the 1981, 1984, 1988 and 1989 seasons. With Young at the controls in 1994, the 49ers defeated San Diego in Super Bowl XXIX—their then-record fifth Super Bowl victory.

Back to the future: Seifert resigned after a 12-4 1996 season that ended with a divisional playoff loss to Green Bay. Inexperienced former University of California Coach Steve Mariucci takes the reins, but he should learn fast with the Young-Rice combination still intact. An aging defense and injury-prone skill-position players offer Mariucci a serious challenge.

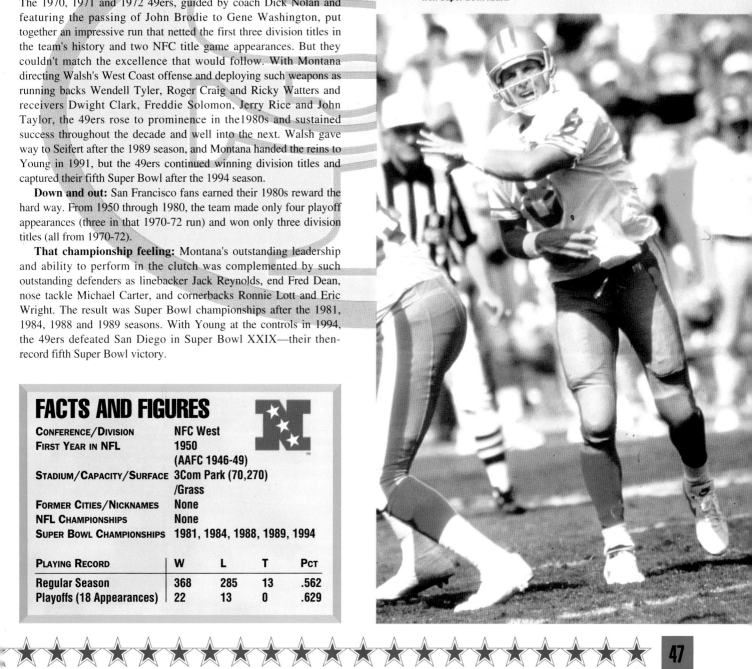

49ers gold: Steve Young was the cornerstone of the NFL's top team in 1994. San Francisco's quarterback was the MVP as the 49ers won Super Bowl XXIX.

FACTS AND FIGURES

CONFERENCE/DIVISION	NFC West
FIRST YEAR IN NFL	1950 (AAFC 1946-49)
STADIUM/CAPACITY/SURFACE	3Com Park (70,270) /Grass
FORMER CITIES/NICKNAMES	None
NFL CHAMPIONSHIPS	None
SUPER BOWL CHAMPIONSHIPS	1981, 1984, 1988, 1989, 1994

PLAYING RECORD	W	L	T	PCT
Regular Season	368	285	13	.562
Playoffs (18 Appearances)	22	13	0	.629

Tampa Bay Buccaneers

ONWARD AND UPWARD

In the beginning: When the Buccaneers were born in 1976 as the baby of Florida attorney Hugh Culverhouse, everybody expected them to suffer the expansion blues. But nobody had envisioned how blue that beginning would be. Under the direction of Coach John McKay, the first-year Bucs failed to win a game. And so did the second-year Bucs until the losing streak had reached an NFL-record 26 games. They finally broke through in the second-to-last game with a 33–14 victory at Tampa Bay and celebrated that success with a season-closing 17–7 home win over St. Louis.

The glory years: Tampa, like Camelot, has enjoyed one, brief, shining moment—a four-year fling started in 1979 when the fourth-year Bucs surprised the football establishment with a 10–6 record, the team's first NFC Central Division title and a playoff run that ended in the NFC championship game, one victory short of a Super Bowl. That season was choreographed by McKay around quarterback Doug Williams, who passed for 2,448 yards, and Ricky Bell, who ran for 1,263 more. A rock-solid defense was centered by Lee Roy Selmon, the team's first-ever draft choice in 1976, linebacker Richard Wood and backs Cedric Brown and Mike Washington. The Bucs sagged back to 5–10–1 in 1980, but they added linebacker Hugh Green and running back James Wilder before bouncing back in 1981 to win another division title and claim the first of consecutive playoff appearances.

Down and out: Since their 1982 first-round playoff loss to Dallas, the Bucs have not been sighted anywhere in the postseason. They rarely have been sighted in the victory column. McKay and successors Leeman Bennett, Ray Perkins, Richard Williamson and Sam Wyche labored in vain to stop a streak that produced 12 straight double-digit losing seasons. When Wyche finally carved out a 7–9 record in 1995, he was fired anyway and Tony Dungy led the Bucs to a familiar 6–10 record in 1996.

That championship feeling: Aside from 1979-82, the Bucs seldom have come close to a winning record, much less a championship. The bright side is that their fans suspect the best is yet to come.

Back to the future: Despite Dungy's first-year struggle, the future actually looks bright. The Bucs finished with a 5–2 flurry in 1996 and quarterback Trent Dilfer began playing like the franchise player Tampa Bay was expecting when it drafted him sixth overall in 1994. Dilfer has a double backfield threat in Errict Rhett and Warrick Dunn and can throw to Horace Copeland and Robb Thomas. A defense featuring Hardy Nickerson in the middle and Donnie Abraham at one corner could be ready to help the Bucs reach for new heights.

On the run: Tampa Bay made big strides forward at the end of 1996 under first-year Coach Tony Dungy, and running back Errict Rhett (above) played his part in the improvement.

FACTS AND FIGURES

CONFERENCE/DIVISION	NFC Central
FIRST YEAR IN NFL	1976
STADIUM/CAPACITY/SURFACE	Houlihan's Stadium (74,301)/Grass
FORMER CITIES/NICKNAMES	None
SUPER BOWL CHAMPIONSHIPS	None

PLAYING RECORD	W	L	T	PCT
Regular Season	100	223	1	.310
Playoffs (3 Appearances)	1	3	0	.250

Washington Redskins

A TOUGH ACT TO FOLLOW

In the beginning: The Team began play in 1932 as the Boston Braves and spent the next four seasons as the Boston Redskins before moving to Washington. The final Boston season produced an Eastern Division title and set the stage for the team's first championship.

The glory years: The Redskins' first sustained success was orchestrated by passing wizard Sammy Baugh, who deployed such offensive weapons as Jack Manders and Cliff Battles en route to two championships and NFL title game appearances in six of 10 seasons from 1936–45. The team would not rediscover such success until Coach George Allen's 1971 arrival triggered another six-year run. Quarterbacks Sonny Jurgensen and Billy Kilmer, running back Larry Brown and wide receiver Charley Taylor keyed a 1972 charge that took the Redskins all the way to the Super Bowl, where they lost to Miami. But everything up to 1981 was just a warmup for the Joe Gibbs era. Over Gibbs' 12 Washington seasons, the Redskins recorded 10 winning records, won four NFC titles and captured three Super Bowl championships—more than any team except San Francisco over that span.

Down and out: From 1943 to 1970, the Redskins managed only seven winning seasons and one playoff appearance. From 1977 to 1981, they failed to qualify for postseason play.

That championship feeling: Baugh's Redskins won titles in 1937 and 1942, but that was it until Gibbs arrived. Gibbs had plenty to work with in his first Super Bowl season: a beefy and talented offensive line called the "Hogs," a powerful running back in John Riggins, a heady quarterback in Joe Theismann and speedy receivers in Art Monk, Charlie Brown and Alvin Garrett. The defense, anchored by end Dexter Manley and tackle Dave Butz, was deep and talented. Those Redskins defeated Miami in Super Bowl XVII and they went on to win two more Super Bowls, one after the 1987 season behind Williams and another after the 1991 campaign behind Mark Rypien. Gibbs retired after one final playoff appearance in 1992.

Back to the future: After a 4–12 disaster in 1993 under Richie Petitbon, Norv Turner took the coaching reins and began reshaping the roster. The 1996 Redskins, with quarterback Gus Frerotte and 1,000-yard rusher Terry Allen operating behind a solid offensive line, just missed the playoffs with a 9–7 record. They should improve steadily with the addition of Cris Dishman to a secondary that already includes veteran Darrell Green, the maturing of receiver Michael Westbrook and defensive help in the middle for linebacker Ken Harvey.

FACTS AND FIGURES

CONFERENCE/DIVISION	NFC East
FIRST YEAR IN NFL	1932
STADIUM/CAPACITY/SURFACE	Jack Kent Cooke Stadium (78,400)/Grass
FORMER CITIES/NICKNAMES	Boston Braves (1932); Boston Redskins (1933-36)
NFL CHAMPIONSHIPS	1937, 1942
SUPER BOWL CHAMPIONSHIPS	1982, 1987, 1991

PLAYING RECORD	W	L	T	PCT
Regular Season	448	392	26	.532
Playoffs (19 Appearances)	21	14	0	.600

Coming attraction: Redskins quarterback Gus Frerotte beat off the challenge of highly-touted Heath Shuler to become the Washington starter, and the offense is now in his hands.

NFL fans

Texas hero: Defensive tackle Bob Lilly was born, raised and educated in Texas, so he was a natural to be the Dallas Cowboys' first-ever draft pick.

Four-ring runner: In addition to winning four Super Bowls rings, Franco Harris ranks as Pittsburgh's all-time rushing leader with 11,950 yards.

They're the one constant in the National Football League's universe, the electricity that illuminates its game. They energize and re-energize it with their special talents, draw attention to it with their brilliance.

Players come and players go, but the stars will shine forever. In our memories. In our hearts. In our record books.

Who can forget the stutter-stepping of Walter Payton? The powerful determination of Jim Brown? The graceful pass-catching artistry of Lynn Swann? The frightful intensity of Dick Butkus and Ray Nitschke? The winning legacies of Otto Graham and Bart Starr?

Because those images stick in our minds and make us lust for more, professional football has grown into the No 1 spectator sport in the United States. One of football's greatest assets has been the impact its star players have on fan interest.

Sports has always needed its superstars and the NFL has provided a steady succession since the arrival of Red Grange, Ernie Nevers and Bronko Nagurski in the 1920s and 1930s. And, conversely, the brilliance of those stars often has been dictated by the needs of the game.

reach for the stars

When rules were made to encourage more passing in the 1930s, quarterbacks like Sammy Baugh and Sid Luckman began mesmerizing a growing fan base with unprecedented aerial displays. When the NFL needed help in its battle with the All-America Football Conference after World War II, runners like Charley Trippi and Steve Van Buren joined such quarterbacks as Bobby Layne and Bob Waterfield in a new talent explosion.

The Cleveland Browns ruled the 1950s with an all-star cast featuring Graham, Lou Groza, Marion Motley, Frank Gatski and Dante Lavelli, and the Green Bay Packers dominated the 1960s behind Starr and supporting stars Paul Hornung, Jerry Kramer, Jim Taylor, Forrest Gregg, Willie Davis and Herb Adderley.

All through football history, the game has been bolstered by unexpected individual feats—athletic performances previously beyond comprehension. When Chicago's Beattie Feathers became the NFL's first 1,000-yard rusher in 1934, everyone gasped. When Brown ran for 1,527 yards in 1958 and 1,863 five years later, everyone was astounded. And when Simpson topped 2,000 yards in 1973, everyone watched in disbelief.

Others claimed the spotlight with great individual performances. Colts quarterback Johnny Unitas threw at least one touchdown pass in 47 straight games from 1956 to 1960. The Bears' Luckman was the first quarterback to pass for seven touchdowns in a single game in 1943. Baltimore's Lenny Moore, one of Unitas' favorite targets, set a record by scoring touchdowns in 18 consecutive games from 1963-65. John Riggins of the Redskins scored 24 touchdowns in the 1983 season. And Walter Payton of the Bears ran for a single-game record 275 yards in 1977.

Miami featured the running back tandem of Larry Csonka, Jim Kiick and Mercury Morris, which led the Dolphins to a perfect 17-0 season in 1972 and consecutive Super Bowl victories. Even more fearsome was the Pittsburgh Steel Curtain that shrouded the NFL in the late 1970s, producing four Super Bowl titles in six years with a defense featuring Mean Joe Greene, LC Greenwood, Mel Blount, Dwight White and the Hall of Fame linebacking duo of Jack Ham and Jack Lambert.

For pure viewing pleasure, you couldn't go wrong with the grace and consistency of receivers like Don Hutson and Paul Warfield, the power and brute force of linemen like Ron Mix and Roosevelt Brown, the strength and intensity of defenders like Bob Lilly and Buck Buchanan, the speed and power of running backs like Riggins, Earl Campbell and Franco Harris and the combination running-passing skills of quarterbacks like Fran Tarkenton and Roger Staubach.

But nobody could fill a spotlight quite like New York Jets quarterback Joe Namath. Broadway Joe's powerful right arm helped the American Football League's Jets prosper in the years leading up to the merger with the NFL and his "I guarantee a victory" speech fueled one of the greatest upsets in sports history—the Jets' 16-7 victory over the Baltimore Colts in Super Bowl III.

The memories, and the stars, indeed will shine forever.

Piloting the Jets: Joe Namath was a New York sportswriter's dream: brash, controversial, glamorous and, most importantly, successful. He "guaranteed" the Jets' Super Bowl III victory.

Troy Aikman

★★★★★ **ENGOYING THE SUPER LIFE**

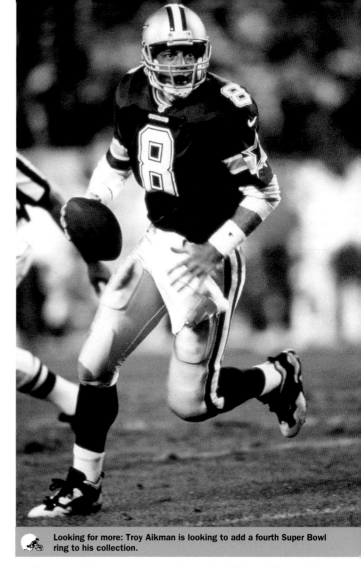

Troy Aikman has experienced life at both ends of the professional football spectrum. His status as quarterback of the three-time Super Bowl-champion Dallas Cowboys is tempered by memories of a humbling 1–15 rookie season—a memory that helps keep everything in perspective.

"I have one 1–15 season in me, and then I'm done," Aikman says. "That made me appreciate the NFL and understand how difficult it is to win."

To say that Aikman, who played collegiately at Oklahoma and UCLA, entered the NFL under difficult circumstances is a massive understatement. As the first overall pick of the 1989 draft, the strong-armed youngster was hailed as the "next Roger Staubach" by down-and-out Cowboys fans. And new Coach Jimmy Johnson fanned the speculation by pushing his $11.2-million quarterback into the heat of battle.

In the 11 games Aikman started as a rookie, the Cowboys were winless and much of his first season was spent on his back, looking up at the world through bleary eyes. The perspective that came from the experience was painful, but it also was invaluable during his transformation from a first-year caterpillar into an NFL butterfly.

When running back Emmitt Smith arrived in 1990 and Johnson began filling key positions around his quarterback (receivers Michael Irvin and Alvin Harper, tight end Jay Novacek, a huge offensive line), life improved quickly. The 1990 Cowboys jumped to 7–9 and the 1991 team, with a poised, mistake-free Aikman as its centerpiece, won 11 of 16 games before suffering a divisional playoff loss to Detroit.

Looking for more: Troy Aikman is looking to add a fourth Super Bowl ring to his collection.

There would be no postseason losses in 1992 or 1993 as Aikman directed the Cowboys to consecutive NFC Championship Game victories over San Francisco and Super Bowl victories over Buffalo. Super Bowl XXVII, a 52–17 rout of the Bills, belonged to Aikman, who completed 22 of 30 passes for 273 yards and four touchdowns en route to MVP honors.

"He can throw the heck out of the football, and he never complains."

ROGER STAUBACH

After a 1994 loss to the 49ers in the NFC Championship Game, the Cowboys, now coached by Barry Switzer, returned to the Super Bowl spotlight in 1995, defeating Pittsburgh, 27–17. Through it all, Aikman has accepted life as the unspectacular director of a machine-like offense that appears to operate on its own—not unlike the Roger Staubach and Bart Starr offenses of yesteryear.

"He can throw the heck out of the football, and he never complains," says Staubach. "He could put up numbers like Dan Marino because he has that much talent."

But the outspoken Aikman prefers the Super Bowls—and he leads his teammates with a team-first attitude that makes such success possible. His 62.9 percent completion percentage defines a career that has produced an 80–44 regular-season record in games he has started. That's not bad when you consider he started off 0–11.

PERSONAL

BIRTHPLACE/DATE   West Covina, Calif./10-11-70
HEIGHT/WEIGHT   6-4, 228

AWARDS

PRO BOWL SELECTIONS   1991-96 seasons
SUPER BOWL MVP   XXVII

CAREER

UNIVERSITY   Oklahoma, UCLA
DRAFT POSITION   1st Round (1st overall), Dallas, 1989
PRO TEAMS   8 Seasons, Dallas Cowbays (1989-96)

RUSHING, RECEIVING RECORD

	PASSING					
	ATT	COMP	YDS	PCT	INT	TD
REGULAR SEASON	3,178	2,000	22,733	62.9	98	110
POSTSEASON	415	276	3,372	66.5	13	22
	RUSHING					
	ATT	YDS	AVG	TD		
REGULAR SEASON	249	845	3.4	6		
POSTSEASON	31	87	2.8	1		

Eric Dickerson

★★★★★★★

MAN ON THE RUN

The first thing you noticed about running back Eric Dickerson was the glide. His feet seemed to hydroplane over a football field like a speedboat barely touching water. When Dickerson exploded through the line, nobody even felt an aftershock.

That glide was only one of Dickerson's gifts. Of more importance were his ability to accelerate through an opening and the unexplainable instinct that allowed him to rush for 13,259 career yards, second only to Walter Payton's all-time record of 16,726.

"I can't remember seeing any back with more talent than Eric," said Hall of Fame running back OJ Simpson midway through the 1984 season. "And that includes myself and Gale Sayers. He is the best I've seen, and I mean ever."

> ## "Every time Eric gets the ball, I say, 'Oh my God, he has a chance to break it.'"
>
> **FORMER RAMS COACH JOHN ROBINSON**

Ironically, Dickerson was on his way to the greatest single-season rushing total in NFL history (2,105 yards) when Simpson offered that assessment. Dickerson's 16-game total would break Simpson's 14-game 2,003-yard effort of 1973—the only other 2,000-yard performance in NFL history.

Dickerson, who was selected out of Southern Methodist University by the Los Angeles Rams with the second overall pick of the 1983 draft, had set the stage for that 1984 explosion with record-shattering rookie totals for rushing attempts (390), yards (1,808) and touchdowns (18).

In the clear: Eric Dickerson set the NFL single-season rushing record in 1984 when he ran for 2,105 yards for the Los Angeles Rams.

PERSONAL

BIRTHPLACE/DATE	Sealy, Tex/9-2-60
HEIGHT/WEIGHT	6-3, 220

AWARDS

PRO BOWL SELECTIONS	1983-84, 1986-89 seasons
SUPER BOWL MVP	None

CAREER

UNIVERSITY	Southern Methodist
DRAFT POSITION	1st Round (2nd overall), L.A. Rams, 1983
PRO TEAMS	11 Seasons, Los Angeles Rams (1983-87); Indianapolis Colts (1987-91); Los Angeles Raiders (1992); Atlanta Falcons (1993)

RUSHING, RECEIVING RECORD

	RUSHING				RECEIVING		
	ATT	**YDS**	**AVG**	**TD**	**NO**	**YDS**	**TD**
REGULAR SEASON	2,996	13,259	4.4	90	281	2,137	6
POSTSEASON	148	724	4.9	3	19	91	1

"Every time Eric gets the ball, I say, 'Oh my God, he has a chance to break it,'" marveled former Rams coach John Robinson. "Whenever he doesn't do something unbelievable, you're disappointed."

Dickerson didn't stop running after 1984. For seven consecutive seasons he passed the 1,000-yard barrier, another NFL record. His lowest total during that span was 1,234.

When relations broke down between Dickerson and the Rams over a contract in 1987, he became the focal point of a different kind of record. He was traded to Indianapolis as part of a three-team, 10-player deal that netted the Rams two players and six draft choices.

The change of scenery did not have an immediate effect on Dickerson's production. He finished off his fifth 1,000-yard season in 1987 and added two more for the Colts before injuries and age began taking their toll.

Dickerson, a six-time Pro Bowl invitee, concluded his career in 1993 after one-season stints in Los Angeles (with the Raiders) and Atlanta.

Tony Dorsett

★★★★★★★★★ **LITTLE BIG MAN**

A t first glance, Tony Dorsett appeared out of place among the big, hard bodies of the National Football League. Most 5-foot-11, 185-pound running backs have an NFL career expectancy of two or three crunching hits.

But Dorsett was not your normal, everyday back. Blessed with incredible balance and an ability to suddenly change direction, he darted, he slashed, he cut against the grain and he masterfully avoided tacklers for 12 seasons en route to 12,739 yards and a third-place ranking on the all-time rushing charts.

Such success was nothing new for Touchdown Tony, who earned his nickname and a Heisman Trophy during four incredible seasons at the University of Pittsburgh. Dorsett broke or tied 14 NCAA records while running for an unprecedented 6,082 career yards, scoring 58 touchdowns and leading the Panthers to an unbeaten record and the 1976 national championship.

When the Dallas Cowboys selected Dorsett with the second overall pick of the 1977 draft, some observers predicted a short career with minimal success. Dorsett had other ideas.

For eight of his first nine seasons, Dorsett topped the 1,000-yard barrier while catching 338 passes. The only season of the nine under 1,000 was 1982, when the schedule was cut to nine games because of a players' strike.

And the Cowboys enjoyed success with Dorsett as their feature back. They reached the NFC Championship Game five times and played in two Super Bowls, winning one (XII). Dorsett's 1,383 postseason rushing yards rank second only to Franco Harris' 1,556.

"No matter what he had to do, he wasn't exerting much effort," marveled Dan Reeves, former Cowboys offensive coordinator and now coach of the New York Giants. "He had the great acceleration that means so much in football. And he could make the full-speed cut."

Dorsett, who was elected to the Pro Football Hall of Fame in 1994, was known for his big-play ability. His 99-yard dash against Minnesota late in the 1982 season stands as the longest run from scrimmage in NFL history.

But Dorsett's most amazing quality might have been his durability. He never sustained a serious injury and he missed just three games in a nine-year stretch from 1977-85. He finished his career at Denver in 1988, playing all 16 games and rushing for 703 yards.

PERSONAL

BIRTHPLACE/DATE	Rochester, Pa/4-7-54
HEIGHT/WEIGHT	5-11/185

AWARDS

PRO BOWL SELECTIONS	1978, 1981-83 seasons
SUPER BOWL MVP	None

CAREER

UNIVERSITY	Pittsburgh
DRAFT POSITION	1st Round (2nd overall), Dallas, 1977
PRO TEAMS	12 Seasons, Dallas Cowboys (1977-87); Denver Broncos (1988)

RUSHING, RECEIVING RECORD

	RUSHING				RECEIVING		
	ATT	YDS	AVG	TD	NO	YDS	TD
REGULAR SEASON	2,936	12,739	4.3	77	398	3,554	13
POSTSEASON	302	1,383	4.6	9	46	403	1

There he goes: Tony Dorsett rushed for 12,739 yards in his career, the third-best total in NFL history. He also ran for 77 touchdowns.

"He had the great acceleration." FORMER FALCONS COACH DAN REEVES

John Elway

★★★   ## ARMED AND DANGEROUS

A ny description of John Elway starts with his arm—that magnificent arm. It's not his only physical tool, but it's certainly the most impressive. "When he's running to his left, he can throw the ball 60 yards on one foot," marveled former Raiders cornerback Mike Haynes. "With a lot of mustard on it."

That arm has been delivering passes to National Football League receivers for 14 often-spectacular seasons. Over that span, Elway has completed 3,633 passes and he joined two other quarterbacks in the exclusive 45,000-yard club (45,034) in 1996.

The arm was so impressive that Elway was being touted as an athletic wonder even before his collegiate days at Stanford. The

PERSONAL
BIRTHPLACE/DATE	Port Angeles, Wash/6-28-60
HEIGHT/WEIGHT	6-3/215

AWARDS
PRO BOWL SELECTIONS	1986-87, 1989, 1991, 1993-94 seasons
SUPER BOWL MVP	None

CAREER
UNIVERSITY	Stanford
DRAFT POSITION	1st Round (1st overall), Baltimore, 1983
PRO TEAMS	14 Seasons, Denver Broncos (1983-96)

PASSING, RUSHING RECORD

	PASSING					
	ATT	**COMP**	**YDS**	**PCT**	**INT**	**TD**
REGULAR SEASON	6,392	3,633	45,034	56.8	205	251
POSTSEASON	422	225	3,245	53.3	17	18
	RUSHING					
	ATT	**YDS**	**AVG**	**TD**		
REGULAR SEASON	686	3,095	4.5	31		
POSTSEASON	71	379	5.3	4		

Stalking horse: John Elway has lost in three Super Bowls, but without his heroics, the Denver Broncos would never have been close to the big game.

Yankees were so impressed with his baseball ability that they picked him first in the 1981 June draft. Over his four seasons for the Cardinal, he delighted football scouts by passing for 9,349 yards and 77 touchdowns.

Baltimore made Elway the first overall choice of the 1983 NFL draft, ahead of such notables as Tony Eason, Jim Kelly, Todd Blackledge, Ken O'Brien and Dan Marino in the "Year of the Quarterback." But he refused to sign with the Colts, forcing a trade that transformed the Denver Broncos from also-rans into contenders.

By 1985, Elway was displaying the leadership abilities that would take the Broncos to five AFC Western Division titles and three AFC championships, a success record marred only by losses in all three Super Bowls. And over the course of Elway's career, he earned a

"There's no question John is the greatest two-minute quarterback ever."

FORMER DENVER AND CURRENT FALCONS COACH DAN REEVES

reputation as one of the great comeback quarterbacks of all time.

"There's no question John is the greatest two-minute quarterback ever," former Broncos coach Dan Reeves once said. "He's got that arm, and the point of a two-minute attack is that everybody in the world knows you're going to throw—and your arm is strong enough to do it anyway."

But "the arm" is not Elway's only weapon. He also is one of the game's most feared scramblers, a reputation Elway attributes to quick feet. His mad dashes have produced 3,095 career rushing yards while helping him avoid rushers and protect his body from hits that other quarterbacks are forced to endure.

"He's got the mobility of Fran Tarkenton and the arm of Joe Namath," said former Arizona Cardinals Coach Buddy Ryan.

A lethal combination.

Brett Favre

★★★★★★★★★★ **A LEADING MAN**

He arrived with a warning label: "Explosive arm, reckless style. Could be hazardous to your team." New Green Bay Coach Mike Holmgren was aware of the critics. So was General Manager Ron Wolf. But Holmgren's new West Coast offense needed a trigger man and young Brett Favre, despite the lack of promise he had shown during his rookie 1991 season with Atlanta, had the physical tools that fit the job description. So Holmgren and Wolf took the plunge, dealing a first-round draft pick to the Falcons for a youngster they hoped could develop into a franchise quarterback.

As five-year plans go, Green Bay's was a doozy. In Favre's fourth season as a starter, he threw for 4,413 yards, fired 38 touchdown

passes, the third-highest total in NFL history, and led the Packers all the way to the NFC Championship Game. A 38–27 loss to Dallas was only a temporary setback.

The 1996 Packers, with Favre throwing for 3,899 yards and 39 touchdowns, advanced to the NFC title game, defeated Carolina 30–13 and ended 29 years of Green Bay frustration with a 35–21 victory over New England in Super Bowl XXXI. Favre crowned his record-tying second straight MVP season with Super Bowl scoring bombs of 54 and 81 yards and a two-yard TD run.

Such success seemed like an elusive dream in 1992 when Favre, who had spent much of his rookie season frustrating Coach Jerry Glanville, accepted the responsibility that comes with the job of starting NFL quarterback. Holmgren's offense was complicated, the learning process was slow and Favre's decision-making received less than passing grades.

In Favre's second Green Bay season, he threw more interceptions (24) than TD passes (19) and struggled through the first half of 1994 with some coaches questioning his future. But Holmgren never wavered and after a 13–10 overtime loss to Minnesota in the season's seventh game, Favre directed a 33–6 rout of Chicago and over his next 41 games threw 101 touchdown passes while leading the team to a 30–11 record. The decision-making improved and the mistakes disappeared when Favre's 4,413-yard breakthrough season opened the eyes of hungry Packers fans.

"Brett had a fantastic year. I think he'll get better, too," said offensive coordinator Sherman Lewis. "He's the leader of the team and that's where it all starts."

Favre's 1996 follow-up season came on the heels of a summer rehabilitation for painkiller abuse and quieted critics who had refused to grant him status among the Joe Montanas, Steve Youngs and Dan Marinos in the NFL's upper quarterback echelon.

Packers fans prefer another comparison—to Bart Starr, the man who guided Green Bay to five NFL championships in the 1960s and wins in the first two Super Bowls. It does seem more appropriate.

In hallowed company: Brett Favre's brilliant 1996 and 1997 seasons for the Green Bay Packers meant he became only the second player to receive back-to-back NFL MVP citations.

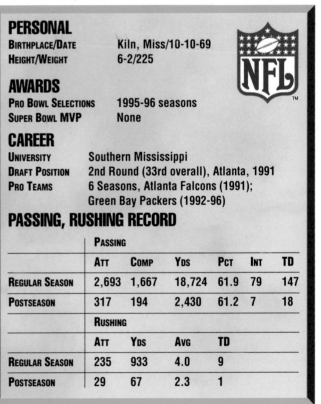

PERSONAL

BIRTHPLACE/DATE	Kiln, Miss/10-10-69
HEIGHT/WEIGHT	6-2/225

AWARDS

PRO BOWL SELECTIONS	1995-96 seasons
SUPER BOWL MVP	None

CAREER

UNIVERSITY	Southern Mississippi
DRAFT POSITION	2nd Round (33rd overall), Atlanta, 1991
PRO TEAMS	6 Seasons, Atlanta Falcons (1991); Green Bay Packers (1992-96)

PASSING, RUSHING RECORD

	PASSING					
	ATT	COMP	YDS	PCT	INT	TD
REGULAR SEASON	2,693	1,667	18,724	61.9	79	147
POSTSEASON	317	194	2,430	61.2	7	18

	RUSHING			
	ATT	YDS	AVG	TD
REGULAR SEASON	235	933	4.0	9
POSTSEASON	29	67	2.3	1

★★★★★★★★★★★★★★★★★★★

John Hannah

A BLOCKING MACHINE

★★★★

PERSONAL
BIRTHPLACE/DATE   Canton, Ga/4-4-51
HEIGHT/WEIGHT   6-3, 260

AWARDS
PRO BOWL SELECTIONS   1976, 1978-85 seasons
SUPER BOWL MVP   None

CAREER
UNIVERSITY   Alabama
DRAFT POSITION   1st Round (4th overall), New England, 1973
PRO TEAMS   13 Seasons, New England Patriots (1973-85)

Contrary to rumors, Herb Hannah did not have a lucrative contract to produce football talent for Paul (Bear) Bryant's Alabama football machine. But it must have seemed that way to Southeastern Conference fans.

Sons John, Charley and David all took turns playing for the Crimson Tide, John earning a consensus All-America citation as an offensive guard and Charley and David earning all-conference honors as defensive tackles. The boys simply were following in the footsteps of their father, who played offensive tackle for Alabama and the New York Giants in the early 1950s.

John and Charley (a combined 520 pounds of muscle) went on to professional careers of their own, but that's where the comparisons end. Charley played 11 solid seasons with Tampa Bay and the Los Angeles Raiders. But John played at a different level over an outstanding 13-year career as a guard with the New England Patriots.

"He's one of the best linemen I've ever played against," said Hall of Fame defensive tackle Randy White, who made his living embarrassing offensive guards. "When you played against John, it was a major challenge. You had to keep your helmet strapped on tight."

There are plenty of defenders who didn't and had it knocked off by the intense Hannah. At 6-feet-3, 260 pounds, he was the outstanding run-blocker of his era. Not surprisingly, the Patriots thrived with a power running attack.

When Hannah, who was elected to the Pro Football Hall of Fame in 1991, stepped on the field, nobody doubted who was in control. "He always wanted to dominate and he did," recalled former Patriots quarterback Matt Cavanaugh. Hannah intimidated opponents quietly, with a businesslike, no-nonsense demeanor that never varied from play to play.

When a defender got out of line or a little too boisterous, Hannah delivered a quick message with his powerful forearm. He was most devastating in pulling situations, when he bulldozed unfortunate defensive ends or linebackers at full speed.

With Hannah leading the charge, the Patriots rushed for an NFL single-season record 3,165 yards in 1978. The 1985 Patriots powered their way to the AFC championship before losing to the Chicago Bears in Super Bowl XX.

When a recurring knee injury forced Hannah's retirement after the Super Bowl, he left with nine Pro Bowl citations and the respect of his coaches and peers. "You had better believe he was the best offensive lineman in the history of the NFL," said Jim Ringo, a Hall of Fame center and Hannah's former line coach.

"He's one of the best linemen I've ever played against."

HALL OF FAME DEFENSIVE TACKLE RANDY WHITE

Center of attention: New England's John Hannah (73) was rarely noticed by fans in the stands. But he was much respected by everybody in the game.

★★★★★★★★★★★★★★★★

Steve Largent

THE CEREBRAL PASS-CATCHER

When Steve Largent's name came up in scouting reports, it usually was accompanied by such words as "heady," "cerebral" and "consistent." But at least one NFL defensive back took his description a step further.

"I call him the Albert Einstein of pass receivers," former Raiders cornerback Lester Hayes once said, "because he's always coming up with some kind of new space age route I've never seen before."

Largent, who caught 819 passes for 13,089 yards and 100 touchdowns over a sterling 14-year career for the Seattle Seahawks, was the thinking man's receiver. What he lacked in speed and athletic grace, he made up for with guile and savvy. Covering the wily Largent was a game of cat and mouse.

"Every time I play him, he pulls a new trick out of his bag," said cornerback Albert Lewis, then with the Chiefs.

"He's always thinking ahead, even though it might not seem that way to you when you cover him," said safety Ronnie Lott. "He might run a certain pattern and you cover him, and you might think that you're doing your job. But basically he's setting you up for the next play."

The essence of Largent's guile might have been that he was more physically gifted than everybody believed. He did not have great straightaway speed, but he had a lateral quickness that allowed him to make defenders look silly. He also had great balance, body control, hand/eye coordination and hands that seldom dropped a pass.

> ## "Every time I play him, he pulls a new trick out of his bag."
>
> ### CORNERBACK ALBERT LEWIS

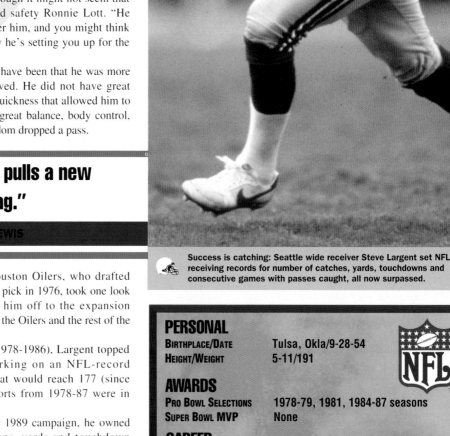

Success is catching: Seattle wide receiver Steve Largent set NFL receiving records for number of catches, yards, touchdowns and consecutive games with passes caught, all now surpassed.

Such qualities were lost on the Houston Oilers, who drafted Largent out of Tulsa with a fourth-round pick in 1976, took one look at him in training camp and shuffled him off to the expansion Seahawks. By 1978, Largent was making the Oilers and the rest of the NFL take note.

For eight of the next nine seasons (1978-1986), Largent topped the 1,000-yard barrier while embarking on an NFL-record consecutive games reception streak that would reach 177 (since broken). His only sub-1,000-yard efforts from 1978-87 were in strike-shortened seasons.

By the time Largent retired after the 1989 campaign, he owned NFL career records for most receptions, yards and touchdown catches—marks that since have been broken. He was elected to the Pro Football Hall of Fame in 1995. The only negative in a career that included seven Pro Bowl invitations was lack of team success. The best the Seahawks managed was an AFC Championship Game loss after the 1983 season.

PERSONAL
BIRTHPLACE/DATE	Tulsa, Okla/9-28-54
HEIGHT/WEIGHT	5-11/191

AWARDS
PRO BOWL SELECTIONS	1978-79, 1981, 1984-87 seasons
SUPER BOWL MVP	None

CAREER
UNIVERSITY	Tulsa
DRAFT POSITION	4th Round (117th overall), Houston, 1976
PRO TEAMS	14 Seasons, Seattle Seahawks (1976-89)

RECEIVING RECORD
	No	YDS	AVG	LG	TD
REGULAR SEASON	819	13,089	16.0	74	100
POSTSEASON	23	433	18.8	56	4

Ronnie Lott

★ ★ ★ ★ **A** DEFENSIVE LEGEND

PERSONAL
BIRTHPLACE/DATE   Albuquerque, NM/5-8-59
HEIGHT/WEIGHT   6-1/200

AWARDS
PRO BOWL SELECTIONS   1981-84, 1986-91 seasons
SUPER BOWL MVP   None

CAREER
UNIVERSITY   Southern California
DRAFT POSITION   1st Round (8th overall), San Francisco, 1981
PRO TEAMS   14 Seasons, San Francisco 49ers (1981-90); Los Angeles Raiders (1991-92); New York Jets (1993-94)
INTERCEPTIONS   Regular Season, 63. Postseason, 9.

The footsteps wide receivers often hear in their worst nightmares belong to Ronnie Lott. Lott, who completed his 14th and final NFL season in 1994 at age 35, is an NFL legend. He's also one of the greatest defensive backs ever to play the game.

"The guy's going to Canton (the Hall of Fame) on rollerskates," said New England Coach Bill Parcells. "I've seen my share of him first-hand. He's one of the best guys that's ever played. You're talking about one of my very favorite players ever."

That's a typical reaction to Lott. Love him, hate him. Love him because he's one of the most competitive, hard-hitting, resourceful players ever to put on a uniform. Hate him for the exact same reasons. He plays the game like the players from yesteryear. Receivers beware.

"When you see Ronnie taking out guys on film, it puts thoughts in the back of your mind," said former Cowboys tight end Doug Cosbie. "You know he's going to hit you and it's not going to be

> **"You know he's going to hit you and it's not going to be a whole lot of fun. It's like a prizefighter who has to face Mike Tyson."**
>
> FORMER COWBOYS TIGHT END DOUG COSBIE

a whole lot of fun. It's like a prizefighter who has to face Mike Tyson."

Lott, who is as soft-spoken off the field as he is crazy on it, plays with passion, throwing his 6-foot-1, 200-pound body at anybody who moves. He intimidates receivers, who often are more interested in protecting their ribs than catching the pass. He intimidates quarterbacks, who have seen him make 63 career interceptions, fifth on the all-time list. Whether covering a speedy receiver, blitzing a quarterback or chasing down an elusive ball carrier, Lott is a master of his art.

Lott, a cornerback and free safety over his outstanding career, was selected out of USC with the eighth overall pick of the 1981 draft. He quickly fit into San Francisco's blueprint for success and led the bruising 49ers defense that helped carve out four Super Bowl championships in the 1980s. Lott, who owns virtually every 49ers pass defense record, did not win any championships in shorter stints with the Los Angeles Raiders and the Jets, but he did earn another Pro Bowl citation with the Raiders in 1991, the 10th time he was honored in his first 11 seasons.

Passing Lottery: Few teams dared to go deep on the San Francisco 49ers when Ronnie Lott was in the defensive backfield. He won four Super Bowl rings.

Dan Marino

★★★★★★

A PASSING FANCY

I t had been billed as the "Year of the Quarterback" and, sure enough, five well-armed college passers were snapped up within the first 24 picks of the NFL draft. John Elway, Todd Blackledge, Tony Eason, Jim Kelly, Ken O'Brien.

In retrospect, it's inconceivable that Dan Marino could be rated sixth on anybody's list of quarterbacks. Over the 13 seasons since he was selected 27th in the 1983 draft, Marino has conducted a record-setting aerial circus while establishing himself as the greatest passer in pro football history.

Former Miami Dolphins Coach Don Shula sometimes had to pinch himself when he thought about his good fortune. Marino, a pro-style quarterback at the University of Pittsburgh, had struggled through a difficult senior year (23 interceptions) while trying to learn a new offense. Five NFL teams backed off.

By the end of the 1983 season, it was clear they had made a big mistake. The rookie warmed up with 173 completions for 2,210 yards and 20 touchdowns. In 1984, he exploded into prominence, setting NFL single-season records for passing yards (5,084) and TD passes (48). The Dolphins rolled to a 14–2 regular-season record and defeated Pittsburgh in the AFC Championship Game before losing to San Francisco in Super Bowl XIX.

While the other first-round quarterbacks either struggled or watched and learned on the sideline, the intense Marino continued to terrorize NFL secondaries with 400-yard passing games and a flurry of TD bombs. He did it with a calm precision and unerring accuracy that shocked Shula.

"How can he play any better," Shula asked after Marino's monster 1984 season. "I don't know. I really don't know."

The poise and confidence Marino displayed in his first two seasons were remarkable. But so was his ability to read defenses and the physical tools he used to pick them apart.

Foremost is the release. "The quickest arm I've ever seen," marveled Shula. With a flick of the wrist, Marino can avoid the rush and deliver a 30-yard pass like a bullet to an open receiver. The release also allows the 6-foot-4 Marino to see the entire field, not just his primary receivers. And the patience keeps his interceptions down, compensating for his one flaw—below-average speed.

As the years pile up, so do the career numbers. In 1996, Marino became pro football's first 50,000-yard passer—he ended the season with 51,636—and he ranks first all-time in completions (4,134), attempts (6,904), touchdown passes (369), 300-yard passing games (52) and numerous other passing categories.

Before he's through, Marino should own his own section of the NFL record book.

"The quickest arm I've ever seen."

FORMER MIAMI COACH DON SHULA

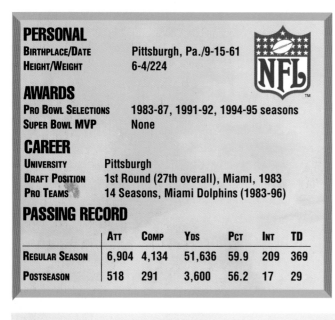

PERSONAL
BIRTHPLACE/DATE Pittsburgh, Pa./9-15-61
HEIGHT/WEIGHT 6-4/224

AWARDS
PRO BOWL SELECTIONS 1983-87, 1991-92, 1994-95 seasons
SUPER BOWL MVP None

CAREER
UNIVERSITY Pittsburgh
DRAFT POSITION 1st Round (27th overall), Miami, 1983
PRO TEAMS 14 Seasons, Miami Dolphins (1983-96)

PASSING RECORD

	ATT	COMP	YDS	PCT	INT	TD
REGULAR SEASON	6,904	4,134	51,636	59.9	209	369
POSTSEASON	518	291	3,600	56.2	17	29

Press release: Dan Marino's passing style is so quick-fire he rarely gets sacked. His quick release demands the Miami Dolphins have fast wide receivers.

Joe Montana

★★★★★ ### NO ORDINARY JOE

When the San Francisco 49ers spent a third-round 1979 draft pick (the 82nd overall) on a young Notre Dame quarterback named Joe Montana, they could not have known the impact of their decision. A struggling franchise was investing in a future legend.

A decade later, the 49ers would be proud owners of four Super Bowl titles and "Montana Magic" would be synonymous with late-game heroics and championship-level performance.

"He's the greatest big-game player I've seen, period."

FORMER 49ERS CENTER RANDY CROSS

It's hard to dispute the facts. After a 16-year career with the 49ers and Kansas City Chiefs, Montana completed 3,409 passes for 40,551 yards. He was a three-time Super Bowl Most Valuable Player, the holder of virtually every Super Bowl passing record; the only quarterback to pass for more than 5,000 postseason yards; an eight-time Pro Bowl invitee—more than any quarterback in history—and he had engineered 31 fourth-quarter career comebacks, including playoffs.

PERSONAL

BIRTHPLACE/DATE	New Eagle, Pa / 6-11-56
HEIGHT/WEIGHT	6-2/205

AWARDS

PRO BOWL SELECTIONS	1981, 1983-85, 1987, 1989-90, 1993 seasons
SUPER BOWL MVP	XVI, XIX, XXIV

CAREER

UNIVERSITY	Notre Dame
DRAFT POSITION	3rd Round (82nd overall), San Francisco, 1979
PRO TEAMS	15 Seasons, San Francisco 49ers (1979-92); Kansas City Chiefs (1993-94)

PASSING, RUSHING RECORD

PASSING

	ATT	COMP	YDS	PCT	INT	TD
REGULAR SEASON	5,391	3,409	40,551	63.2	139	273
POSTSEASON	734	460	5,772	62.7	21	45

RUSHING

	ATT	YDS	AVG	TD
REGULAR SEASON	457	1,676	3.7	20
POSTSEASON	63	310	4.9	2

Not bad for a quarterback with only slightly above-average arm strength and speed. The Montana legend was built around quick feet, a quicker mind and the determination and ability to succeed when everything is on the line.

"He is clearly the best quarterback in football today and maybe the best in many years," marveled former 49ers coach Bill Walsh after watching Montana direct a Super Bowl XIX victory over Miami.

"I just hope now they'll stop saying, 'He's right up there with the best,'" former 49ers center Randy Cross said after Montana's 10-yard touchdown pass to John Taylor with 34 seconds remaining had given the 49ers a 20–16 victory over Cincinnati in Super Bowl XXIII. "He's the greatest big-game player I've seen, period."

After a serious elbow injury sidelined Montana for the entire 1991 season and all but one game in 1992, he resurrected his career in Kansas City, where he was greeted like a conquering hero. Trying to guide the Chiefs to their first Super Bowl since 1970, Montana got them as far as the 1993 AFC Championship Game before they stumbled at Buffalo. A 1994 Kansas City playoff appearance resulted in a quick out.

Expressing regret over his inability to produce that one last bit of Super Bowl magic, a 38-year-old Montana retired in the spring of 1995, taking with him a legacy as one of the great big-game players in NFL history.

Redefining the position: For many people, Joe Montana is the greatest quarterback in NFL history. His three Super Bowl MVP awards are a record.

Anthony Muñoz

★★★ ## POWER IN THE TRENCHES

PERSONAL
BIRTHPLACE/DATE Ontario, Calif/8-19-58
HEIGHT/WEIGHT 6-6/285

AWARDS
PRO BOWL SELECTIONS 1981-91 seasons
SUPER BOWL MVP None

CAREER
UNIVERSITY Southern California
DRAFT POSITION 1st Round (3rd overall), Cincinnati, 1980
PRO TEAMS 13 Seasons, Cincinnati Bengals (1980-92)

Who's the greatest offensive tackle of all time? Hall of Fame tackle Mike McCormack has a good idea. "Anthony Muñoz was the epitome of what an NFL offensive lineman should be," he said. "I've never seen one better."

McCormack's view is supported by defensive end Greg Townsend, a two-time Pro Bowl performer for the Los Angeles Raiders. "He's the best tackle I've ever seen," Townsend said.

From his days as an All-American at USC through his 13-year career with the Cincinnati Bengals, Muñoz earned such accolades from impressed viewers. The late Paul Brown, one of the greatest judges of football talent in NFL history, recalled watching Muñoz play for the Trojans in the 1980 Rose Bowl against Ohio State. "The guy was so big and so good it was a joke," he said.

With Brown providing that reference, the Bengals selected Muñoz with the third overall pick of the 1980 draft and he quickly began throwing his 285 pounds around with enthusiastic abandon.

Muñoz, showing amazing agility and foot quickness for his 6-foot-6 frame, dominated defenders with his "attack" philosophy. "He has a defensive mentality on offense," Townsend once said. "He has this killer instinct to get his man and put him away."

Whether opening holes for Cincinnati runners or dropping back to protect the quarterback, Muñoz usually won the war of the trenches. He was like an impenetrable wall. His quickness, toughness and consistency impressed teammates and opponents alike, earning him 11 invitations to the Pro Bowl. From 1980-91, he was snubbed only once—his rookie season.

No pussycat: Offensive tackle Anthony Muñoz was a first-round draft pick in 1980 by the Cincinnati Bengals. He was voted to 11 Pro Bowls.

"He has this killer instinct to get his man and put him away."

DEFENSIVE END GREG TOWNSEND

With Muñoz providing an offensive anchor, the Bengals rose to prominence, losing to San Francisco in Super Bowl XVI (26–21) and Super Bowl XXIII (20–16)—the only close calls for the 49ers in their five Super Bowl victories.

But of all of his awards, Muñoz said he was most proud of the 1991 NFL Man of the Year citation that annually honors role models, both on and off the field. Muñoz has been active in many charitable activities, including drug and alcohol programs in the Cincinnati area.

When he retired after the 1992 season, a collective sigh of relief could be heard from NFL defensive coordinators who never saw the charitable side of this football giant.

Walter Payton

★★★★★★

MR. VERSATILITY

He was known affectionately as "Sweetness." But the Walter Payton who graced National Football League fields for 13 record-setting seasons was anything but. Payton, the Chicago Bears' primary offensive weapon from 1975-87 and the most prolific running back in the history of the game, was a collision waiting to happen, a defense's worst nightmare. Not only would Payton slash his 5-foot-10, 200-pound body through the tiniest of cracks in a defensive line and outsprint speedy linebackers to the corner, he would dish out punishing hits to destructive-minded tacklers.

San Diego Chargers General Manager Bobby Beathard called Payton the most complete player who ever played in the NFL. Mike Ditka, Payton's coach for six seasons, seconded that notion.

"He's the most gifted athlete I've ever seen," Ditka said. For all of his individual success, which included a record 275-yard rushing effort against Minnesota in 1977, Payton labored for a mediocre team much of his career. The Bears earned wild-card playoff spots in 1977 and 1979, but otherwise were also-rans until awakening in the mid-1980s.

Payton did go out in a blaze of glory. The Bears won NFC Central Division championships from 1984-87 and Payton was able to showcase his talents in Super Bowl XX, a 46–10 Bears victory over New England.

Payton retired as the holder of 23 team records and 8 NFL marks, including 110 rushing touchdowns. The 10-time 1,000-yard rusher also played in nine Pro Bowls. He was elected to the Pro Football Hall of Fame in 1993.

"He's the most gifted athlete I've ever seen."

FORMER BEARS COACH MIKE DITKA

But Payton's legacy goes beyond the record 16,726 rushing yards (3,467 ahead of second-place Eric Dickerson) he compiled after coming out of Jackson State as the fourth overall draft pick in 1975. The black-shirted No. 34 also was one of professional football's most versatile talents—and one of its most willing to sacrifice for his team.

"As far as blocking, tackling, running, durability, intelligence, throwing, he does it all," said Bill Tobin, the Colts director of operations and a former Bears executive, a few years ago.

Tobin wasn't exaggerating. During the prime of Payton's career, scouts considered him the best blocking back in the league. Payton played in 174 consecutive regular-season games from his rookie 1975 season through 1986. He caught 492 NFL passes for 4,538 yards and set the NFL record for combined yardage (rushing, receiving and kick returns) with 21,803. And he even threw eight career touchdown passes and served as the Bears' backup punter and placekicker.

PERSONAL

BIRTHPLACE/DATE	Columbia, Miss / 7-25-54
HEIGHT/WEIGHT	5-10/200

AWARDS

PRO BOWL SELECTIONS	1976-80, 1983-86 seasons
SUPER BOWL MVP	None

CAREER

UNIVERSITY	Jackson State
DRAFT POSITION	1st Round (4th overall), Chicago, 1975
PRO TEAMS	13 Seasons, Chicago Bears (1975-87)

RUSHING, RECEIVING RECORD

	RUSHING				RECEIVING		
	ATT	YDS	AVG	TD	NO	YDS	TD
REGULAR SEASON	3,838	16,726	4.4	110	492	4,538	15
POSTSEASON	180	632	3.5	2	22	178	0

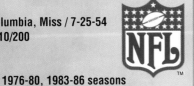

Running Bear: Former Chicago running back Walter Payton owns the NFL career rushing record (16,726 yards) and he seems likely to keep it for many years.

Jerry Rice

★★★★★★★★★

THE NATURAL

He wasn't anything special. He dropped passes, ran bad routes and sometimes looked out of control. Jerry Rice, the San Francisco 49ers' 1985 first-round draft pick out of tiny Mississippi Valley State University, looked like your average, everyday rookie wide receiver.

Until, that is, a late-season Monday night game when Rice exploded into national prominence with a 10-catch, 241-yard performance against the Los Angeles Rams. Over the next 11 seasons, Rice would help carry the 49ers to three Super Bowl championships while cementing his claim as the greatest wide receiver in the history of the game.

"I really want to be the all-time best receiver ever to play in the NFL."

JERRY RICE

The more-confident Rice that 49ers Coach Bill Walsh unleashed on the National Football League in 1986 was a devastating offensive weapon. He was a perfect combination of size, speed, grace and agility. Using his 6-foot-2 frame and long arms against smaller defensive backs, he pulled in the difficult passes. Fearless over the middle and sure-handed in a crowd, Rice had an extra gear that could separate him from the swiftest defender.

"He had the Paul Warfield grace, the Charley Taylor determination, the hands of (Fred) Biletnikoff," recalled teammate Ronnie Lott, an understanding defensive back. "He had the Dwight Clark work attitude. I just knew right away some good things were going to happen. I just didn't expect so many good things."

Rice had the same vision. "I really want to be the all-time best receiver ever to play in the NFL," he said early in his career.

It didn't take long to figure out that could really happen. Working in the 49ers' sophisticated offense and receiving passes from such quarterbacks as Joe Montana and Steve Young, Rice began piling up big numbers. When the 49ers completed their 1995 season, Rice owned virtually every receiving record.

He became the most prolific touchdown maker in NFL history, passing Walter Payton and Jim Brown, during San Francisco's 1994 Super Bowl run. In 1995 he passed Art Monk as the all-time leader in receptions and became the first player to pass the 1,000-catch barrier a year later. He also ranks first all-time in touchdown receptions (154) and receiving yards (16,377) and he set the single-season yardage record in 1995 with 1,848. Rice also owns every major postseason, Super Bowl and Pro Bowl mark.

And he's only 34. By the time Rice is finished, he could warrant a special section in the NFL's record book. "He is not a normal human being," former teammate Randy Cross once said. He was right about that.

Perfect reception: San Francisco 49ers wide receiver Jerry Rice is generally acknowledged as the greatest wide receiver in the history of the NFL.

PERSONAL

BIRTHPLACE/DATE	Starkville, Miss./10-13-62
HEIGHT/WEIGHT	6-2/200

AWARDS

PRO BOWL SELECTIONS	1986-96 seasons
SUPER BOWL MVP	XXIII

CAREER

UNIVERSITY	Mississippi Valley State
DRAFT POSITION	1st Round (16th overall), San Francisco 49ers, 1985
PRO TEAMS	12 Seasons, San Francisco 49ers (1985-96)

RUSHING, RECEIVING RECORD

	RUSHING			
	ATT	YDS	AVG	TD
REGULAR SEASON	80	624	7.8	10
POSTSEASON	7	44	6.3	0

	RECEIVING				
	NO	YDS	AVG	LG	TD
REGULAR SEASON	1,050	16,377	15.6	96t	154
POSTSEASON	120	1,742	14.5	72t	18

★★★★★★★★★★★★★★★★

Barry Sanders

★ ★ ★ ★ ★ ★ ★ ★

THE LION KING

I f Detroit's Barry Sanders is not the best running back in the National Football League, he's certainly the most exciting. Many coaches and players believe he's both. "He makes you stand on your toes any time he gets the ball," former Lions Coach Wayne Fontes says. "You watch because you feel something big's about to happen."

Watching Sanders carry the ball is an adventure. Every run is filled with stops, starts, head fakes, jukes, quick cuts and broken tackles. Whether it nets one yard or 90, it electrifies the crowd—home or road. Sanders' quickness is startling, his balance and power inconceivable.

"Barry can flat-out embarrass anyone," says linebacker and former teammate Chris Spielman. And Sanders has embarrassed plenty of his opponents en route to three rushing titles, a record eight straight 1,000-yard seasons and a 1,883-yard effort in 1994—the fourth-highest rushing total in NFL history.

The incredible quickness is complemented by a set of powerful legs that allow Sanders to break tackles and regain his balance when it appears he is going down.

PERSONAL

BIRTHPLACE/DATE	Wichita, Kan./7-16-68
HEIGHT/WEIGHT	5-8/200

AWARDS

PRO BOWL SELECTIONS	1989-96 seasons
SUPER BOWL MVP	None

CAREER

UNIVERSITY	Oklahoma State
DRAFT POSITION	1st Round (3rd overall), Detroit, 1989
PRO TEAMS	8 Seasons, Detroit Lions (1989-96)

RUSHING, RECEIVING RECORD

	RUSHING				RECEIVING		
	ATT	YDS	AVG	TD	NO	YDS	TD
REGULAR SEASON	2,384	11,725	4.9	84	281	2,309	7
POSTSEASON	73	321	4.4	1	16	68	0

When he does get free, he has breakaway speed.

Nobody could have guessed that a squatty 5-foot-8, 200-pound body with tree-trunk legs would carry Sanders so far. But by his junior year at Oklahoma State University, he was confounding college defenses en route to the 1988 Heisman Trophy and 13 NCAA rushing and scoring records. When Sanders announced he would bypass his senior season, the Lions

> ## "He makes you stand on your toes any time he gets the ball."
>
> **FORMER LIONS COACH WAYNE FONTES**

were waiting with the third overall pick of the draft.

The quiet, soft-spoken Sanders has been a worthy investment. He was unsure of his role in Detroit's run-and-shoot offense when he joined the team in 1989, but a 1,470-yard, 14-touchdown rookie season eliminated the doubts and 24 receptions for 282 yards enhanced his reputation as a versatile performer. That pattern would continue.

And Sanders, who already holds virtually every Lions career rushing record, would lead the playoff-starved team to a pair of NFC Central Division titles and four postseason appearances, giving him god-like status in Detroit. But his admirers are not confined to the Motor City.

"He's very special," said former Chicago coach Mike Ditka. "He reminds me of another player we used to have named Walter Payton."

That's pretty select company.

Hard to stop: One of the most amazing things about Barry Sanders' rushing style is the number of tacklers he avoids, both in a crowd and the open field.

★ ★ ★ ★ ★ ★ ★ ★ ★ ★ ★ ★ ★

Mike Singletary

★ ★ ★ ★ ★ ★ ★

ANOTHER BUTKUS

PERSONAL
BIRTHPLACE/DATE   Houston, Tex / 10-9-58
HEIGHT/WEIGHT   6-0/230

AWARDS
PRO BOWL SELECTIONS   1983-92 seasons
SUPER BOWL MVP   None

CAREER
UNIVERSITY   Baylor
DRAFT POSITION   2nd Round (38th overall), Chicago, 1981
PRO TEAMS   12 Seasons, Chicago Bears (1981-92)
SACKS   Regular Season, 19. Postseason, 1.

Mike Singletary, a Baylor University middle linebacker with professional aspirations, knew something that the National Football League scouts didn't know. "He was dead serious, very businesslike," said former Bears scout Jim Parmer, referring to a pre-draft interview. "He looked right at me and said, 'Mr Parmer, if you draft me, I'm going to be the best linebacker in the National Football League.' "

Despite Singletary's suspect size (6-foot, 230 pounds) and below-average speed, Parmer was impressed enough to recommend that the Bears take a chance. They grabbed him on the second round of the 1981 draft and nobody ever regretted the decision.

What the youngster lacked in size and speed, he made up for with intensity and determination. Singletary, the youngest of ten children who grew up in a Houston ghetto, simply willed himself into becoming a great player and maintained his high level of play for 12 NFL seasons.

Singletary's aggressiveness fed off the intensity, drawing comparisons to another great Bears middle linebacker. "He plays like (Dick) Butkus did," said former Bears coach Mike Ditka. Former teammate Jim Osborne, a defensive tackle, seconded that notion. "I haven't seen a linebacker play with his intensity since I played with Butkus," he said.

What Singletary couldn't do when he joined the Bears, he quickly learned. He discovered ways to fight through blocks, he worked at covering backs on pass defense and he spent hours studying film and learning tendencies that would help him on the field. When he made a mistake, you could bet your life it would never happen again.

Nobody could match the work ethic and Singletary's desire to play at all times—and all costs. Over his 12 seasons, he missed only two games and once, when he noticed that the tip of one of his fingers was dangling by a thread of flesh, he had it taped and returned to the field.

But Singletary's influence was more than physical. The son of a preacher, he liked giving inspirational speeches to his teammates and continuously exhorted them to work harder. The Bears' hard work paid off with seven playoff appearances during Singletary's career and a victory in Super Bowl XX.

Singletary, who was named 1990 NFL Man of the Year for his off-field community service, made 10 Pro Bowl appearances before retiring after the 1992 season.

> ## "He looked right at me and said, 'Mr. Parmer, if you draft me, I'm going to be the best linebacker in the National Football League.' "
>
> **FORMER BEARS SCOUT JIM PARMER**

Midway Mayhem: Chicago linebacker Mike Singletary was the key to the Bears' famed 46 Defense, which terrorized the NFL in their Super Bowl XX season.

Emmitt Smith

★★★★

RUSHING ROULETTE

In retrospect, it seems incredible that 16 teams could have passed up Emmitt Smith in the 1990 National Football League draft. But then how can you explain destiny? The Dallas Cowboys enthusiastically grabbed the Florida running back with the 17th pick and laid the foundation for rapid reconstruction of a franchise.

Smith would fuel the Cowboys' rise with three consecutive rushing titles after a 937-yard rookie season. The Cowboys, who had finished 1–15 the year before his arrival, improved to 7–9 and 11–5 before dominating the NFL with consecutive Super Bowl championships after the 1992 and 1993 seasons and another after the 1995 campaign.

Did anybody envision such production from Smith, who left Florida with a year of eligibility remaining?

"Of course not, I'm no genius," said Cowboys running backs coach Joe Brodsky. "But if you look past the size, look past the fact that he's not as fast running straight down a track as you'd like a guy to be, you'd see a complete football player with magnificent strength in his thighs and hips."

That strength is used like a weapon by the no-nonsense Smith, who disdains the Barry Sanders-like jukes and fakes and runs through potential tacklers. He also has superb instincts that allow him to pick his holes, peripheral vision that Smith claims allows him to see both sidelines and the quickness to bolt to daylight. "He's the best north-south runner I've ever seen," said former Coach Jimmy Johnson, who directed the first two Super Bowl winners.

But the intangibles are what make Smith so special. Such as his fierce dedication to winning and his ability to play when most mortal men would prefer the sideline.

Smith was still competing with the Rams' Jerome Bettis for the 1993 rushing title when the Cowboys squared off with the New York Giants in a season finale that would decide the NFC East title. Midway through the game, he was tossed to the hard turf, separating his left shoulder. Smith was in terrible pain when Brodsky and Johnson told him to pack it in.

He refused. Smith carried 13 more times with the separated shoulder, the Cowboys won and he finished 57 yards ahead of Bettis. The inspired

"He's the best north-south runner I've ever seen."

FORMER DALLAS COACH JIMMY JOHNSON

Cowboys went on to win the Super Bowl, with Smith earning MVP honors.

Smith ran for 1,484 yards in 1994, but both he and the Cowboys fell short in their title defenses. That wasn't the case in 1995 when he led the league with 1,773 yards and the Cowboys captured their third Super Bowl in four years.

PERSONAL

BIRTHPLACE/DATE	Pensacola, Fla./5-15-69
HEIGHT/WEIGHT	5-9/209

AWARDS

PRO BOWL SELECTIONS	1990-96 seasons
SUPER BOWL MVP	XXVIII

CAREER

UNIVERSITY	Florida
DRAFT POSITION	1st Round (17th overall), Dallas, 1990
PRO TEAMS	7 Seasons, Dallas Cowboys (1990-96)

RUSHING, RECEIVING RECORD

	RUSHING				RECEIVING		
	ATT	YDS	AVG	TD	NO	YDS	TD
REGULAR SEASON	2,334	10,160	4.4	108	348	2,200	7
POSTSEASON	318	1,413	4.4	18	44	318	2

Star of Texas: Emmitt Smith has become the mainstay of the Dallas Cowboys' running attack. He led the NFL in rushing three straight years from 1991 to 1993.

★ ★ ★ ★ ★ ★ ★ ★ ★ ★ ★ ★ ★ ★ ★ ★ ★

Lawrence Taylor

★★★★★★★★

THE PROTOTYPE

PERSONAL
BIRTHPLACE/DATE   Williamsburg, Va / 2-4-59
HEIGHT/WEIGHT   6-3/243

AWARDS
PRO BOWL SELECTIONS   1981-90 seasons
SUPER BOWL MVP   None

CAREER
UNIVERSITY   North Carolina
DRAFT POSITION   1st Round (2nd overall), New York Giants, 1981
PRO TEAMS   13 Seasons, New York Giants (1981-93)
SACKS   Regular Season, 132.5, 2nd on all-time list. Postseason, 6.5.

He stood 6-feet-3, weighed 243 pounds and ran the field like a speedy wide receiver. It was a massive understatement to call Lawrence Taylor, with his menacing glare and riveting eyes, imposing.

His defensive presence made quarterbacks drop snaps, blockers jump offsides and coaches reconstruct game plans. When the New York Giants selected Taylor with the second overall pick of the 1981 draft, they turned loose a monster who would terrorize overmatched offensive coordinators for the next 13 seasons.

Taylor, more than anything, was the prototype outside linebacker. He dominated offensive linemen, chased down speedy running backs on the opposite side of the field and slammed quarterbacks to the turf like rag dolls, often fighting through triple-team blocks to reach them. In his rookie season, he earned defensive player of the year honors, an NFL first. By his second season, he already was the standard by which future outside linebackers would be judged.

"There are very few defensive players who can win a game by themselves," said television commentator John Madden, a former Raiders coach. "Lawrence Taylor is the most dominant defensive player I've seen... Taylor takes a game over by sheer force."

Former Philadelphia Eagles coach Dick Vermeil once called Taylor the most difficult player he ever coached against.

Not bad for a Williamsburg, Va, kid who didn't even play football until his third year of high school. After receiving consensus All-America honors as a senior at North Carolina, Taylor was sent off to search and destroy in the NFL wars.

> ## "Lawrence Taylor is the most dominant defensive player I've seen... Taylor takes a game over by sheer force."
>
> **TELEVISION COMMENTATOR JOHN MADDEN**

And the Giants, with big No 56 serving as their defensive anchor, stood tall after two decades of mediocrity. They qualified for the playoffs in 1981, 1984 and 1985 and won Super Bowls after the 1986 and 1990 seasons.

When he retired in January 1994, he ranked second on the all-time sacks list (132.5) and had collected ten Pro Bowl invitations.

Redefining the position: New York Giants linebacker Lawrence Taylor set new standards for the way linebacking should be played.

Reggie White

THE MINISTER OF DEFENSE

O n the field, Reggie White is a modern-day Rambo, dedicated to mayhem and destruction under the green-and-gold banner of the Green Bay Packers. Off the field, Reggie White is a humanitarian, an anti-drugs spokesman, an ordained minister dedicated to fighting the destructive forces that prey on society.

Will the real Reggie White please stand up—all 6-feet-5, 295 pounds of him?

The Reggie White who prowls football fields on Sunday afternoons is the most dominant defensive end in the National Football League, one of the best ever to play. He dictates offensive strategy, shuts down running games, chases down ballcarriers with his sprinter speed and powers his way through double and triple-team blocks to terrorize quarterbacks.

"Reggie's the real deal," says Packers defensive line coach Larry Brooks. "His best qualities are his strength and his speed. And the bigger the game, the bigger he plays. When he gets to playing, it just shows—he's a force."

And a sack machine. Not counting the $23^1/2$ he recorded in his first two professional seasons in the now-defunct United States Football League, White has 165.5 career sacks—more than any player in NFL history. And he constantly forces nervous quarterbacks to rush throws or scamper prematurely out of the pocket.

But White's biggest contribution might be the problems he creates for offensive coaches just by being on the field. For eight dominating seasons with the Philadelphia Eagles and four in Green Bay, White has attracted double and triple-team attention, freeing teammates to make big plays. In 1993, his first season with Green Bay, the Packers improved from a No. 23 defensive ranking to No. 2. When White left the Eagles in 1992, he became the most sought-after free agent in NFL history.

"Reggie's the real deal."

PACKERS DEFENSIVE LINE COACH LARRY BROOKS

PERSONAL

BIRTHPLACE/DATE	Chattanooga, Tenn./12-19-61
HEIGHT/WEIGHT	6-5/295

AWARDS

PRO BOWL SELECTIONS	1986-96 seasons
SUPER BOWL MVP	None

CAREER

UNIVERSITY	Tennessee
DRAFT POSITION	1st Round (4th overall), Philadelphia, 1984 Supplemental Draft
PRO TEAMS	14 Seasons, Memphis USFL (1984-85); Philadelphia Eagles (1985-92); Green Bay Packers (1993-96)
SACKS	165.5, 1st on all-time list

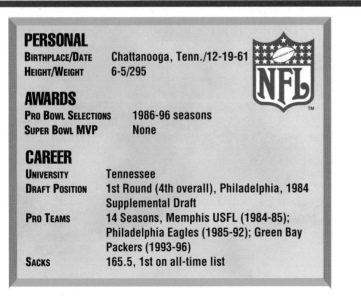

At long last: Reggie White, the NFL's all-time sack leader, desperately wanted a Super Bowl ring before he retired and, in 1997, he got one.

But the former University of Tennessee star has a "Dr. Jekyll" side to his "Mr. Hyde." In 1992, the NFL Players Association named him winner of the prestigious Byron (Whizzer) White Humanitarian Award for service to team, community and country. He is involved in numerous charitable activities and regularly takes his ministry to churches and street corners.

White's full impact on the Packers can be measured in Pro Bowl (11) and playoff appearances and the 1996 Super Bowl championship that ended the team's three decades of frustration. The Packers qualified for the playoffs in each of his first four seasons, reached the NFC Championship Game in 1995 and completed their revival a year later with a victory over New England in Super Bowl XXXI.

Kellen Winslow

★★★★★ **BETTER TO RECEIVE**

PERSONAL
BIRTHPLACE/DATE   St Louis, Mo / 11-5-57
HEIGHT/WEIGHT   6-5/250

AWARDS
PRO BOWL SELECTIONS   1980-83, 1987 seasons
SUPER BOWL MVP   None

CAREER
UNIVERSITY   Missouri
DRAFT POSITION   1st Round (13th overall), San Diego, 1979
PRO TEAMS   9 Seasons, San Diego Chargers (1979-87)

RECEIVING RECORD

	NO	YDS	AVG	LG	TD
REGULAR SEASON	541	6,741	12.5	67t	45
POSTSEASON	28	380	13.6	33t	4

Kellen Winslow did not get the basic training that usually precedes Hall of Fame careers. But when he finally got his hands on a football, he wouldn't let go. Winslow, one of seven children raised by an East St Louis family, was not allowed to play football until his senior year in high school. His mother was afraid he would get hurt.

But her 6-foot-5, 250-pound son would make it through that season, four years at the University of Missouri and part of his rookie campaign with the San Diego Chargers before her fear would be warranted. And even the broken leg Winslow suffered in 1979 would be only a temporary setback.

When the Chargers grabbed Winslow with the 13th pick of the 1979 draft, they saw him as a perfect fit for an innovative, wide-open passing attack dubbed "Air-Coryell" in honor of Coach Don Coryell. Winslow, because of his size, deceptive speed and glue-like hands, was the final piece to the puzzle. He was the prototype tight end, the man who would re-define the position. He would be used like an extra wide receiver rather than in the traditional blocking and occasional receiving roles.

With Dan Fouts at quarterback, John Jefferson and Charlie Joiner at wide receiver and Winslow at tight end, the Chargers were virtually unstoppable. In 1980, Jefferson, Joiner and Winslow became the first trio in NFL history to catch passes for more than 100 yards in a game and 1,000 yards in a season. Winslow, working his magic over the middle like no one before him, led the league in catches in 1980 (89) and 1981 (88).

He tied an NFL record in 1981 by catching five touchdown passes in a game with the Raiders and helped the Chargers reach the AFC Championship Game after the 1980 and 1981 seasons.

"Kellen Winslow was the finest tight end ever to play football and one of the most dominant players of his era," Fouts said. "You could put the ball anywhere and you knew he'd come up with it."

Winslow made four consecutive Pro Bowl appearances before a career-threatening knee injury sidelined him in 1984. Defying odds, he made the painful journey through rehabilitation and earned another Pro Bowl citation in 1987 before ending his career with 541 catches for 6,741 yards.

"You could put the ball anywhere and you knew he'd come up with it."

FORMER SAN DIEGO QUARTERBACK DAN FOUTS

Tightly charged: San Diego's All-Pro tight end Kellen Winslow (80) cuts between San Francisco defensive backs Dwight Hicks (22) and Ronnie Lott (42).

Steve Young

★★★ ## OUT OF THE SHADOW

From his college days as a record-setting quarterback at Brigham Young University to that 1991 season when he officially became Joe Montana's successor as quarterback of the 49ers, Steve Young had been trapped in no-win situations.

First as quarterback of the Los Angeles Express of the dying United States Football League, then as quarterback of the NFL's lowly Tampa Bay Buccaneers. Even when Young was traded to San Francisco in 1987, he watched from the bench as Montana directed the 49ers to Super Bowl victories after the 1988 and '89 seasons.

When he finally got his chance in 1991, Young found that his battle against Montana's legacy and fan expectations was more difficult than the weekly skirmishes on the field. The only way to survive, he finally decided, was to be himself.

When Young is "being himself," opposing defenses are in trouble. His rifle left arm is selective and accurate. When he can't find a Jerry Rice or John Taylor open downfield, he tucks the ball under his arm and sprints for big yardage. If Young is not the best scrambling quarterback in football history, he's close. And he complements his physical abilities with intelligence, resourcefulness, modesty and a willingness to spread credit for his team's success.

Finally armed and dangerous, Young proceeded to win an unprecedented four consecutive passing titles, firing 108 touchdown passes and running for 17 more. When he finished the 1994 regular season, he was the highest rated passer in NFL history.

But that was not enough. Young finally punched a hole in Montana's massive shadow on Super Sunday 1995 when he fired a Super Bowl-record six touchdown passes in the 49ers' 49–26 victory over San Diego, one more than Montana had thrown in Super Bowl XXIV against Denver. He also was named Super Bowl MVP as the 49ers won their fifth championship.

"The 1990s belong to Steve Young and he deserves that moment."

49ERS PRESIDENT CARMEN POLICY

Only the powerful Dallas Cowboys of 1992 and 1993 kept Young and the 49ers from becoming the first team to win three consecutive Super Bowls. And 49ers President Carmen Policy put Young's accomplishments into perspective.

"Joe was a huge part of what made the 49ers great," he said. "He is the 1980s and that should be unblemished and untarnished. By the same token, the 1990s belongs to Steve Young and he deserves that moment unblemished and untarnished."

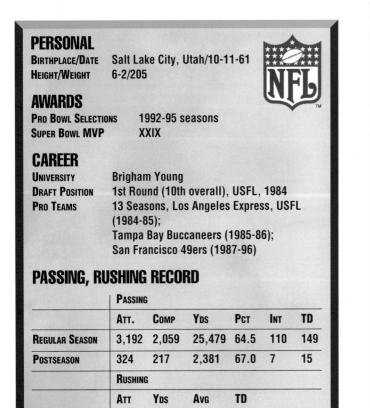

PERSONAL
BIRTHPLACE/DATE Salt Lake City, Utah/10-11-61
HEIGHT/WEIGHT 6-2/205

AWARDS
PRO BOWL SELECTIONS 1992-95 seasons
SUPER BOWL MVP XXIX

CAREER
UNIVERSITY Brigham Young
DRAFT POSITION 1st Round (10th overall), USFL, 1984
PRO TEAMS 13 Seasons, Los Angeles Express, USFL (1984-85);
Tampa Bay Buccaneers (1985-86);
San Francisco 49ers (1987-96)

PASSING, RUSHING RECORD

	Passing					
	ATT.	COMP	YDS	PCT	INT	TD
REGULAR SEASON	3,192	2,059	25,479	64.5	110	149
POSTSEASON	324	217	2,381	67.0	7	15
	Rushing					
	ATT	YDS	AVG	TD		
REGULAR SEASON	591	3,529	6.0	34		
POSTSEASON	81	512	6.3	7		

No dropoff: Steve Young replaced the legendary Joe Montana as San Francisco's quarterback and won four consecutive NFL passing titles.

A super way to end every

***

I t's a media monster, a celebration, a near religious experience. For one super Sunday in January, the entire world stops to watch football. It's called the Super Bowl and it has become the most anticipated sports event of the year.

It wasn't always so Super. When the Kansas City Chiefs and Green Bay Packers squared off in January 1967, reducing football's seven-year war to a bragging-rights battle that finally would produce a clear-cut winner, it was dubbed the "AFL-NFL World Championship Game." Officially.

Unofficially, a more colorful name was circulating through the press box at Los Angeles' Memorial Coliseum, courtesy of Kansas City owner and American Football League founder Lamar Hunt. As the story goes, Hunt was inspired one day by the name "Super Ball," a bouncy rubber ball that his children played with. In a meeting to work on details for the championship game, he referred to it as the "Super Bowl," and it caught on in private and then in public.

Skeptical just how "super" this annual series was going to be, the NFL deferred on Hunt's colorful new name. The skepticism was short-lived. After the powerful Packers had dominated the Chiefs and Oakland Raiders in the first two title games, Joe Namath and the New York Jets pumped life into the AFL-NFL feud in 1969 when they deflated the powerful Baltimore Colts and the Chiefs followed suit a year later by dismantling Minnesota's supposedly invincible machine. Hunt's "Super Bowl" was here to stay.

The idea of an inter-league championship game was but a hazy fantasy in 1959 when Hunt, a Texas oilman who had been thwarted in his attempts to bring an NFL franchise to Dallas, began piecing together an ownership puzzle that would become the AFL. The NFL had fought this kind of war before, but not against Lamar Hunt and his band of deep-pocketed associates.

When the NFL located a new franchise in Dallas and succeeded in running Hunt out of his own backyard, he simply took his Dallas Texans' AFL team to Kansas City in 1963. From 1960 to 1966, a costly war was waged for players and respect—and the all-important television contracts. When the AFL signed a $36-million, five-year deal with NBC-TV in 1964, guaranteeing its perseverance at least through the decade, the rival leagues were motivated to begin serious peace talks that would lead to a 1966 merger agreement.

Although the AFL and NFL would not merge under a common banner until 1970, the agreement did set up a common draft and a yearly AFL-NFL championship game that would begin after the 1966 season.

Most of the 61,946 fans who showed up January 15, 1967, at the Coliseum (only two-thirds of capacity), and the 60 million-plus who watched on the simultaneous CBS and NBC broadcasts viewed the Packers-Chiefs inaugural as a curiosity piece. The question was not who would win, but by how much. The answer was 35-10 and NFL fans smugly said, "I told you so."

It was more of the same the following year when Vince Lombardi's Packers routed the Raiders. But little did anybody know that the Packers simply were setting the stage for Namath, who would almost single-handedly change curiosity to passion and give personality to an event that would never be lacking for that quality again.

Crimson tide: Super Bowl III MVP Joe Namath attended the University of Alabama, as did the MVP in Super Bowls I and II, Bart Starr.

72

season

★★★★★ ## THE SUPER BOWL

The colorful, flamboyant Namath strutted and pranced around Miami in the week preceding Super Bowl III, guaranteeing a Jets victory over the powerful Colts and expounding on the superior talents of AFL quarterbacks. His behavior was outlandish, his victory prediction illogical. The Colts were listed as 18-point favorites.

But when Namath and the Jets delivered a 16-7 victory, the football establishment was shocked. And when the Chiefs followed by beating the Vikings, the AFL took its place as a football equal. Super Bowl V would be the first under a common umbrella.

The Super Bowl, which is played two weeks after the conference championship games, has grown from that humble beginning into a media celebration. The last two were televised into more than 140 countries with estimated worldwide audiences of 750 million. By kickoff, everybody is well-versed on the teams and the players have been relentlessly dissected and analyzed for two weeks.

Critics who point out that the Super Bowl has been burdened by one-sided mismatches can't deny it also has been blessed by many outstanding individual performances. Quarterbacks like Bart Starr, Joe Namath, Len Dawson, Jim Plunkett, Doug Williams, Terry Bradshaw, Joe Montana and Steve Young have written personal legacies that will be difficult to top. So have running backs like John Riggins, Timmy Smith, Tony Dorsett, Marcus Allen and Emmitt Smith and receivers like Max McGee, Jerry Rice and John Stallworth.

But the most lasting legacy belongs to Lombardi, whose name is imprinted on the Super Bowl Trophy—the symbol for what has become the greatest show on earth.

Key figure: Kansas City Chiefs owner Lamar Hunt was instrumental in the AFL–NFL merger that led to the Super Bowl.

Holy Grail: The Lombardi Trophy, for winning the Super Bowl, is the prize all 30 NFL teams dream of collecting when the season starts.

First World Championship Game AFL vs NFL

TM/©1966 NFL

JAN 15, 1967, AT THE LOS ANGELES COLISEUM
PACKERS 35, CHIEFS 10

★★★★★★★★★★★★★★★★★★

SCORING SUMMARY

	1	2	3	4	Total
KANSAS CITY	0	10	0	0	10
GREEN BAY	7	7	14	7	35

GB	McGee 37 pass from Starr (Chandler kick)
KC	McClinton 7 pass from Dawson (Mercer kick)
GB	Taylor 14 run (Chandler kick)
KC	FG Mercer 31
GB	Pitts 5 run (Chandler kick)
GB	McGee 13 pass from Starr (Chandler kick)
GB	Pitts 1 run (Chandler kick)

★★★★★★

After seven years of bitter hostilities, the AFL-NFL war was fought head-to-head, mano a' mano for the first time amid the glitz and hoopla of television cameras, blaring bands and skyward-rising pigeons.

Most of the 60-million-plus television viewers and 61,946 fans at the Los Angeles Coliseum were drawn more by curiosity than expectations of a competitive championship game. How could the 7-year-old Chiefs possibly compete with Vince Lombardi's noble and powerful Packers, who would be carrying the 47-year-old banner of the NFL? Judging by the final score, they couldn't.

But that score was deceiving. Throughout a competitive first half, quarterbacks Bart Starr and Len Dawson battled on even terms and the Packers carried only a 14-10 lead into halftime. Green Bay scored on Starr's 37-yard touchdown pass to Max McGee and Jim Taylor's 14-yard run. The Chiefs countered with Dawson's seven-yard pass to Curtis McClinton and Mike Mercer's 31-yard field goal.

The game's turning point might have come in the locker room when Lombardi, hoping to pressure Dawson, ordered his defense to blitz. Early in the second half, Dawson, under pressure, wobbled a pass toward the sideline that Packers safety Willie Wood picked off and returned 50 yards to the 5. Elijah Pitts scored on the next play for a 21-10 lead and the Packers were off to the races.

Starr, who completed 16 of 23 passes for 250 yards to earn MVP honors, added a 13-yard TD pass to McGee, and Pitts ran one yard for a fourth-quarter touchdown to complete the scoring. The Green Bay defense harried Dawson into a 5-for-12 second-half performance that doomed the Chiefs.

The NFL's football crown was safe for at least another year.

★★★★★

Super charged: Max McGee races to the end zone to score Green Bay's and the NFL's first Super Bowl touchdown.

SUPER BOWL II

JAN 14, 1968, AT THE ORANGE BOWL, MIAMI
PACKERS 33, RAIDERS 14

★★★★★★★★★★★★★★★★

The Packers, playing inspired football in what they suspected would be Vince Lombardi's last game as Green Bay coach, blitzed the overmatched Raiders early and proudly carried the NFL banner to their fifth championship of the decade.

With quarterback Bart Starr performing flawlessly en route to his second straight MVP citation and Don Chandler kicking four field goals, the Packers were never challenged. Starr's public dissection of Oakland's defense was viewed by 75,546 reverential fans at Miami's Orange Bowl.

Repeating the dose: Green Bay quarterback Bart Starr was named MVP in Super Bowls I and II. He's now in the Pro Football Hall of Fame.

SCORING SUMMARY

GREEN BAY	3	13	10	7—33
OAKLAND	0	7	0	7—14

GB	FG Chandler 39
GB	FG Chandler 20
GB	Dowler 62 pass from Starr (Chandler kick)
OAK	Miller 23 pass from Lamonica (Blanda kick)
GB	FG Chandler 43
GB	Anderson 2 run (Chandler kick)
GB	FG Chandler 31
GB	Adderley 60 interception return (Chandler kick)
OAK	Miller 23 pass from Lamonica (Blanda kick)

The Packers didn't waste any time, scoring on their first three possessions. Chandler kicked two field goals to open the scoring and Starr made it 13-0 when he picked up a Raiders blitz and fired a stunning 62-yard bomb to Boyd Dowler. After the Raiders cut the margin with a 23-yard Daryle Lamonica-to-Bill Miller touchdown pass, Chandler kicked a 43-yard field goal for a 16-7 halftime lead.

Things only got worse for the Raiders. Donny Anderson's two-yard third-quarter run and Chandler's 31-yard field goal lifted the lead to 26-7 and set up cornerback Herb Adderley for the coup de grace. In the fourth quarter, Adderley picked off a pass by Lomonica, followed crunching blocks by defensive tackles Henry Jordan and Ron Kostelnik and raced 60 yards for a touchdown. Another 23-yard Lamonica-to-Miller TD pass was too little, too late.

The game, which drew football's first $3-million gate, indeed was Lombardi's last as Green Bay coach and marked the end of a great dynasty.

PACKERS ICE COWBOYS

It was decision time. Quarterback Bart Starr and Coach Vince Lombardi discussed strategy on the Green Bay sideline with the 1967 NFL championship riding on the next play. The Packers, trailing 17-14, were 2 feet away from their third straight crown and fifth in seven seasons. They also were 16 seconds away from defeat.

The scene was frozen Lambeau Field in Green Bay and 50,861 shivering fans watched in anticipation. The next play would decide the "Ice Bowl," a game played in 13-below-zero temperatures with a stiff wind making it feel more like minus 35.

Starr returned to the Green Bay huddle and relayed the decision to his teammates. There would be no field-goal attempt. They would gamble. Lombardi and Starr had agreed on a quarterback sneak, although, in the huddle, Starr called for a handoff to fullback Chuck Mercein.

But Starr took the snap, followed guard Jerry Kramer and dove into the end zone, completing the 68-yard drive. Packers 21, Cowboys 17. Green Bay would represent the NFL in Super Bowl II.

Starr's gamble ended a dramatic test of nerves and endurance. After Green Bay had taken a 14-0 lead on two Starr TD passes to Boyd Dowler, the Cowboys had fought back to take a fourth-quarter lead on Danny Reeves' 50-yard halfback pass to Lance Rentzel.

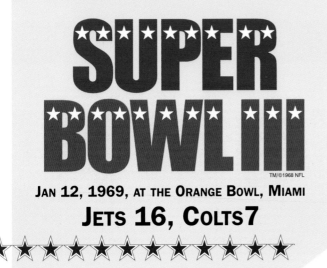

SUPER BOWL III

TM/©1968 NFL

JAN 12, 1969, AT THE ORANGE BOWL, MIAMI
JETS 16, COLTS 7

★★★★★★★★★★★★★★★★★

NYJ	Snell 4 run (Turner kick)
NYJ	FG Turner 32
NYJ	FG Turner 30
NYJ	FG Turner 9
BAL	Hill 1 run (Michaels kick)

The AFL was badly in need of a savior after two lopsided World Championship Game defeats. What it got was a brash victory prediction from a young New York Jets quarterback. "We're going to win on Sunday, I guarantee it," announced Joe Namath when he appeared before the Miami Touchdown Club on the Thursday before the game. Those amazing words circulated quickly and twice-humiliated AFL officials cringed. Namath's guarantee probably would have an inspirational effect on the powerful, once-beaten Colts (15-1 overall), who already were listed as 18-point favorites.

That appeared to be the case as the Colts moved to the New York 19-yard line early in the opening quarter. But Lou Michaels missed a 27-yard field goal. Again the Colts threatened after recovering a fumble at the Jets 12. But an Earl Morrall

pass was picked off by Randy Beverly in the end zone, one of three first-half interceptions Morrall would throw. Suddenly, the momentum shifted.

Namath's passing and the power running of Matt Snell moved the Jets into scoring position midway through the second quarter and Snell's four-yard TD run gave them a 7-0 halftime lead.

The fired-up New York defense smothered the bewildered Colts in the second half. It forced a first-possession fumble that set up Jim Turner's 32-yard field goal and Namath, who would earn MVP honors for his 206-yard passing performance, moved his team in position for two more Turner field goals.

Only a late Johnny Unitas-led drive that resulted in a one-yard Jerry Hill touchdown run kept Baltimore from being shut out. The Colts, badly outplayed and humiliated, watched in disbelief as Namath walked off the field after the game, his forefinger held high signaling the obvious.

The Jets, and the AFL, were No 1 and the new league had its savior—as well as a large dose of respectability.

Keeping his promise: Joe Namath delivered on his guarantee that the New York Jets would defeat the heavily-favored Baltimore Colts in Super Bowl III.

SUPER BOWL IV

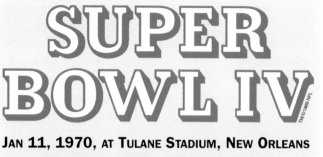

JAN 11, 1970, AT TULANE STADIUM, NEW ORLEANS

CHIEFS 23, VIKINGS 7

★★★★★★★★★★★★★★★

SCORING SUMMARY				
MINNESOTA	0	0	7	0—7
KANSAS CITY	3	13	7	0—23

KC	FG Stenerud 48
KC	FG Stenerud 32
KC	FG Stenerud 25
KC	Garrett 5 run (Stenerud kick)
MIN	Osborn 4 run (Cox kick)
KC	Taylor 46 pass from Dawson (Stenerud kick)

The NFL, anxious to avenge the indignation suffered by the Colts, sent another powerful representative into the fourth edition of the Super Bowl. Minnesota, which had lost only two regular-season games, was listed as a two-touchdown favorite over the AFL's Chiefs, who were making their second appearance in the extravaganza.

Not only did the Chiefs have to contend with the Vikings' quick-strike offense and rugged defensive line dubbed "The Purple People Eaters," they had to do so under a cloud of suspicion. In the week preceding the game, Chiefs quarterback Len Dawson was named as one of several players who would be called to testify in a federal investigation into sports gambling.

Dawson, who later was cleared of any wrong-doing, was devastated by the reports. Players and coaches were angered by the timing. It was a distraction that could have killed what little chance the Chiefs were given of pulling an upset.

But it didn't. The Chiefs, confident and surprisingly ready to play, dramatically turned the tables on the Vikings and gave the AFL its second straight Super Bowl upset, tying the young series at two games apiece.

Utilizing Dawson's short, precision passing and a defense that stuffed Minnesota's powerful running game, the Chiefs methodically dominated the game. Three Jan Stenerud field goals opened the scoring and Mike Garrett's five-yard second-quarter run gave Kansas City a 16-0 halftime lead.

Dave Osborn's four-yard third-quarter TD run gave the Vikings temporary hope, but Dawson and wide receiver Otis Taylor took care of that on the Chiefs' next possession. Dawson fired a six-yard out pattern to Taylor, who broke two tackles and raced a total of 46 yards for the clinching touchdown.

Minnesota's futility was dramatized in the fourth period when quarterback Joe Kapp, battered and injured, had to be helped off the field after being sacked. There was no such exit for Dawson, who walked off the field a conquering hero.

★★★★★★★★★★★★

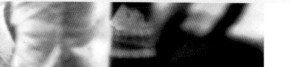

Super cool: Kansas City quarterback Len Dawson was linked to a gambling investigation before Super Bowl IV, but on game day he delivered.

SUPER BOWL V

JAN 17, 1971, AT THE ORANGE BOWL, MIAMI
COLTS 16, COWBOYS 13

★★★★★★★★★★★★★★★

SCORING SUMMARY

	1	2	3	4	
BALTIMORE	0	6	0	10	—16
DALLAS	3	10	0	0	—13

DAL	FG Clark 14
DAL	FG Clark 30
BAL	Mackey 75 pass from Unitas (kick blocked)
DAL	Thomas 7 pass from Morton (Clark kick)
BAL	Nowatzke 2 run (O'Brien kick)
BAL	FG O'Brien 32

This was both the worst and the best of the Super Bowls to date. The worst: The teams combined for 11 turnovers in a penalty-filled contest that neither team appeared capable of winning. The best: Baltimore's Jim O'Brien kicked a 32-yard field goal with five seconds remaining, ending the tightest of the five Super Bowls on an exciting note.

This was the first Super Bowl featuring teams under the single NFL banner. Baltimore represented the new American Conference, Dallas the National Conference. It was played before 79,204 fans at Miami's Orange Bowl.

The comedy of errors started early when Ron Gardin fumbled a punt return (the first of seven Colts turnovers) and the Cowboys converted it into Mike Clark's 14-yard field goal. Clark's 30-yard kick made it 6-0 in the second quarter.

But the Colts struck back when a Johnny Unitas pass was deflected to tight end John Mackey, who ran the rest of the way for a 75-yard touchdown pass play. O'Brien's conversion kick was blocked, leaving the game tied. Dallas regained the lead in the second quarter on Craig Morton's seven-yard touchdown pass to Duane Thomas.

The game's key play occurred early in the second half when Dallas drove to the Baltimore 2-yard line, only to lose the ball on a Thomas fumble. Another turnover, Rich Volk's interception of a Morton pass, set up Baltimore's tying touchdown, a two-yard run by Tom Nowatzke.

O'Brien's game winner was set up by a Mike Curtis interception.

Last kick drama: Baltimore won Super Bowl V when rookie Jim O'Brien's kick with five seconds remaining sailed through the uprights from 32 yards away.

SUPER BOWL VI

TM/©1971 NFL

JAN 16, 1972, AT TULANE STADIUM, NEW ORLEANS
COWBOYS 24, DOLPHINS 3

★★★★★★★★★★★★★★★

SCORING SUMMARY

DALLAS	3	7	7	7—24
MIAMI	0	3	0	0—3

DAL	FG Clark 9
DAL	Alworth 7 pass from Staubach (Clark kick)
MIA	FG Yepremian 31
DAL	D. Thomas 3 run (Clark kick)
DAL	Ditka 7 pass from Staubach (Clark kick)

The Cowboys, who had fumbled and bumbled their way through Super Bowl V, were much more efficient against the young Dolphins. Dominating both the offensive and defensive lines, they rushed for a Super Bowl-record 252 yards while holding Miami to 185 total yards and no touchdowns.

It wasn't pretty, but it was effective.

The Cowboys jumped on top in the opening quarter when Miami fullback Larry Csonka, who had not fumbled all season, lost control of the ball near midfield, setting up a nine-yard Mike Clark field goal. Dallas added to its lead in the second quarter when Roger Staubach, who completed 12 of 19 passes en route to MVP honors, culminated a 76-yard drive with a seven-yard TD toss to Lance Alworth. That was all the Cowboys would need.

Garo Yepremian gave the Dolphins brief hope when he drilled a 31-yard field goal just before halftime, but the Cowboys would regain control on their first possession of the second half. With Duane Thomas doing most of the damage against the tiring Miami defense, the Cowboys powered the ball 71 yards and scored on Thomas' three-yard run for a 17-3 lead. Staubach's seven-yard fourth-quarter TD strike to tight end Mike Ditka closed out the scoring.

Thomas rushed for a game-high 95 yards, atoning for his untimely fumble against Baltimore in Super Bowl V. The Cowboys did some atoning of their own and silenced critics who said they couldn't win the big game. Dallas had lost to the Packers in the 1966 and 1967 NFL Championship Games before losing to the Colts in Super Bowl V.

★★★★★

No choke: Dallas finally proved it could win the big game in Super Bowl VI; Duane Thomas rushed for a touchdown in the defeat of Miami.

SUPER BOWL VII

TM/©1972 NFL

Jan 14, 1973, at the Los Angeles Coliseum
DOLPHINS 14, REDSKINS 7

★ ★ ★ ★ ★ ★ ★ ★ ★ ★ ★ ★ ★ ★ ★

It appeared Miami's "No-Name Defense" would write the perfect ending to the Dolphins' perfect season. It had stuffed, throttled and denied the Redskins for more than three quarters and was on the verge of posting the first shutout in Super Bowl history.

But fate would not let that script play out. With Coach Don Shula's Dolphins leading 14-0 and about to put the wraps on the first undefeated, untied season in the NFL's 53-year history, little placekicker Garo Yepremian lined up for a 42-yard field goal attempt that everybody thought would clinch the Dolphins' date with destiny.

But when Yepremian kicked the ball squarely into defensive lineman Bill Brundige, it deflected back, took a big hop and landed in his arms. Instead of falling on the ball, Yepremian saw several massive bodies charging toward him and desperately tried to heave it forward. The ball slipped out of his hand to cornerback Mike Bass, who grabbed it and ran 49 yards for a touchdown with 2:07 remaining.

With the shoutout gone and the victory no longer secure, the Dolphins were forced to hunker down one more time. Washington regained possession with 1:14 remaining and the Miami defense swarmed Redskins quarterback Billy Kilmer, ending the game, fittingly, with a nine-yard sack.

The victory, Miami's record-setting 17th, was accomplished like most of its other 16—efficiently. With an offense featuring the three-pronged running attack of Larry Csonka, Jim Kiick and Mercury

THE IMMACULATE RECEPTION

The young, defensive Steelers, playing in only the franchise's second playoff game, were looking for respect. What they got was a miracle.

It appeared the Steelers' playoff adventure would be short when Oakland quarterback Ken Stabler, a fourth-quarter replacement for ineffective starter Daryle Lamonica, scrambled 30 yards for a touchdown with 1:13 remaining in a 1972 AFC divisional-round battle. Stabler's run capped an 80-yard drive and gave the Raiders their first lead of the day, 7-6.

The Steelers were in trouble. Quarterback Terry Bradshaw, trying to get them in field-goal position, completed two short passes to the Pittsburgh 40-yard line before missing on three in a row. Facing a fourth down with 22 seconds remaining, Bradshaw avoided heavy pressure, then spotted Frenchy Fuqua streaking downfield and fired the ball.

Raiders defensive back Jack Tatum reached Fuqua at the same moment as the ball and the ball bounced backward off one or both of them, apparently ending the threat. But just before the ball hit the turf at the Oakland 42, Pittsburgh running back Franco Harris, running full speed, reached down, grabbed the ball off his shoetops and raced toward the goal line.

Harris fought off a desperation shove from defender Jimmy Warren and scored standing up—with five seconds remaining. Final score: Steelers 13, Raiders 7.

SCORING SUMMARY

MIAMI	7	7	0	0—14
WASHINGTON	0	0	0	7—7

MIA	Twilley 28 pass from Griese (Yepremian kick)
MIA	Kiick 1 run (Yepremian kick)
WAS	Bass 49 fumble recovery return (Knight kick)

Morris and quarterback Bob Griese directing a controlled passing game, the Dolphins were usually in command.

They jumped on the Redskins in the opening quarter when Griese connected with Howard Twilley on a 28-yard touchdown pass and extended the lead to 14-0 on Kiick's one-yard second-quarter run. The rest of the game belonged to the defense.

Csonka picked up a clock-killing 112 yards for Miami, but MVP honors went to safety Jake Scott, who picked off two passes—one a drive-killer in the Miami end zone.

Big play: Miami's Jake Scott had two interceptions, this one in the end zone.

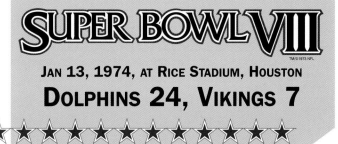

SUPER BOWL VIII

TM/©1973 NFL

JAN 13, 1974, AT RICE STADIUM, HOUSTON
DOLPHINS 24, VIKINGS 7

★★★★★★★★★★★★★★

SCORING SUMMARY					
MINNESOTA	0	0	0	7	7
MIAMI	14	3	7	0	24

MIA	Csonka 5 run (Yepremian kick)
MIA	Kiick 1 run (Yepremian kick)
MIA	FG Yepremian 28
MIA	Csonka 2 run (Yepremian kick)
MIN	Tarkenton 4 run (Cox kick)

★★★★★★★★★★★★★★★★★★

I t wasn't the end to a perfect season, but Don Shula's Dolphins became only the second team to win consecutive Super Bowls. And nobody in the professional football world would deny that this team was just as dominant as the oh-so-perfect Dolphins of 1973.

This Super Bowl was a mismatch from the opening kickoff. It pitted a Minnesota run defense that ranked 23rd during the regular season against a relentless Miami ground attack. The Dolphins wasted little time probing the Vikings' weakness, putting together consecutive 62 and 56-yard touchdown drives while controlling the ball for 11 minutes of the opening quarter.

The first touchdown was scored by bulldozing fullback Larry Csonka, who would add a third-quarter TD and finish his MVP outing with a Super Bowl-record 145 yards. Csonka's five-yard run and Jim Kiick's one-yarder gave the Dolphins a 14-0 lead before the Vikings even managed a first down.

A 28-yard Garo Yepremian field goal increased the margin to 17-0 before halftime and Csonka's two-yard third-quarter run made the score 24-0 before Vikings quarterback Fran Tarkenton broke the shutout with a four-yard fourth-quarter run.

The victory, which was forged before 71,882 fans at Houston's Rice Stadium, lifted the Dolphins' final record to 15-2 and their two-season mark to 32-2—the best back-to-back finishes in NFL history. Only the 1966 and 1967 Green Bay Packers had won back-to-back Super Bowls. Conversely, the Vikings became the first team to lose two Super Bowls.

Minnesota Csonked: Larry Csonka scored two touchdowns in Super Bowl VIII as the Miami Dolphins won their second straight championship, defeating the Vikings 24-7.

SUPER BOWL IX

TM/©1974 NFL

JAN 12, 1975, AT TULANE STADIUM, NEW ORLEANS
STEELERS 16, VIKINGS 6

★★★★★★★★★★★★★★★★

A new team crashed, Pittsburgh, the Super Bowl party, but its patriarch was a familiar face in football circles. Art Rooney, who founded the team in 1933, had been waiting 42 years for his first championship

The Steelers of Coach Chuck Noll gave it to him. Competing against a Vikings team that was looking for its first Super Bowl victory after two losses, Noll had twin weapons at his disposal—a smothering, "Steel Curtain" defense and running back Franco Harris. The Vikings were in trouble.

Neither team could get untracked in a defensive first half that ended with the unlikely score of 2-0. Pittsburgh scored a safety when Fran Tarkenton's handoff hit running back Dave Osborn on the hip, and the ball bounded into the Minnesota end zone, where Tarkenton fell on it. He was touched down by Pittsburgh end Dwight White for a safety.

Minnesota made its second critical mistake when Bill Brown took the second-half kickoff, returned it two yards and fumbled, setting up Pittsburgh on the Vikings' 30-yard line. Four plays later, Harris swept left end for nine yards and a touchdown.

The Vikings finally broke through in the fourth quarter when Matt Blair blocked a Bobby Walden punt and Terry Brown recovered in the end zone. But Steelers quarterback Terry Bradshaw answered with a clock-eating 66-yard drive that culminated with a four-yard, game-sealing TD pass to Larry Brown.

Harris, who was named MVP, ran for a Super Bowl-record 158 yards. The Steelers defense, led by tackle Mean Joe Greene, linebackers Jack Lambert and Jack Ham and cornerback Mel Blount, held the Vikings to 119 total yards, 17 on the ground, and intercepted three passes.

Big play: Larry Brown's (87) four-yard touchdown reception of Terry Bradshaw's pass insured Pittsburgh's first Super Bowl win, 16-6, and Minnesota's second straight loss.

SUPER BOWL X

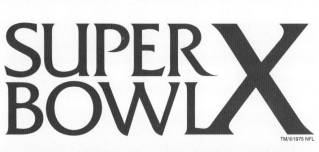

TM/©1975 NFL

JAN 18, 1976, AT THE ORANGE BOWL, MIAMI
STEELERS 21, COWBOYS 17

★★★★★★★★★★★★★★★

The "Steel Curtain" continued to shroud the NFL, but Cowboys quarterback Roger Staubach did manage to poke a few holes in it. When all was said and done, however, the Steelers had given long-suffering Pittsburgh fans their second consecutive championship.

The Cowboys sent a quick message that it would not be easy—a 29-yard touchdown pass from Staubach to Drew Pearson one play after a fumbled punt attempt on Pittsburgh's first offensive series. It marked the first time all season the Steelers had surrendered first-quarter points.

It didn't take Pittsburgh long to get them back. Quarterback Terry Bradshaw moved the Steelers 67 yards on their next possession, a drive that ended with a seven-yard touchdown pass to Randy Grossman. The Steelers fell behind again in the second quarter on a 36-yard field goal by Dallas' Toni Fritsch.

The Cowboys maintained their 10-7 advantage until the Steelers struck for 14 fourth-quarter points on an unusual scoring combination—a safety, two Roy Gerela field goals and a 64-yard Bradshaw bomb to Lynn Swann. Pittsburgh led 21-10 with 3:02 left to play.

But Staubach was not finished. He quickly moved the Cowboys 80 yards, completing the drive with a 34-yard TD pass to Percy Howard. Then, after the Steelers were forced to give the ball up on downs with 1:22 remaining, he moved the Cowboys to the Pittsburgh 38 before throwing a goal-line pass that was picked off by Steelers safety Glen Edwards.

Pittsburgh's Swann, who caught four passes for 161 yards, was named MVP.

ROGER SAYS HAIL MARY

Dallas quarterback Roger Staubach had been in desperate situations before. He knew this one called for extraordinary measures.

"I guess it's a 'Hail Mary' pass," he said after firing a 50-yard touchdown bomb to Drew Pearson, giving the Cowboys an unlikely 17-14 victory over Minnesota in a 1975 NFC Divisional Playoff Game. "You throw it up and pray he catches it."

Staubach and the Cowboys had been thwarted all day by the Vikings' Purple People Eaters defense and fell behind, 14-10, when Minnesota's Brent McClanahan ran one yard for a touchdown with 5:24 remaining.

With less than a minute left and facing fourth down on his own 25-yard line, Staubach bought new life for Dallas with a 25-yard pass to Pearson. But with 32 seconds remaining, the Cowboys decided it was time to go for broke.

Staubach heaved the second-and-10 pass toward the end zone, again looking for Pearson. But this time the pass was underthrown and Pearson came out of the end zone for the ball. He snatched it away from defenders Nate Wright and Terry Brown and rolled into the end zone with 24 seconds remaining.

Vikings players and Coach Bud Grant screamed for offensive pass interference as the stunned Minnesota crowd watched in disbelief. The touchdown stood.

SCORING SUMMARY

	1	2	3	4	Total
DALLAS	7	3	0	7	—17
PITTSBURGH	7	0	0	14	—21

DAL	D. Pearson 29 pass from Staubach (Fritsch kick)
PIT	Grossman 7 pass from Bradshaw (Gerela kick)
DAL	FG Fritsch 36
PIT	Safety, Harrison blocked Hoopes' punt through end zone
PIT	FG Gerela 36
PIT	FG Gerela 18
PIT	Swann 64 pass from Bradshaw (kick failed)
DAL	P. Howard 34 pass from Staubach (Fritsch kick)

Graceful Swann: This falling 53-yard catch by Lynn Swann was one of four for 161 yards by the Pittsburgh receiver, who was the game's MVP.

SUPER BOWL XI

JAN 9, 1977, AT THE ROSE BOWL, PASADENA, CAL

RAIDERS 32, VIKINGS 14

★★★★★★★★★★★★★★

SCORING SUMMARY

OAKLAND	0	16	3	13—32
MINNESOTA	0	0	7	7—14

OAK	FG Mann 24
OAK	Casper 1 pass from Stabler (Mann kick)
OAK	Banaszak 1 run (kick failed)
OAK	FG Mann 40
MIN	S. White 8 pass from Tarkenton (Cox kick)
OAK	Banaszak 2 run (Mann kick)
OAK	Brown 75 interception return (kick failed)
MIN	Voigt 13 pass from Lee (Cox kick)

Nine years after getting flogged by Green Bay in Super Bowl II, the Raiders claimed football's biggest prize. But their victory was obscured by the shadow of Minnesota's futility—a record four Super Bowl losses in eight years.

The Vikings, seeking redemption under the close scrutiny of 81 million television viewers and 103,438 fans at the Rose Bowl in Pasadena, Cal, got a first-quarter break when Fred McNeill blocked a Ray Guy punt and recovered at the Oakland 3-yard line. But on a second-down play, Brent McClanahan fumbled, Oakland's Willie Hall recovered and momentum shifted dramatically.

Quarterback Ken Stabler quickly drove the Raiders 90 yards to an Errol Mann field goal. Two more second-quarter possessions produced a one-yard Stabler-to-Dave Casper touchdown pass and a one-yard Pete Banaszak TD run. Not only had the Raiders jumped to a 16-0 halftime lead, they had dominated the Vikings: 16-4 in first downs, 288-86 in total yards, 166-27 in rushing yards and 122-59 in passing yards.

The Vikings were better in the second half, but not much. After another Mann field goal, quarterback Fran Tarkenton hit Sammy White with an eight-yard scoring pass to cut the deficit to 19-7. But two Oakland interceptions iced the victory. One set up Banaszak's two-yard TD run and cornerback Willie Brown returned another 75 yards for a score.

Coach John Madden watched his Raiders amass a Super Bowl-record 429 yards and Clarence Davis rush for 137. Fred Biletnikoff earned MVP honors with four receptions for 79 yards.

★★★★★★★★

Pulling 'em in: Watched by a record crowd, Oakland won its first Super Bowl, handing Minnesota its fourth defeat, thanks to Fred Biletnikoff's four receptions.

SUPER BOWL XI

TM/©1977 NFL

JAN 15, 1978, AT LOUISIANA SUPERDOME, NEW ORLEANS
COWBOYS 27, BRONCOS 10

★★★★★★★★★★★★★★

SCORING SUMMARY

DALLAS	10	3	7	7—27
DENVER	0	0	10	0—10

DAL	Dorsett 3 run (Herrera kick)
DAL	FG Herrera 35
DAL	FG Herrera 43
DEN	FG Turner 47
DAL	Johnson 45 pass from Staubach (Herrera kick)
DEN	Lytle 1 run (Turner kick)
DAL	Richards 29 pass from Newhouse (Herrera kick)

Denver quarterback Craig Morton knew it wasn't going to be easy. But he never dreamed it would be so bad. Harried, battered and abused by his former teammates, Morton completed only 4 of 15 passes, threw four interceptions and watched the final 20 minutes from the sideline as good friend Roger Staubach directed the Cowboys to victory in the first indoor Super Bowl game.

The 75,583 fans who packed the New Orleans Superdome watched the Cowboys ride their defensive horses. Not only did the Dallas defense throttle Morton, it held the Broncos to 156 total yards, forced eight total turnovers, including four fumbles, and set up ten points. Defensive end Harvey Martin and tackle Randy White were so dominating they were named co-MVPs.

The Cowboys converted two of their interceptions into first-quarter points—Tony Dorsett's three-yard touchdown run and Efren Herrera's 35-yard field goal. Herrera connected from 43 yards in the second period to give the Cowboys a 13-0 halftime advantage that could have been a lot higher considering the Broncos had turned the ball over seven times and managed two first downs.

Morton made Dallas fans a little nervous when he drove the Broncos to a 47-yard Jim Turner field goal after the second-half kickoff. But Staubach answered with a 45-yard TD pass to Butch Johnson.

When a one-yard Rob Lytle run cut the deficit back to 10 points (20-10) late in the third quarter, Dallas administered the coup de grace—Robert Newhouse's 29-yard touchdown bomb to Golden Richards on a halfback pass.

Dallas double-dip: Two defensive linemen, end Harvey Martin (79) and tackle Randy White (54), shared the MVP award after the Cowboys defeated Denver 27-10.

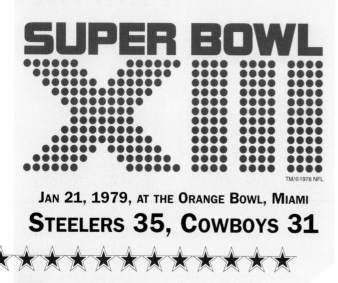

SUPER BOWL XIII

TM/©1978 NFL

JAN 21, 1979, AT THE ORANGE BOWL, MIAMI

STEELERS 35, COWBOYS 31

★★★★★★★★★★★★★★★★★

The bruising "Steel Curtain" defense received most of the credit for Pittsburgh's first two Super Bowl triumphs, but victory No 3 belonged to the offense. Specifically to quarterback Terry Bradshaw, who threw for 318 yards and a record four touchdowns while earning MVP honors.

Bradshaw mesmerized a packed house at Miami's Orange Bowl with three touchdown strikes in a wild first half that produced a 21-14 Pittsburgh lead. Two of those strikes were to John Stallworth—a 28-yarder that gave the Steelers a 7-0 lead and a 75-yard bomb that tied the game at 14. The third, a seven-yarder to Rocky Bleier, gave Pittsburgh a lead it never relinquished.

The Cowboys, who had taken their 14-7 lead on Roger Staubach's 39-yard pass to Tony Hill and linebacker Mike Hegman's 37-yard romp with a fumble recovery, closed to within 21-17 on Rafael Septien's 27-yard third-quarter field goal. But the Steelers blew the game open with two touchdowns in a 19-second span of the fourth quarter.

Franco Harris's 22-yard run accounted for one and Bradshaw's 18-yard strike to Lynn Swann produced the other after a Dallas fumble. With 6:51 remaining, the Steelers were in control, 35-17. Or so everybody thought.

The ever-dangerous Staubach connected on a seven-yard TD strike to Billy Joe DuPree with 2:27 remaining and passed four yards to Butch Johnson for another score with 22 seconds left after the Cowboys recovered an onside kick. The victory wasn't sealed until another onside kick failed after the final touchdown.

Going all the way: Pittsburgh wide receiver John Stallworth (82) made this 75-yard touchdown reception from Terry Bradshaw in the Steelers' 35-31 victory over Dallas.

JAN 20, 1980, AT THE ROSE BOWL, PASADENA, CAL
STEELERS 31, RAMS 19

★★★★★★★★★★★★★★★★★★

A funny thing happened to the Steelers on their way to the coronation: they almost got crowned. Pittsburgh, seeking to become the first four-time Super Bowl winner and stake its claim as the greatest team of all time, needed a 73-yard fourth-quarter touchdown pass from Terry Bradshaw to dispatch a Rams team that had finished 9-7 during the regular season.

The Rams, who had been listed as 11-point underdogs, made Pittsburgh's run to immortality a difficult one. Moving the ball consistently against the "Steel Curtain" defense, the Rams surprisingly forged a 13-10 halftime lead on Cullen Bryant's one-yard run and two Frank Corral field goals. When the Steelers grabbed a 17-13 third-quarter lead on Bradshaw's 47-yard touchdown pass to Lynn Swann, everybody expected the Rams to do a quick fade. What they did was score quickly.

It took quarterback Vince Ferragamo only four plays to move the Rams 77 yards and reclaim the lead. Fifty of those yards came on a pass to Billy Waddy. The final 24 came on running back Lawrence McCutcheon's pass to Ron Smith.

With the Steelers trailing 19-17, Bradshaw decided it was time to think big. With less than 13 minutes remaining and buried on the Pittsburgh 27-yard line, Bradshaw sent Stallworth deep, hit him in stride at the Rams 34 and watched him race untouched toward the end zone for a 24-19 lead. Back in control, Bradshaw later connected with Stallworth on the same play for a 45-yard gain that set up a clinching touchdown—Franco Harris' one-yard run.

Unfazed by the closeness of their fourth Super Bowl victory in six years, the Steelers tried to answer the question on everybody's mind.

 Bradshaw's best again: Pittsburgh quarterback Terry Bradshaw collected his second straight Super Bowl MVP award after the Steelers' fourth triumph, 31-19 over the Rams.

SCORING SUMMARY

LOS ANGELES	7	6	6	0—	19
PITTSBURGH	3	7	7	14—	31

PIT	FG Bahr 41
LA	Bryant 1 run (Corral kick)
PIT	Harris 1 run (Bahr kick)
LA	FG Corral 31
LA	FG Corral 45
PIT	Swann 47 pass from Bradshaw (Bahr kick)
LA	Smith 24 pass from McCutcheon (kick failed)
PIT	Stallworth 73 pass from Bradshaw (Bahr kick)
PIT	Harris 1 run (Bahr kick)

"Winning a fourth Super Bowl should put us in a special category," said cornerback Mel Blount. "I think this is the best team ever assembled. They talk about Vince Lombardi and the Packers, but I think the Chuck Noll era is even greater."

Despite throwing three interceptions, Bradshaw earned his second consecutive MVP award.

★★★★★★★★★★★★★★★★★★★★★★★★★★★★★★★

SUPER BOWL XV

JAN 25, 1981, AT LOUISIANA SUPERDOME, NEW ORLEANS

RAIDERS 27, EAGLES 10

★★★★★★★★★★★★★★★★

Quarterback Jim Plunkett completed his Cinderella season with a three-touchdown performance against the Eagles and the Raiders completed their Cinderella playoff run by becoming the first wild-card team to win a Super Bowl.

The veteran Plunkett, who had been buried on the Oakland bench for more than two years, took over for injured starter Dan Pastorini in Game 5 of the 1980 regular season. The reborn former Heisman Trophy winner led the Raiders to nine victories in his 11 starts and a wild-card playoff berth, a death sentence for all but one previous Super Bowl hopeful (the 1975 Cowboys, who lost in Super Bowl X).

SCORING SUMMARY

OAKLAND	14	0	10	3—27
PHILADELPHIA	0	3	0	7—10

OAK	Branch 2 pass from Plunkett (Bahr kick)
OAK	King 80 pass from Plunkett (Bahr kick)
PHI	FG Franklin 30
OAK	Branch 29 pass from Plunkett (Bahr kick)
OAK	FG Bahr 46
PHI	Krepfle 8 pass from Jaworski (Franklin kick)
OAK	FG Bahr 35

But the Raiders swept through three playoff games and made their victory over the Eagles look easy. Plunkett threw a pair of touchdown passes to Cliff Branch (2 and 29 yards) and connected with running back Kenny King on an 80-yard bomb that broke the Eagles' back.

On the final play from scrimmage of the opening quarter with the Raiders already leading 7-0, a scrambling Plunkett fired to King on the left sideline, just over the outstretched arm of Eagles cornerback Herman Edwards, and King ran untouched for the longest touchdown play in Super Bowl history.

Leading 14-3 at halftime, the Raiders struck for ten third-quarter points to seal the victory. Plunkett, who completed 13 of 21 passes for 261 yards, earned MVP honors, but Raiders linebacker Rod Martin made a major contribution by intercepting a Super Bowl-record three Ron Jaworski passes.

Dick Vermeil's Eagles scored on Jaworski's eight-yard pass to Keith Krepfle and Tony Franklin's 30-yard field goal.

Wild at heart: Jim Plunkett's (16) two first-quarter touchdown passes helped the Oakland Raiders become the first wild card team to win the Super Bowl.

SUPER BOWL XVI

TM/©1981 NFL

JAN 24, 1982, AT PONTIAC SILVERDOME ,PONTIAC, MICH

49ERS 26, BENGALS 21

★★★★★★★★★★★★★★★

SCORING SUMMARY

	1	2	3	4 — Total
SAN FRANCISCO	7	13	0	6—26
CINCINNATI	0	0	7	14—21

SF	Montana 1 run (Wersching kick)
SF	Cooper 11 pass from Montana (Wersching kick)
SF	FG Wersching 22
SF	FG Wersching 26
CIN	Anderson 5 run (Breech kick)
CIN	Ross 4 pass from Anderson (Breech kick)
SF	FG Wersching 40
SF	FG Wersching 23
CIN	Ross 3 pass from Anderson (Breech kick)

When the 49ers squared off against the Bengals in a battle of first-time Super Bowl participants, nobody knew what to expect. And that's exactly what 81,270 fans at the Pontiac Silverdome got—the unexpected.

Such as San Francisco's Super Bowl-record 92-yard drive that produced a second-quarter touchdown; Ray Wersching's record-tying four field goals; the 49ers' record 20-0 halftime lead, courtesy of three point-producing Cincinnati turnovers; a valiant Bengals comeback that fell just short, and a game-saving goal-line stand by the 49ers.

Coach Bill Walsh's 49ers appeared headed for an easy day when quarterback Joe Montana, the game's MVP, scored on a one-yard run and fired an 11-yard scoring pass to Earl Cooper, culminating the 92-yard drive. But the biggest blows were delivered when Wersching kicked two field goals in the final 18 seconds of the first half, the second after a fumbled kickoff.

The Bengals were down, but not out. Cincinnati quarterback Ken Anderson, who would set a Super Bowl record for completions

(25), scored on a five-yard third-quarter run and then directed the Bengals to a first-and-goal at the San Francisco 3. Fullback Pete Johnson reached the one on first down, but the Bengals failed on three tries from there. Johnson was stopped on a fourth-down plunge.

Having missed on that opportunity, Anderson threw a four-yard fourth-quarter touchdown pass to Dan Ross, cutting the deficit to 20-14. But two fourth-quarter Wersching field goals stretched the 49ers' advantage to 26-14, and another Anderson-to-Ross TD pass with 16 seconds remaining was too little, too late.

A SUPER LEAP FOR THE 49ERS

Time was running out for the 49ers in their bid to reach the team's first Super Bowl. Only 4:54 remained in their 1981 NFC Championship Game battle with Dallas and they were 89 yards away from a potential winning touchdown.

If a situation ever was made for Joe Montana, this was it. With his team trailing 27-21, the San Francisco quarterback began a march that would end with one of the most exciting plays in football history.

Mixing runs and passes and masterfully working the clock, Montana took the 49ers deep into Cowboys territory, finally setting up on third-and-three at the Dallas 6-yard line. Only a minute remained.

Montana, who had thrown earlier touchdown passes to Freddie Solomon and Dwight Clark, took the snap, rolled right and felt the pressure of three Dallas defenders. As he neared the sideline, he fired a high pass that appeared to be out of everybody's reach. But the 6-foot-4 Clark, stationed in the back of the end zone, jumped high and snared the ball with a fingertip catch. Ray Wersching's extra point made it final: 49ers 28, Cowboys 27. The victory sent the 49ers to their first Super Bowl. The Cowboys had set up Montana's heroics when Danny White fired a 21-yard fourth-quarter TD pass to Doug Cosbie for the 27-21 lead.

Ray of light: San Francisco was never headed in Super Bowl XVI, and kicker Ray Wersching's four field goals were a record for the game.

SUPER BOWL XVII

Jan 30, 1983, at the Rose Bowl, Pasadena, Cal

REDSKINS 27, DOLPHINS 17

★★★★★★★★★★★★★★★★

It was the "Hogs" versus the "Killer Bees," Washington's huge offensive line versus Miami's swarming defense. In the end, size and strength won out. The unmentioned factors in that equation were bulldozing Redskins running back John Riggins and a Washington defense that did a little swarming of its own. Riggins earned MVP honors by rushing for a Super Bowl-record 166 yards, 43 coming on a fourth-and-one final-quarter touchdown romp that decided the game.

Miami's 17-13 fourth-quarter advantage was forged in a big-play first half that featured a 76-yard touchdown pass from David Woodley to Jimmy Cefalo and an electrifying 98-yard kickoff return by Fulton Walker after Washington had tied the game at 10–10 Walker's TD was the first on a kick return in Super Bowl history.

But the second half was all downhill for the Dolphins, who could penetrate the Washington defense for only 34 total yards. Neither Woodley nor backup quarterback Don Strock completed a second-half pass. It was just a matter of time.

The Redskins sliced their 17-10 halftime deficit to four on Mark Moseley's third-quarter field goal and took control in the final period when Riggins bolted off tackle for his dramatic game-winner. Quarterback Joe Theismann completed the scoring with his second TD pass, a six-yarder to Charlie Brown.

The championship was the first for a Washington team since 1942.

★★★★★★★

SCORING SUMMARY

MIAMI	7	10	0	0—17
WASHINGTON	0	10	3	14—27

MIA	Cefalo 76 pass from Woodley (von Schamann kick)
WAS	FG Moseley 31
MIA	FG von Schamann 20
WAS	Garrett 4 pass from Theismann (Moseley kick)
MIA	Walker 98 kickoff return (von Schamann kick)
WAS	FG Moseley 20
WAS	Riggins 43 run (Moseley kick)
WAS	Brown 6 pass from Theismann (Moseley kick)

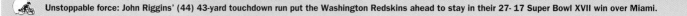

Unstoppable force: John Riggins' (44) 43-yard touchdown run put the Washington Redskins ahead to stay in their 27-17 Super Bowl XVII win over Miami.

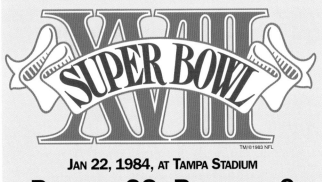

JAN 22, 1984, AT TAMPA STADIUM

RAIDERS 38, REDSKINS 9

★★★★★★★★★★★★★

SCORING SUMMARY

WASHINGTON	0	3	6	0—9
LA RAIDERS	7	14	14	3—38

RAI	Jensen recovered blocked punt in end zone (Bahr kick)
RAI	Branch 12 pass from Plunkett (Bahr kick)
WAS	FG Moseley 24
RAI	Squirek 5 interception return (Bahr kick)
WAS	Riggins 1 run (kick blocked)
RAI	Allen 5 run (Bahr kick)
RAI	Allen 74 run (Bahr kick)
RAI	FG Bahr 21

It might not have been exciting, but it was impressive. The Raiders dominated the defending-champion Redskins in every phase of the game and piled up the most points and biggest margin of victory so far in Super Bowl history.

The first half belonged to the Los Angeles defense, which shut down the Redskins' powerful running attack, pressured quarterback Joe Theismann and produced a pair of touchdowns.

The first came when Derrick Jensen broke through the Washington line, blocked a Jeff Hayes punt and fell on the ball in the end zone. The second was a back-breaker. Seven seconds before halftime, linebacker Jack Squirek intercepted a Joe Theismann pass and returned it five yards for a score. Those big plays, sandwiched around Jim Plunkett's 12-yard scoring pass to Cliff Branch, gave the Raiders a 21-3 halftime lead.

The second half belonged to Raiders running back Marcus Allen, who scored a pair of touchdowns, earned MVP honors and easily outdistanced Washington running back John Riggins in their head-to-head duel. Allen finished with a Super Bowl-record 191 rushing yards, including a creative 74-yard third-quarter touchdown jaunt that iced the Raiders' victory. Ironically, he broke the rushing mark set a year earlier by Riggins (166).

Not only did the Raiders hold Riggins to 64 yards, his first sub-100-yard performance in seven postseason games, they also shut down a Redskins team that had won 11 consecutive games and outscored opponents by more than 250 points.

The Super Bowl victory was the third for the Raiders, their first since moving from Oakland to Los Angeles.

Into the hole: Los Angeles Raiders running back Marcus Allen bursts into the Washington defense with a Super Bowl XVIII MVP performance at Tampa Stadium.

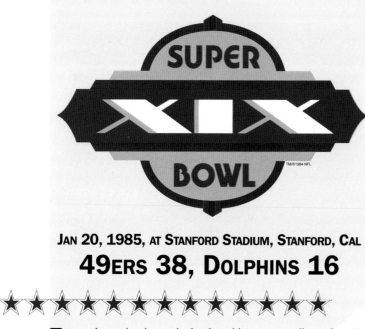

SUPER XIX BOWL

TM/©1984 NFL

49ERS 38, DOLPHINS 16

★★★★★★★★★★★★★

SCORING SUMMARY

MIAMI	10	6	0	0	—16
SAN FRANCISCO	7	21	10	0	—38

MIA	FG von Schamann 37
SF	Monroe 33 pass from Montana (Wersching kick)
MIA	D. Johnson 2 pass from Marino (von Schamann kick)
SF	Craig 8 pass from Montana (Wersching kick)
SF	Montana 6 run (Wersching kick)
SF	Craig 2 run (Wersching kick)
MIA	FG von Schamann 31
MIA	FG von Schamann 30
SF	FG Wersching 27
SF	Craig 16 pass from Montana (Wersching kick)

It was becoming increasingly clear this was no ordinary Joe. And when the dust had cleared on the 19th Super Bowl, Joe Montana had entrenched his name among the great big-game quarterbacks of football history.

Montana, who had won MVP honors in Super Bowl XVI, was nothing short of amazing in this one-sided duel with Dolphins quarterback Dan Marino. Montana completed 24 of 35 passes for a Super Bowl-record 331 yards and three touchdowns. He also scored on a six-yard run, scrambled for 59 yards and directed a diversified San Francisco offense that compiled a record 537 total yards.

It appeared early that Montana and the 49ers would be in for a real shootout. Marino quickly drove the Dolphins to a Uwe von Schamann field goal and answered Montana's 33-yard TD pass to Carl Monroe with a six-play drive that ended with a two-yard scoring pass to Dan Johnson for a 10-7 Miami lead.

But while the 49ers continued to move relentlessly up and down the field, San Francisco defensive coordinator George Seifert made adjustments that slowed Marino to a crawl. The Dolphins would manage only two field goals, one set up by a fumble, the rest of the way.

But Montana was not a one-man show. He received excellent support from Roger Craig (three touchdowns), Wendell Tyler and Dwight Clark, while Marino was forced to operate as a one-man offense. He completed 29 of 50 passes for 318 yards, but he also was sacked four times and harassed unmercifully.

★★★★★★★★★★★★★★

Glory grab: Roger Craig, making an acrobatic catch of this Joe Montana pass, became the first man to score three touchdowns in one Super Bowl.

JAN 26, 1986, AT LOUISIANA SUPERDOME, NEW ORLEANS

BEARS 46, PATRIOTS 10

★ ★ ★ ★ ★ ★ ★ ★ ★ ★ ★ ★ ★ ★

SCORING SUMMARY

CHICAGO	13	10	21	2—46
NEW ENGLAND	3	0	0	7—10

NE	FG Franklin 36
CHI	FG Butler 28
CHI	FG Butler 24
CHI	Suhey 11 run (Butler kick)
CHI	McMahon 2 run (Butler kick)
CHI	FG Butler 24
CHI	McMahon 1 run (Butler kick)
CHI	Phillips 28 interception return (Butler kick)
CHI	Perry 1 run (Butler kick)
NE	Fryar 8 pass from Grogan (Franklin kick)
CHI	Safety, Waechter tackled Grogan in end zone

The big, bad, bragging Bears of Mike Ditka, featuring one of the greatest defenses in NFL history, were way too much for the conservative and outmanned Patriots in the 20th Super Bowl. The problem for New England was very basic.

The Patriots were a running team and nobody had been able to run on the Bears all season. Chicago ranked first against the run and in total defense, third against the pass. The once-beaten Bears had allowed 118 total rushing yards and no points in their previous two playoff contests.

The game opened on a curious note. On the Bears' second play, Walter Payton fumbled and New England's Larry McGrew recovered on the Chicago 19. Three plays later, 1:19 into the game, Tony Franklin gave the Patriots a 3-0 lead with a 36-yard field goal.

That was New England's best moment. The Chicago defense dropped a blanket on the Pats and quarterback Jim McMahon began carving them up offensively. By the end of the first quarter, it was 13-3. By halftime, the Bears led 23-3. A three-touchdown third period, highlighted by cornerback Reggie Phillips' 28-yard interception return, stretched the lead out of sight.

When all was said and done, statistics told a grim story for New England fans. The Patriots had managed only 123 total yards, seven on the ground. The Bears' 46 points were the most in Super Bowl history, as was the 36-point margin of victory. Chicago ran up 408 yards against a respected New England defense.

Behind you: New England's Steve Grogan is about to be sacked by Bears' defensive end Richard Dent, MVP in Chicago's 46-10 Super Bowl XX rout.

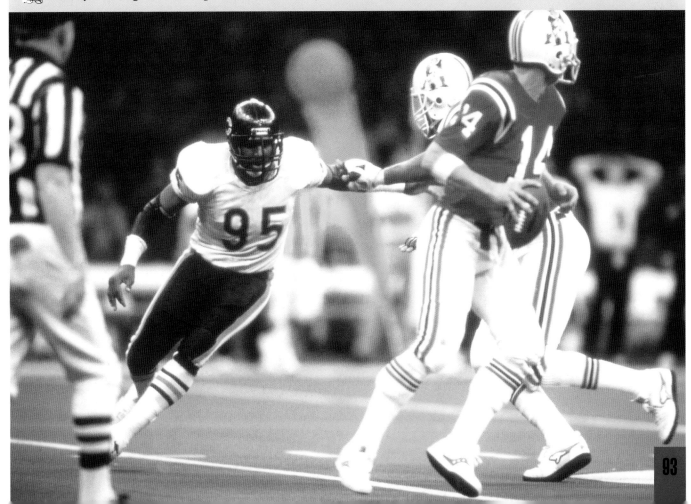

Super Bowl XXI

JAN 25, 1987, THE ROSE BOWL, PASADENA, CAL

GIANTS 39, BRONCOS 20

★★★★★★★★★★★★★★★★

SCORING SUMMARY

DENVER	10	0	0	10	—20
NY GIANTS	7	2	17	13	—39

DEN	FG Karlis 48
NYG	Mowatt 6 pass from Simms (Allegre kick)
DEN	Elway 4 run (Karlis kick)
NYG	Safety, Martin tackled Elway in end zone
NYG	Bavaro 13 pass from Simms (Allegre kick)
NYG	FG Allegre 21
NYG	Morris 1 run (Allegre kick)
NYG	McConkey 6 pass from Simms (Allegre kick)
DEN	FG Karlis 28
NYG	Anderson 2 run (kick failed)
DEN	V Johnson 47 pass from Elway (Karlis kick)

★★★★★★★★★★★★★★

It was supposed to be John Elway versus the rugged New York defense. The only question was whether the strong-armed Broncos quarterback could do enough damage to offset the physical superiority of the heavily favored Giants.

But, like so many big-game plots, this one didn't play out. Elway did give the Giants first-half fits and the New York defense did shut down the Broncos in the second half, but one of the game's other players stole the show.

Giants quarterback Phil Simms, who had played all season in the shadow of a defense featuring super linebacker Lawrence Taylor, didn't get lost in anybody's shadow on this day. He completed 22 of 25 passes for 268 yards and three touchdowns. His 88 percent accuracy was a Super Bowl record, as was his stretch of ten consecutive completions.

The game opened as expected with Elway firing and scrambling and the Broncos reached halftime with a 10-9 lead. It could have been more, but Rich Karlis missed two short field goals and the Giants made a dramatic goal-line stand.

There was nothing dramatic about the third quarter—it was raw power. Simms fired a 13-yard touchdown pass to Mark Bavaro and drove the Giants to a field goal and a one-yard Joe Morris TD run. Simms' six-yard fourth-quarter scoring pass to Phil McConkey stretched the lead to 33-10 before the Broncos could score again.

How good was Simms? "Almost every pass landed exactly where I wanted it," he said. "I've never played better. I told everyone before the game I was smoking."

Close to perfection: New York's Phil Simms, the game's MVP, saw only three of his 25 passing attempts fall incomplete as the Giants beat Denver 39-20.

SCORING SUMMARY

	1	2	3	4 — Total
WASHINGTON	0	35	0	7—42
DENVER	10	0	0	0—10

DEN	Nattiel 56 pass from Elway (Karlis kick)
DEN	FG Karlis 24
WAS	Sanders 80 pass from Williams (Haji-Sheikh kick)
WAS	Clark 27 pass from Williams (Haji-Sheikh kick)
WAS	Smith 58 run (Haji-Sheikh kick)
WAS	Sanders 50 pass from Williams (Haji-Sheikh kick)
WAS	Didier 8 pass from Williams (Haji-Sheikh kick)
WAS	Smith 4 run (Haji-Sheikh kick)

JAN 31, 1988, AT JACK MURPHY STADIUM, SAN DIEGO
REDSKINS 42, BRONCOS 10

★★★★★★★★★★★★

It was more than just a Super Bowl. It was a social milestone. Doug Williams would carry Washington's banner as the first black quarterback to play in the Super Bowl, and he would do it better than any quarterback before him—black or white.

The Broncos never had a chance, even after John Elway had thrown a 56-yard touchdown pass to Ricky Nattiel on Denver's first play from scrimmage; even after Rich Karlis' 24-yard field goal had stretched the advantage to 10-0. The Broncos were merely setting the stage for Williams.

Early in the second quarter, Williams went to work. First he fired an 80-yard bomb to wide receiver Ricky Sanders, matching the longest TD pass in Super Bowl history. Then he fired 27 yards to Gary Clark for another score. After rookie Timmy Smith had reeled off a 58-yard run for Washington's third touchdown of the quarter, Williams hit Sanders again, this time for 50 yards. With the Redskins now leading 28-10, Williams capped the record-setting second-quarter blitz with an eight-yard TD pass to Clint Didier.

The 35-point explosion buried the Broncos and guaranteed Williams game MVP honors. And his record 340-yard, four-touchdown passing performance overshadowed the outstanding effort of Smith, who ran for a Super Bowl-record 204 yards and finished the game with two touchdowns.

Lost in all the offensive fireworks was the play of a Redskins defense that persevered through a tough first quarter and shut down Elway and the Broncos the rest of the way.

Quarter master: Doug Williams was Super Bowl XXII, MVP, throwing four touchdown passes in the second quarter of the Washington Redskins' 42-10 defeat of Denver.

SUPER BOWL XXIII

TM/©1988 NFL

JAN 22, 1989, AT JOE ROBBIE STADIUM, MIAMI
49ERS 20, BENGALS 16

★★★★★★★★★★★★★★★★★

It had to happen. Sooner or later there would be another truly super Super Bowl. After a long string of one-sided games dominated by teams from the NFC, football's showcase event needed a shot of adrenalin. What it also got was a big dose of "Montana Magic."

Bill Walsh's 49ers, trying to win their third Super Bowl of the decade, appeared to be doomed when they took possession at their own eight-yard line with 3:10 remaining. The Bengals led 16-13 and the 49ers had been uncharacteristically checked by the bend-but-don't-break Cincinnati defense.

But nobody had to tell the 49ers that this script was perfect for Joe Montana, the greatest pressure quarterback of the era. "When you see Joe do it in the clutch as much as we have, you think he can do it every time," said tackle Bubba Paris.

Montana, operating without a huddle, proceeded to carve up the Bengals with uncanny precision. Mixing passes and runs while masterfully working the clock, he marched the 49ers 92 yards, completing the most electrifying drive in Super Bowl history with a ten-yard scoring strike to John Taylor with 34 seconds remaining.

Montana finished with a Super Bowl-record 357 passing yards, but most of them were garnered between the 20s. Only one of his previous passes had produced points—a 14-yard fourth-quarter strike to Jerry Rice. That touchdown tied the game at 13 after the Bengals had jumped ahead on Stanford Jennings' 93-yard kickoff return.

Before Jennings' burst, the game had been a defensive battle of the kickers—Mike Cofer hitting two field goals for San Francisco, Jim Breech two for Cincinnati. After Rice's touchdown, Breech added a third that gave the Bengals their 16-13 lead.

Despite Montana's late heroics, MVP honors went to Rice, who caught 11 passes for a Super Bowl-record 215 yards. The victory was the fifth straight for the NFC and seventh in eight years.

★★★★★★★★★★★★★★★★★

Lull before the storm: MVP Jerry Rice had 11 receptions for a game record 215 yards in San Francisco's 20-16 Super Bowl XXIII victory over Cincinnati.

JAN 28, 1990, AT LOUISIANA SUPERDOME, NEW ORLEANS
49ERS 55, BRONCOS 10

SCORING SUMMARY

	1	2	3	4	
SAN FRANCISCO	13	14	14	14	—55
DENVER	3	0	7	0	—10

SF	Rice 20 pass from Montana (Cofer kick)
Den	FG Treadwell 42
SF	Jones 7 pass from Montana (kick failed)
SF	Rathman 1 run (Cofer kick)
SF	Rice 38 pass from Montana (Cofer kick)
SF	Rice 28 pass from Montana (Cofer kick)
SF	Taylor 35 pass from Montana (Cofer kick)
Den	Elway 3 run (Treadwell kick)
SF	Rathman 4 run (Cofer kick)
SF	Craig 1 run (Cofer kick)

One year after choreographing the most exciting finish in Super Bowl history, Joe Montana powered the 49ers to the game's most one-sided mismatch. As a result, San Francisco joined Pittsburgh as the only four-time winners of football's showcase event and the Broncos joined Minnesota as the only four-time losers.

Denver's hopes of ending that futility vanished with three first-half flicks of Montana's wrist and a one-yard run by Tom Rathman. On the 49ers' first possession, Montana fired a 20-yard scoring pass to Jerry Rice. He followed that with a seven-yarder to Brent Jones and a 38-yarder to Rice. It was 27-3 at halftime, and 34-3 early in the second half when Rice caught his third TD pass, a 28-yarder.

When the dust cleared, Montana had completed 22 of 29 passes for 297 yards and a Super Bowl-record five touchdowns. Rice caught seven of those passes for 148 yards. The performance earned Montana a record third Super Bowl MVP award and padded an unbelievable postseason in which he completed 63 of 85 passes (no interceptions) for 800 yards and 11 touchdowns. Not surprisingly, the 49ers won their three playoff games by 100 points.

The 49ers' four Super Bowl victories were accomplished in nine years, three more than it took the Steelers to win their four. San Francisco's first three wins were coached by Bill Walsh, the fourth by George Seifert, who took the reins when Walsh retired after Super Bowl XXIII.

The Broncos, who suffered their third Super Bowl loss in four years, were outgained 461 yards to 167.

Four-timer: San Francisco routed Denver 55-10 in Super Bowl XXIV, the team's fourth triumph, while quarterback Joe Montana collected his third MVP award.

SUPER BOWL XXV

TM/©1990 NFL

JAN 27, 1991, AT TAMPA STADIUM
GIANTS 20, BILLS 19

★★★★★★★★★★★★★★★★★★★

SCORING SUMMARY

BUFFALO	3	9	0	7—19
NY GIANTS	3	7	7	3—20

NYG	FG Bahr 28
BUF	FG Norwood 23
BUF	D. Smith 1 run (Norwood kick)
BUF	Safety, B. Smith tackled Hostetler in end zone
NYG	Baker 14 pass from Hostetler (Bahr kick)
NYG	Anderson 1 run (Bahr kick)
BUF	Thomas 31 run (Norwood kick)
NYG	FG Bahr 21

After the Bills responded with Thurman Thomas' 31-yard go-ahead TD run, Matt Bahr kicked a 21-yard field goal to put New York ahead 20-19 and set up Norwood's memorable miss.

But the game really was won and lost in the trenches. The Giants played almost a perfect game, controlling the ball for 40 minutes, 33 seconds. The Bills had the ball for less than eight minutes in the second half.

Anderson, who rushed for 102 yards, was named most valuable player. Thomas ran for 135 yards in a losing cause.

After six consecutive Super Bowl victories by NFC teams, Buffalo kicker Scott Norwood stood near midfield considering the responsibility that had been placed on his shoulders. The clock showed eight seconds remaining, the Bills trailed by a point and Norwood had it within his power to give the AFC a much-needed victory.

It wasn't to be. In one of the most electrifying moments in Super Bowl history, Norwood stepped into a 47-yard field-goal attempt that would pull millions of fans to the edge of their seats. The ball sailed high, long—and wide right with four seconds left. The Giants were Super Bowl winners for a second time, by the narrowest margin in the classic's 25-year history.

The game was a matchup of contrasting styles. The high-powered Bills, who had scored 95 points in two playoff victories with their no-huddle offense, were pitted against a physical Giants team that relied on a run-oriented, ball-control offense.

And after Buffalo had jumped to a 12-3 second-quarter lead on a Norwood field goal, Don Smith's one-yard run and a safety, the Giants settled into their game plan, which was to keep the Bills' offense off the field.

The Giants trimmed the lead in the second quarter on Jeff Hostetler's 14-yard TD pass to Stephen Baker and moved ahead in the third on a 75-yard drive that consumed 9:29 before Ottis Anderson ran over from the 1 for a 17-12 lead.

Giant strides: Super Bowl XXV MVP Ottis Anderson is chased by Buffalo linebacker Ray Bentley, en route to his game-high 102 yards.

JAN 26, 1992, AT THE METRODOME, MINNEAPOLIS

REDSKINS 37, BILLS 24

TM/© 1990 NFL

SCORING SUMMARY

WASHINGTON	0	17	14	6—37
BUFFALO	0	0	10	14—24

WAS	FG Lohmiller 34
WAS	Byner 10 pass from Rypien (Lohmiller kick)
WAS	Riggs 1 run (Lohmiller kick)
WAS	Riggs 2 run (Lohmiller kick)
BUF	FG Norwood 21
BUF	Thomas 1 run (Norwood kick)
WAS	Clark 30 pass from Rypien (Lohmiller kick)
WAS	FG Lohmiller 25
WAS	FG Lohmiller 39
BUF	Metzelaars 2 pass from Kelly (Norwood kick)
BUF	Beebe 4 pass from Kelly (Norwood kick)

B uffalo fans who were expecting their Bills to avenge a one-point 1991 Super Bowl loss to the Giants were in for a rude awakening. By halftime, the Redskins had pinched them back to reality and plotted the course for their third Super Bowl championship in ten seasons.

After a scoreless first quarter, it was never close. The Redskins, who had squandered scoring opportunities on their first two possessions, posted 17 second-quarter points—three on a 34-yard Chip Lohmiller field goal, seven on Mark Rypien's ten-yard pass to Earnest Byner and seven more on Gerald Riggs' one-yard run—for a 17-0 halftime lead.

At that point, the Redskins had outgained the high-powered Bills, 264 yards to 31. And things only got worse when linebacker Kurt Gouveia intercepted Jim Kelly's first pass of the second half and returned it to Buffalo's 2-yard line, setting up another Riggs TD run.

The Bills rallied with ten third-quarter points, but Rypien's 30-yard touchdown pass to Gary Clark and two more Lohmiller field goals sealed the verdict. Two late Kelly TD passes only made the score respectable.

The Redskins rolled up 417 total yards, 292 on the passing of Rypien, the game's MVP. Conversely, the Bills' Thurman Thomas, who had led the AFC with 1,407 rushing yards, was held to 13 while Kelly was forced to throw a Super Bowl-record 58 passes, four of which were intercepted.

The victory lifted Redskins Coach Joe Gibbs into elite status. He became only the third three-time Super Bowl winner, joining Chuck Noll, who won four, and Bill Walsh.

Defense ripped to shreds: Mark Rypien was named Most Valuable Player in Super Bowl XXVI after throwing touchdown passes to Earnest Byner and Gary Clark.

JAN 31, 1993, AT THE ROSE BOWL, PASADENA, CAL
COWBOYS 52, BILLS 17

★★★★★★★★★★★★★★★★★

I n their first Super Bowl appearance since the 1978 season (Super Bowl XIII), the Cowboys overpowered the frustrated Bills, who lost for the third year in a row. Buffalo committed nine turnovers that Dallas converted into 35 points.

The Cowboys, who won their third Super Bowl in a record sixth appearance, recovered five fumbles and intercepted four passes after Buffalo had taken a quick 7-0 lead on Thurman Thomas' two-yard run. That early Buffalo touchdown was set up by a blocked punt.

BUFFALO STAMPEDES HOUSTON

To say the Buffalo Bills were forced away from their game plan is something of an understatement. When Houston safety Bubba McDowell intercepted a Frank Reich pass and ran it back 58 yards for a third-quarter touchdown, the Oilers enjoyed a comfortable 35-3 lead in a 1992 AFC Wild-Card Playoff Game at Buffalo.

No NFL team had ever come back from such a deficit and a pair of third-quarter Reich touchdown passes did not seem overly significant. But a combination of Houston mistakes and two more quick Buffalo scores cut Houston's lead to 35-31 heading into the final quarter.

The sellout crowd watched in disbelief as Reich, filling in for injured Jim Kelly, completed the amazing comeback with a 17-yard TD strike to Andre Reed, giving the Bills a 38-35 advantage with 3:08 left. The stunned Oilers did manage a valiant 63-yard drive of their own, resulting in Al Del Greco's game-tying field goal with 12 seconds remaining.

But they were just delaying the inevitable. The game ended in overtime, 41-38, when Buffalo's Nate Odomes intercepted a Warren Moon pass to set up Steve Christie's winning 32-yard field goal. The Oilers had built their big lead on Moon's four first-half TD passes, two to Haywood Jeffires.

SCORING SUMMARY

BUFFALO	7	3	7	0—17
DALLAS	14	14	3	21—52

Buf — Thomas 2 run (Christie)
Dal — Novacek 23 pass from Aikman (Elliott)
Dal — Jones 2 fumble recovery return (Elliott)
Buf — FG Christie 21
Dal — Irvin 19 pass from Aikman
Dal — Irvin 18 pass from Aikman
Dal — FG Elliott 20
Buf — Beebe 40
Dal — Harper
Dal —
Buf —
Dal — Norton

Dallas pulled even when quarterback Troy Aikman passed 23 yards to tight end Jay Novacek after a James Washington interception and took the lead for good when defensive tackle Jimmie Jones picked up a Kelly fumble and ran two yards for a touchdown.

It was that kind of a day for Buffalo players and fans.

Late in the second quarter Aikman fired 19 and 18-yard touchdown passes to Michael Irvin 18 seconds apart for a 28-10 halftime lead. The second score was set up by a Thomas fumble. The Cowboys scored three touchdowns in 2:33 of the fourth quarter, the finale on linebacker Ken Norton's nine-yard fumble return.

Dallas' victory, the ninth straight for an NFC team, completed the Cowboys' swift rise to prominence under Coach Jimmy Johnson. Dallas had finished 1-15 in 1989, Johnson's first season.

Cowboys running back Emmitt Smith ran for 108 yards and a touchdown in his first Super Bowl appearance, but Aikman claimed MVP honors with a 22-of-30 passing performance that netted 273 yards and four touchdowns.

Cowboys' explosion: Dallas, quarterbacked by Troy Aikman, defeated the Bills 52-17, the Cowboys' third Super Bowl triumph, and first of the post-Tom Landry era.

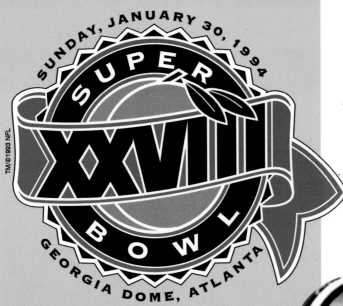

SUNDAY, JANUARY 30, 1994

SUPER BOWL

XXVIII

GEORGIA DOME, ATLANTA

TM/©1993 NFL

SCORING SUMMARY				
DALLAS	6	0	14	10—30
BUFFALO	3	10	0	0—13

Dal	FG Murray 41
Buf	FG Christie 54
Dal	FG Murray 24
Buf	Thomas 4 run (Christie kick)
Buf	FG Christie 28
Dal	Washington 46 fumble return (Murray kick)
Dal	E. Smith 15 run (Murray kick)
Dal	E. Smith 1 run (Murray kick)
Dal	FG Murray 20

JAN 30, 1994, AT THE GEORGIA DOME, ATLANTA

COWBOYS 30, BILLS 13

★★★★★★★★★★★★★★★★

The Cowboys joined the Steelers and 49ers as four-time Super Bowl winners, while the Bills, the first team to earn four Super Bowl berths in a row, became the first to lose four in a row. However, the Bills went down with a fight. They played well enough, in fact, to forge a 13-6 halftime advantage and they trailed by only a touchdown (20-13) before the Cowboys put the game away with a 10-point final quarter.

The Cowboys' best offensive weapon was running back Emmitt Smith, who rushed for a game-high 132 yards and two touchdowns en route to MVP honors. Smith did most of his damage in the second half, rushing for 91 yards and scoring on runs of 15 yards and one yard—the touchdowns that broke a 13-13 tie and sealed the victory.

But it was a big defensive play that turned the momentum in Dallas' favor. Trailing by seven points with 55 seconds gone in the second half, defensive tackle Leon Lett stripped Thurman Thomas of the ball and safety James Washington picked it up. Washington weaved through traffic for 46 yards and a touchdown.

On their next possession, the Cowboys drove for another score with Smith rushing for 61 of the 64 yards. Eddie Murray contributed three field goals to the Dallas cause while Steve Christie booted a Super Bowl-record 54-yarder for Buffalo.

★★★★★★★★★★★★★★★★★

 Just Super: Emmitt Smith injured his shoulder four weeks before Super Bowl XXVIII, but when it mattered he was ready and picked up the MVP award.

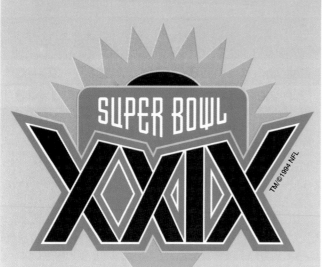

SUPER BOWL XXIX

TM/© 1994 NFL

JAN 29, 1995, AT JOE ROBBIE STADIUM, MIAMI

49ERS 49, CHARGERS 26

★★★★★★★★★★★★★★★

The ghost of Joe Montana wouldn't go away. So San Francisco quarterback Steve Young arranged an exorcism. It would be performed on Super Sunday during a game that would pit football's best offense against the heaviest underdog in Super Bowl history.

It's not like Young really had anything to prove. Since taking over as starting quarterback from Montana in 1991, he had won four straight NFL passing titles and moved ahead of Montana as the game's all-time highest-rated passer. His 1994 season was brilliant: 3,969 passing yards, a 70.3 percent completion rate, 35 TD passes, 293 rushing yards. With Young pulling the trigger, the high-powered 49ers had averaged more than 31 points per game.

But something was missing. Montana had won four Super Bowls; Young had never gotten the 49ers past the NFC Championship Game. The exorcist was ready and the Chargers never had a prayer.

Young completed 24 of 36 passes for 325 yards and a Super Bowl-record six touchdowns, breaking Montana's mark of five. His MVP performance also included a game-high 49 rushing yards. Ten of Young's completions and three of his touchdown passes went to Jerry Rice, who finished the day as the holder of every major receiving record in Super Bowl history.

How complete was San Francisco's domination? Young fired a 44-yard scoring pass to Rice on the game's third play. He hit running back Ricky Watters with a 51-yard TD pass 4:55 into the first quarter. He added scoring tosses of five yards to William Floyd and eight yards to Watters before halftime and connected with Rice again in the third quarter for a 42-10 lead after Watters had run nine yards for a touchdown.

The highlight for San Diego, a first-time Super Bowl participant, was a 98-yard kickoff return for a touchdown by Andre Coleman after Rice's second touchdown.

When all was said and done, the 49ers had their record fifth Super Bowl victory, the NFC had its 11th in a row and Young had his "Big One." The ghost was gone.

SCORING SUMMARY				
SAN DIEGO	7	3	8	8—26
SAN FRANCISCO	14	14	14	7—49

SF	Rice 44 pass from Young (Brien kick)
SF	Watters 51 pass from Young (Brien kick)
SD	Means 1 run (Carney kick)
SF	Floyd 5 pass from Young (Brien kick)
SF	Watters 8 pass from Young (Brien kick)
SD	FG Carney 31
SF	Watters 9 run (Brien kick)
SF	Rice 15 pass from Young (Brien kick)
SD	Coleman 98 kickoff return (Seay pass from Humphries)
SF	Rice 7 pass from Young (Brien kick)
SD	Martin 30 pass from Humphries (Pupunu pass from Humphries)

Young at heart: San Francisco became the first five-time Super Bowl champion, routing the San Diego Chargers, 49-26. Steve Young threw a Super Bowl-record six touchdown passes.

SUNDAY, JANUARY 28, 1996
SUPER
XXX
BOWL
SUN DEVIL STADIUM, ARIZONA

TM/©1995 NFL

JAN 28, 1996, AT SUN DEVIL STADIUM, TEMPE
COWBOYS 27, STEELERS 17

★★★★★★★★★★★★★★★

Everybody agreed. The only way to unplug the Dallas Cowboys' offensive machine was to harness the triple-threat tandem of quarterback Troy Aikman, running back Emmitt Smith and wide receiver Michael Irvin.

The Pittsburgh Steelers did exactly that-and still lost. The new era Steel Curtain limited Aikman to 15 pass completions, Smith to 49 yards and Irvin to five catches, but the Cowboys still had enough horses to pull out their third Super Bowl victory in four years and the NFC's 12th in a row and 14th in 15 years.

The victory was especially sweet for much-maligned Dallas Coach Barry Switzer, who had replaced Jimmy Johnson after the team's 1993 championship and generated a storm of controversy with his comments and sideline decisions. It was also redemption for a franchise that had fallen twice in Super Bowls to the powerful Pittsburgh teams of the 1970s.

The Steelers entered Super Bowl XXX as heavy underdogs and quickly fell behind 13-0 on two Chris Boniol field goals and Aikman's three-yard touchdown pass to tight end Jay Novacek. The touchdown was set up by Aikman's 47-yard strike to cornerback-turned-receiver Deion Sanders.

But the rest of the game belonged to the Steelers-statistically. After quarterback Neil O'Donnell's second-quarter six-yard pass to Yancey Thigpen had cut the deficit to 13-7, the Pittsburgh defense took over. In the second half, the Steelers outgained the Cowboys 201 yards to 61, ran 52 plays to their 19 and controlled the ball for 21 minutes, 20 seconds.

But they were outscored 14-10, thanks to Dallas cornerback Larry Brown's two untimely interceptions of O'Donnell passes.

The first came midway through the third quarter and Brown returned it 44 yards to the Pittsburgh 18. It took Aikman two plays to get it into the end zone—a 17-yard pass to Irvin and Smith's one-yard run—increasing the Dallas lead to 20-7.

The Steelers struck back on Norm Johnson's fourth-quarter field goal and surprised the Cowboys by recovering an on-side kick. Nine plays later, Bam Morris' one-yard run and Johnson's extra-point kick cut the deficit to 20-17 with 6:36 remaining.

The Steelers, with the momentum suddenly in their favor and O'Donnell having completed 13 of his last 14 passes, got the ball

SCORING SUMMARY				
DALLAS	10	3	7	7—27
PITTSBURGH	0	7	0	10—17

DAL	FG Boniol 42
DAL	Novacek 3 pass from Aikman (Boniol kick)
DAL	FG Boniol 35
PIT	Thigpen 6 pass from O'Donnell (Johnson kick)
DAL	Smith 1 run (Boniol kick)
PIT	FG Johnson 46
PIT	Morris 1 run (Johnson kick)
DAL	Smith 4 run (Boniol kick)

back and began what they hoped would be the game-winning drive. But on Pittsburgh's second play, O'Donnell's pass into the right flat was picked off by Brown, who returned the ball 33 yards to the Steelers 6-yard line. Smith scored the game-securing touchdown two plays later on a four-yard run.

Brown was named MVP in Dallas' record-tying fifth Super Bowl victory and Cowboys defensive end Charles Haley competed in his record fifth Super Bowl triumph. The loss was Pittsburgh's first in five Super Bowl appearances.

Brownout: When Cowboys defensive back Larry Brown made this fourth-quarter interception of a Neil O'Donnell pass and returned it to the 6-yard line, a Dallas victory was all but assured.

SUPER BOWL XXXI

SCORING SUMMARY

NEW ENGLAND	14	0	7	0—21
GREEN BAY	10	17	8	0—35

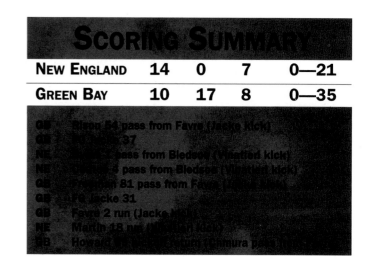

GB — Rison 54 pass from Favre (Jacke kick)
GB — FG Jacke 37
NE — Byars 1 pass from Bledsoe (Vinatieri kick)
NE — Coates 4 pass from Bledsoe (Vinatieri kick)
GB — Freeman 81 pass from Favre (Jacke kick)
GB — FG Jacke 31
GB — Favre 2 run (Jacke kick)
NE — Martin 18 run (Vinatieri kick)
GB — Howard 99 kickoff return (Chmura pass from Favre)

JAN 26, 1997, AT LOUISIANA SUPERDOME, NEW ORLEANS

PACKERS 35, PATRIOTS 21

★★★★★★★★★★★★★★★★★

Vince Lombardi might not have approved of the method. But he would have appreciated the result. Throwing caution to the wind and the ball to his fleet of speedy receivers, Packers quarterback Brett Favre keyed a Super Bowl victory over the Patriots that returned the NFL championship to Green Bay after a 29-year absence.

When Lombardi-coached Packers teams captured five NFL titles and two Super Bowls during the 1960s, they did it with methodical precision and raw power. Finesse wasn't a big part of Lombardi's game plan.

But Mike Holmgren drew up his strategy around the strong right arm of Favre, who rewarded his coach with touchdown bombs of 54 yards to Andre Rison and 81 yards to Antonio Freeman before scoring another on a two-yard scramble in the second quarter. But the coup de grace was delivered without Favre's help. After the Patriots had pulled to within 27–21 late in the third quarter on an 18-yard Curtis Martin run, little Desmond Howard broke New England's back.

Howard, who had set up 10 early points with long punt returns, took the ensuing kickoff at the 1-yard line and headed toward a seam in the middle of the field. A block by Lamont Hollinquest and a missed tackle opened the gate for Howard, who sprinted a record 99 yards for the

touchdown and then watched Favre pass to Mark Chmura for a two-point conversion. The Patriots, their momentum sapped, were beaten.

It appeared early that the Packers' road to a 13th consecutive NFC Super Bowl victory would be smooth and almost effortless. On Green Bay's second offensive play, Favre caught the Patriots in a blitz and fired deep to Rison, who caught the ball at the New England 20 and raced home for the first score. An interception of Patriots quarterback Drew Bledsoe on the next possession set up a 37-yard Chris Jacke field goal that made it 10–0.

But any thoughts of another Super blowout died quickly when Bledsoe put together two quick drives of his own and fired a one-yard TD pass to Keith Byars and a four-yarder to Ben Coates for a 14–10 lead.

The Packers regained control in a 17-point second quarter that was highlighted by Freeman's 81-yard bomb, the longest scoring play from scrimmage in Super Bowl history. The Packers held their 27–14 lead until Martin ran for his touchdown and set the stage for Howard, who was named Super Bowl MVP.

Favre concluded his big day with 14 completions in 27 attempts for 246 yards. Bledsoe was 25-of-48 for 253.

Turning point: With three blockers in front of him, Desmond Howard embarks on a Super Bowl-record 99-yard kickoff return that knocked the heart out of the New England Patriots and ensured that the Green Bay Packers' 29-year wait for a third Super Bowl was over.

Super Bowl results

GAME	DATE	SITE	WINNER	LOSER	SCORE
I	1-15-67	Los Angeles	Green Bay	Kansas City	35-10
II	1-14-68	Miami	Green Bay	Oakland	33-14
III	1-12-69	Miami	NY Jets	Baltimore	16-7
IV	1-11-70	New Orleans	Kansas City	Minnesota	23-7
V	1-17-71	Miami	Baltimore	Dallas	16-13
VI	1-16-72	New Orleans	Dallas	Miami	24-3
VII	1-14-73	Los Angeles	Miami	Washington	14-7
VIII	1-13-74	Houston	Miami	Minnesota	24-7
IX	1-12-75	New Orleans	Pittsburgh	Minnesota	16-6
X	1-18-76	Miami	Pittsburgh	Dallas	21-17
XI	1- 9-77	Pasadena	Oakland	Minnesota	32-14
XII	1-15-78	New Orleans	Dallas	Denver	27-10
XIII	1-21-79	Miami	Pittsburgh	Dallas	35-31
XIV	1-20-80	Pasadena	Pittsburgh	LA Rams	31-19
XV	1-25-81	New Orleans	Oakland	Philadelphia	27-10
XVI	1-24-82	Pontiac	San Francisco	Cincinnati	26-21
XVII	1-30-83	Pasadena	Washington	Miami	27-17
XVIII	1-22-84	Tampa	LA Raiders	Washington	38-9
XIX	1-20-85	Stanford	San Francisco	Miami	38-16
XX	1-26-86	New Orleans	Chicago	New England	46-10
XXI	1-25-87	Pasadena	NY Giants	Denver	39-20
XXII	1-31-88	San Diego	Washington	Denver	42-10
XXIII	1-22-89	Miami	San Francisco	Cincinnati	20-16
XXIV	1-28-90	New Orleans	San Francisco	Denver	55-10
XXV	1-27-91	Tampa	NY Giants	Buffalo	20-19
XXVI	1-26-92	Minneapolis	Washington	Buffalo	37-24
XXVII	1-31-93	Pasadena	Dallas	Buffalo	52-17
XXVIII	1-30-94	Atlanta	Dallas	Buffalo	30-13
XXIX	1-29-95	Miami	San Francisco	San Diego	49-26
XXX	1-28-96	Tempe	Dallas	Pittsburgh	27-17
XXXI	1-26-97	New Orleans	Green Bay	New England	35-21

Fun in the sun

★★★★★★★★★★★★

PRO BOWL FINDS LIFE IN HAWAII'S EMBRACE

The Pro Bowl is not your average, everyday all-star game. It never has been. Since its 1939 debut as the brainchild of Washington Redskins owner George Preston Marshall, football's postseason classic has groped and searched for an identity that only recently has taken shape.

That shape began emerging from the shadows of a formless past in 1980 when the Pro Bowl, looking for a new home and a

warm embrace, found both in Hawaii, the event's first non-league site. It was a perfect fit. The NFL needed enthusiasm and atmosphere for its traveling all-star show. The islands, with a strong base of football fans, wanted a professional sports event they could call their own.

"The game became much bigger there than it ever could have in an NFL city, because it was the only opportunity for the fans of Hawaii

Fun in the sun: The beautiful Aloha Stadium in Hawaii has been the setting for the Pro Bowl since 1980. This game is usually a sellout.

to see NFL players in person," said Joe Rhein, a former NFL official who helped coordinate the first 10 Hawaiian Pro Bowls.

With exotic beaches and ideal weather providing the perfect backdrop for the culmination of a long football season, attitudes toward the Pro Bowl did an abrupt about-face. Players who had pleaded injuries and dropped out of previous Pro Bowl games found the lure of an all-expense-paid week in paradise too much to resist. So did mainland tourists, who didn't need that much of an excuse to begin with. And the Hawaiians filled the pre-game week with cultural events and activities that only enhanced their reputation as exquisite hosts.

Today's Pro Bowl, which annually attracts sellout crowds at Honolulu's Aloha Stadium, is light years removed from the loosely organized exhibition played in January, 1939, pitting the defending-champion New York Giants against a team of other NFL all-stars. The Giants won that game, 13-10, before an estimated crowd of 20,000 at Wrigley Field in Los Angeles—a stadium built for baseball. That format continued for four more games, played at Los Angeles' Gilmore Stadium, New York's Polo Grounds and Philadelphia's Shibe Park drawing an attendance best of 21,624.

When the game was put on hold because of World War II, the format was reassessed. The all-star classic (now bearing the Pro Bowl banner) re-emerged as a bigger and better product in 1951, pitting the American Conference against the National Conference in the huge Los Angeles Coliseum. The format would change to East versus West in 1954, but the game would remain in Los Angeles until 1972.

It was a tenuous existence. The Pro Bowl seemed incapable of matching the charm of baseball's midsummer classic and fans never embraced the format. The game could not be played at midseason for fear of injuries; it seemed anticlimactic as a postscript to the NFL's championship season. And the indifference displayed by many players only made matters worse. A Pro Bowl-record crowd of 72,250 flocked to the Coliseum in 1959, but that stood in stark contrast to the sub-20,000 crowds of 1952 and 1967.

After the 1970 merger, the Pro Bowl became a battle between stars from the AFC and NFC. It also became a traveling show, similar to the concept baseball employs for its All-Star Game. With the league convinced that the regional concept was outdated in this era of mass marketing and coast-to-coast television coverage, the Pro Bowl made stops at Texas Stadium, Kansas City's Arrowhead Stadium, Miami's Orange Bowl, the Louisiana Superdome, Seattle's Kingdome, Tampa Stadium and back to the LA Coliseum before finding its way to Hawaii. Paradise found.

Energized by life in the tropics, the Pro Bowl has joined the baseball and NBA All-Star games as show-stopping classics. The game now offers $20,000 to members of the winning team, $10,000 to the losers. That winning incentive was $600 in 1951, $5,000 in 1978.

Local welcome: Cheerleaders at the Pro Bowl take on a different look as the hula dancers entertain the fans before the 1989 game.

The Pro Bowl also has become more fan-friendly. The game's players, who are selected by a combination vote of players, coaches and fans, are relaxed and approachable. There's plenty for everybody to see and do. And everything about the game carries the flavor of the islands, from pre-game Hula dancers to halftime pageantry featuring Hawaiian themes. It has become difficult to separate the Pro Bowl from Hawaii's cultural traditions.

As far as NFL officials are concerned, that's the way it should be.

Pro Bowl classics

1939

NY GIANTS 13, ALL-STARS 10

Bringing George Preston Marshall's dream of an NFL all-star game to life, the defending-champion Giants rallied for ten fourth-quarter points and pulled out a three-point decision over a team of NFL and independent professional All-Stars.

The winning points were scored with five minutes remaining on an 18-yard field goal by Ward Cuff after the Giants had tied the game on Ed Danowski's 22-yard touchdown pass to Chuck Gelatka.

The All-Stars scored their only touchdown in the third quarter on a stunning 70-yard pass from Sammy Baugh (Redskins) to Lloyd Cardwell (Lions).

1956

EAST 31, WEST 30

This battle of big plays was not decided until the West's Bert Rechichar missed a final-second field-goal attempt. He had connected from 46 yards in the third quarter.

The West's Jack Christiansen (Lions) returned the opening kickoff 103 yards for a touchdown and the East's Ollie Matson (Cardinals)

Revenge is sweet: Joe Theismann put the misery of Washington's Super Bowl defeat a week earlier behind him, to have an MVP day in the Pro Bowl in 1984. His NFC team won, 45-3.

returned the second-half kickoff 91 yards for another score. Matson also scored on a 15-yard run and West quarterback Ed Brown (Bears) fired a 73-yard TD pass to Billy Howton (Packers).

In addition to his two touchdowns, Matson rushed for 83 yards, returned two punts for 57 yards and brought back two kickoffs for 137. Lou Groza (Browns) kicked a 50-yard field goal for the East.

1962

WEST 31, EAST 30

Jim Brown (Browns) ran 70 yards for a go-ahead touchdown with 5:20 remaining, but his fumble with less than 2 minutes to play set up the West's winning touchdown.

The final drive was engineered by the master—Johnny Unitas (Colts). Working without a timeout, Unitas marched the West to the East 12-yard line, scrambled away from the rush and found Jon Arnett (Rams) wide open in the end zone with 10 seconds on the clock. Unitas had connected earlier on a 16-yard TD pass to Colts teammate Raymond Berry.

Brown, who was voted the game's outstanding back, rushed for a game-high 120 yards.

1971

NFC 27, AFC 6

The first post-merger Pro Bowl game matched the American Conference against the National Conference in a new format. The game was tightly contested until a Cowboys defensive back stole the spotlight in the final quarter.

With the NFC guarding a 13-6 lead, Mel Renfro fielded an AFC punt at his own 18-yard line and ran it back 82 yards for a touchdown. Later in the period, Renfro iced the victory by returning a punt 56 yards for another touchdown.

The NFC's other TD came in the third quarter on a 23-yard pass from John Brodie (49ers) to Dave Osborn (Vikings).

1975

NFC 17, AFC 10

James Harris (Rams), a Pro Bowl injury replacement for Fran Tarkenton (Vikings), came off the bench and rallied the NFC with two fourth-quarter touchdown passes.

With the AFC protecting a 10-3 advantage, Harris fired an eight-yard TD strike to Mel Gray (Cardinals). He connected with Charley Taylor (Redskins) on an eight-yard touchdown pass 1:24 later after Ken Houston (Redskins) recovered an AFC fumble.

The AFC's only touchdown was scored on a 32-yard third-quarter pass from Bob Griese to Miami teammate Paul Warfield.

1976

NFC 23, AFC 20

Mike Boryla (Eagles), who entered the game with only 5:39 remaining, fired scoring passes to two Cardinals receivers and rallied the NFC to an unlikely victory.

Boryla took over with the NFC trailing, 20-9. He connected with Terry Metcalf on a 14-yard scoring pass and fired the winner to Mel Gray (an eight-yarder) with 1:09 remaining. The NFC victory tied the series at 3-3.

Despite Boryla's late heroics, outstanding player honors went to Houston's Billy (White Shoes) Johnson, who scored a touchdown on a 90-yard punt return and set up a field goal with a 55-yard return. Johnson amassed a whopping 233 return yards.

1980

NFC 37, AFC 27

In a game that included seven future Hall of Famers, NFC running back Chuck Muncie (Saints) stole the show. Muncie ran for two touchdowns (1 and 11 yards) and threw a 25-yard TD pass to Tony Hill (Cowboys).

The game, the first at Honolulu's Aloha Stadium, also featured an 86-yard punt return for a touchdown by Wally Henry (Eagles) in his first—and only—Pro Bowl appearance. The game marked the final NFL appearance for outstanding Cowboys quarterback Roger Staubach, who retired.

1984

NFC 45, AFC 3

The NFC rolled to a Pro Bowl-record 45 points behind the record performance of quarterback Joe Theismann (Redskins). Theismann completed 21 of 27 pass attempts for 242 yards and three touchdowns. The 21 completions and three TD passes were Pro Bowl records.

One of Theismann's scoring passes was caught by William Andrews (Falcons), who also caught a two-yard TD pass from Joe Montana (49ers). Safety Nolan Cromwell (Rams) added spice to the victory with a 44-yard interception return for a touchdown.

1986

NFC 28, AFC 24

Phil Simms of the New York Giants fired three second-half touchdown passes and rallied the NFC to the biggest comeback victory in Pro Bowl history. The NFC trailed 24-7 at halftime and appeared to be in a hopeless situation.

But the NFC defense clamped down and Simms threw scoring strikes to Art Monk (Redskins), Doug Cosbie (Cowboys) and Jimmie Giles (Buccaneers), the winner with 2:47 remaining.

The AFC built its early lead on a two-yard Marcus Allen (Raiders) run, Allen's 51-yard TD pass to Wes Chandler (Chargers) and an 11-yard TD pass from Ken O'Brien (Jets) to Louis Lipps (Steelers).

 On a roll: Jacksonville's Mark Brunell (8) earned the MVP award at the 1997 Pro Bowl as the AFC defeated the NFC 26–23 in overtime.

FLASHES AND DASHES

Some flashes and dashes from the 50-game history of the NFL's postseason all-star game:

■ In 1951, the first game of the "modern" Pro Bowl series, Cleveland quarterback Otto Graham ran for two touchdowns and passed for another as the American Conference posted a 28-27 victory over the National Conference at the Los Angeles Memorial Coliseum.

■ The 1963 and 1966 games belonged to incomparable Cleveland running back Jim Brown. In 1963, Brown ran for 144 yards and scored a pair of touchdowns in a 30-20 East victory. Three years later, playing his final professional game, Brown ran for three touchdowns in a 36-7 East triumph.

■ Chicago's Gale Sayers was named the outstanding back in 1967, 1968 and 1970, even though his West team won only two of the games.

■ Miami's Garo Yepremian set a Pro Bowl record in 1974 by kicking five field goals, including the winner with 21 seconds remaining. Yepremian accounted for all of the AFC's points in a 15-13 victory.

■ Detroit's Eddie Murray tried to match Yepremian in 1981, but his fifth field-goal attempt, a 37-yarder, hit the crossbar with 22 seconds remaining. Murray had connected on his other four attempts in a 21-7 NFC victory.

■ Believe it or not, 49ers quarterback Joe Montana struggled through a horrid game in 1982, a week after earning MVP honors in Super Bowl XVI. Montana completed only 4 of 14 passes for 23 yards and threw an interception. His backup, Steve Bartkowski (Falcons), wasn't much better, completing 3 of 15 for 49 yards with an interception. Needless to say, their NFC team lost 16-13.

■ Art Still, a 6-foot-7, 260-pound defensive end, decided the 1985 Pro Bowl when he picked up a fumble and rumbled 83 yards for a fourth-quarter touchdown, wiping out a 14-12 NFC advantage in an eventual 22-14 AFC victory.

1995

AFC 41, NFC 13

After trailing 10-0 early, the AFC exploded behind a record-setting ground attack. The AFC outgained the NFC, 400-41, on the ground and rookie Marshall Faulk (Colts) and Chris Warren (Seahawks) both topped the AFC-NFC Pro Bowl rushing mark (112 yards) set by OJ Simpson in 1973.

Faulk finished the game with 180 yards, including 49 for a touchdown on a fake punt. Warren, who had scored on an 11-yard run, was watching Faulk from the bench after leaving the game with 127 rushing yards.

Tight end Eric Green (Steelers) caught a pair of TD passes—one from John Elway (Broncos) and one from Jeff Hostetler (Raiders).

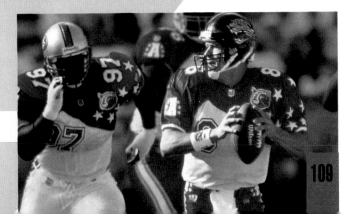

All-time Pro Bowl results

Date	Result	Outstanding Player(s)
1-15-39	Giants 13, All-Stars 10	
1-14-40	Packers 16, All-Stars 7	
12-29-40	Bears 28, All-Stars 14	
1- 4-42	Bears 35, All-Stars 24	
12-27-42	All-Stars 17, Redskins 14	
1-14-51	American Conference 28, National Conference 27	Otto Graham (Browns)
1-12-52	National Conference 30, American Conference 13	Dan Towler (Rams)
1-10-53	National Conference 27, American Conference 7	Don Doll (Lions)
1-17-54	East 20, West 9	Chuck Bednarik (Eagles)
1-16-55	West 26, East 19	Billy Wilson (49ers)
1-15-56	East 31, West 30	Ollie Matson (Cardinals)
1-13-57	West 19, East 10	Bert Rechichar (Colts)
		Ernie Stautner (Steelers)
1-12-58	West 26, East 7	Hugh McElhenny (49ers)
		Gene Brito (Redskins)
1-11-59	East 28, West 21	Frank Gifford (Giants)
		Doug Atkins (Bears)
1-17-60	West 38, East 21	Johnny Unitas (Colts)
		Big Daddy Lipscomb (Colts)

Best of the best: The intimidating visage of 49ers wide receiver Jerry Rice has become a Pro Bowl tradition.

1-15-61	West 35, East 31	Johnny Unitas (Colts)
		Sam Huff (Giants)
1-14-62	West 31, East 30	Jim Brown (Browns)
		Henry Jordan (Packers)
1-13-63	East 30, West 20	Jim Brown (Browns)
		Big Daddy Lipscomb (Steelers)
1-12-64	West 31, East 17	Johnny Unitas (Colts)
		Gino Marchetti (Colts)
1-10-65	West 34, East 14	Fran Tarkenton (Vikings)
		Terry Barr (Lions)
1-16-66	East 36, West 7	Jim Brown (Browns)
		Dale Meinert (Cardinals)
1-22-67	East 20, West 10	Gale Sayers (Bears)
		Floyd Peters (Eagles)
1-21-68	West 38, East 20	Gale Sayers (Bears)
		Dave Robinson (Packers)
1-19-69	West 10, East 7	Roman Gabriel (Rams)
		Merlin Olsen (Rams)
1-18-70	West 16, East 13	Gale Sayers (Bears)
		George Andrie (Cowboys)
1-24-71	NFC 27, AFC 6	Mel Renfro (Cowboys)
		Fred Carr (Packers)
1-23-72	AFC 26, NFC 13	Jan Stenerud (Chiefs)
		Willie Lanier (Chiefs)
1-21-73	AFC 33, NFC 28	OJ Simpson (Bills)
1-20-74	AFC 15, NFC 13	Garo Yepremian (Dolphins)
1-20-75	NFC 17, AFC 10	James Harris (Rams)
1-26-76	NFC 23, AFC 20	Billy Johnson (Oilers)
1-17-77	AFC 24, NFC 14	Mel Blount (Steelers)
1-23-78	NFC 14, AFC 13	Walter Payton (Bears)
1-29-79	NFC 13, AFC 7	Ahmad Rashad (Vikings)
1-27-80	NFC 37, AFC 27	Chuck Muncie (Saints)
2-1-81	NFC 21, AFC 7	Eddie Murray (Lions)
1-31-82	AFC 16, NFC 13	Kellen Winslow (Chargers)
		Lee Roy Selmon (Buccaneers)
2-6-83	NFC 20, AFC 19	Dan Fouts (Chargers)
		John Jefferson (Packers)
1-29-84	NFC 45, AFC 3	Joe Theismann (Redskins)
1-27-85	AFC 22, NFC 14	Mark Gastineau (Jets)
2-2-86	NFC 28, AFC 24	Phil Simms (Giants)
2-1-87	AFC 10, NFC 6	Reggie White (Eagles)
2-7-88	AFC 15, NFC 6	Bruce Smith (Bills)
1-29-89	NFC 34, AFC 3	Randall Cunningham (Eagles)
2-4-90	NFC 27, AFC 21	Jerry Gray (Rams)
2-3-91	AFC 23, NFC 21	Jim Kelly (Bills)
2-2-92	NFC 21, AFC 15	Michael Irvin (Cowboys)
2-7-93	AFC 23, NFC 20 (OT)	Steve Tasker (Bills)
2-6-94	NFC 17, AFC 3	Andre Rison (Falcons)
2-5-95	AFC 41, NFC 13	Marshall Faulk (Colts)
2-4-96	NFC 20, AFC 13	Jerry Rice (49ers)
2-2-97	AFC 26, NFC 23 (OT)	Mark Brunell (Jaguars)

Picking and hoping

★ ★ ★ ★ ★ ## COLLEGE DRAFT HAS BECOME A NATIONAL PHENOMENON

The football draft, known officially as the NFL Annual Selection Meeting, is not a recent innovation. NFL teams have been drafting college players to replenish their rosters since 1936, using a system very similar to the one they use today.

But the draft as an event is a recent phenomenon—an extravagant media happening with trimmings and trappings befitting a gala Hollywood event. The action is slow, the results are indecisive and the drama is infrequent and overplayed, but nobody can deny the grip football's talent auction holds on the American psyche.

On a weekend afternoon in late April, millions of hard-core football fanatics position themselves for a bird's-eye view of the much-anticipated selection process. Fans gather in a New York City ballroom, to cheer and jeer live announcements of their teams' picks. The rest tune into ESPN, assured of getting all the news from New York as well as hours and hours of "expert" analysis, interviews with everybody from agents to players' parents and live camera shots from

teams' war rooms, where decisions are made and phoned to New York. The ultimate moments come during the much-anticipated first round when Commissioner Paul Tagliabue steps to the New York microphone and announces another selection.

Nothing is analyzed, predicted and more rigorously debated than the NFL draft. "Draftniks" come out of the woodwork after every Super Bowl to study team weaknesses, analyze film and sift through scouting reports on the top college players. Draft guides are published, mock drafts are conducted and predictions of first-round selections are offered amid rumors of draft-day trades and position-switching deals. It's a fan's attempt to act as coach, general manager and football expert for a day.

Beyond the hype and prediction mania, the draft really is an opportunity for teams to reload, rebuild and recover past glories. They spend hundreds of thousands of dollars scouting college players and looking for the next Dick Butkus. Sometimes they find someone

Center stage: The podium stands vacant, waiting for commissioner Paul Tagliabue to approach and announce another draft selection.

would bring more parity to the game. Teams agreed to draft in inverse order of their previous season's standing and the Eagles kicked off the process by grabbing University of Chicago halfback Jay Berwanger with the first pick. Ironically, Berwanger, winner of college football's first Heisman Trophy, refused to sign, even after the Eagles traded his rights to the Chicago Bears.

There have been variations in draft procedures, but the basic format remains the same. From 1947-58, "bonus choices" were awarded with the winner of a lottery getting the first pick. That winner dropped out of the lottery with the process continuing each year until every team had made a "bonus choice." In 1976, the draft was moved from winter to spring, allowing more time for player evaluation. Drafts also have gotten shorter, from 30 rounds in the 1940s and 1950s, to 12 in the 1970s, and seven in 1995, 1996 and 1997. For television, the event was switched first to a Sunday-Monday format, then in 1995 to a Saturday-Sunday format.

There's a lot more money at stake today, too. Whereas Berwanger might have commanded a $5,000 contract in 1936, today's first-round picks expect millions of dollars. Every player's attributes are broken down and analyzed, from vertical leaps and 40-yard times to attitude and desire. Teams, anxious to hedge their investment, conduct pre-draft workouts and interviews, with every coach and personnel director knowing that a first-round mistake could cost their teams millions of dollars as well as fans and victories. They also know that some of the best picks have been made in the later rounds, necessitating thorough preparation, not to mention perseverance.

It all adds up to a kind of drama nobody could have foreseen 40 years ago when drafts were reported with agate type in the back of sports sections. Today's drafts garner major headlines and with that hype comes pressure—to pick wisely or face the consequences. Two things are at stake: pride and the future of 30 franchises.

And everybody is watching.

Top pick: Orlando Pace became an instant millionaire when, as the No. 1 pick of the 1997 draft, he agreed terms with the St. Louis Rams.

close, more often they find something less. In the world of computers and scouting combines, the art of picking future stars remains an inexact science.

Fundamentally, the draft is no different than the selection process used in 1936 when NFL leaders adopted the suggestion of Philadelphia Owner Bert Bell for a talent-distribution system that

High-flying Jet: The no.1 pick of the 1996 draft, Keyshawn Johnson (19), made some great plays for his team, the New York Jets, but the team endured another trying season.

In search of parity

★★★★★★★ **REBUILDING OF NFL FORTUNES IS AS EASY AS 1-2-3**

The NFL draft was adopted as a means of bringing parity to professional football. With weaker teams getting first choice of available college seniors, it stood to reason they would be able to plug holes with star-quality players, close the talent gap with stronger teams and become more competitive. That would in turn make the game more attractive to fans.

That basic premise has withstood the test of time, although many No 1 and 2 overall picks have fallen well short of stardom and many teams with preferred drafting position have fallen well short of improvement. The draft is not a scientific given: it's a combination of scouting, preparation, judgment—and luck. Even in this age of computerized player analysis and sophisticated scouting procedures, very good players are often found in the middle or late rounds.

Scouting was very crude in 1936, when a Bert Bell brainstorm developed into football's first draft. Bell, who owned the Philadelphia Eagles, last-place finishers in 1935, made the first pick and eight others in the 81-player auction—but failed to sign any of them. He eventually traded the rights to top pick Jay Berwanger to Chicago, but the Bears, like the Eagles, could not lure him onto the field.

Bell's inability to sign any of his draft picks was a simple case of miscommunication—there was little in those days between professional teams and top college stars. In a more graphic illustration of unsophisticated scouting procedures, the Washington Redskins drafted UCLA halfback Cal Rossi in the first round of the 1946 draft—and also in the 1947 draft. It seems the Redskins had mistakenly believed Rossi was eligible in 1946—his junior season.

Such snafus were part of the learning process. As the draft evolved, the lines of communication opened and teams became more

Inexact science: Every NFL team passed on Notre Dame quarterback Joe Montana before he was drafted by San Francisco in the third round in 1979.

aware of its importance as a means of restocking and rebuilding. Draft choices became prize possessions. The draft-day operation also became more sophisticated with teams wheeling and dealing for picks and position while trying to project opponents' moves. Draft day under the tell-all scrutiny of ESPN cameras and the national media has become a game of cat and mouse.

But the object remains the same: finding players who will make your team stronger. When that happens, division titles and championships often follow.

A review of 62 years worth of drafts reveals some fascinating subplots that add color to a black-and-white selection process:

THE BONUS CHOICES

From 1947 through 1958, the NFL opened its annual drafts with "bonus choices" that were awarded through a lottery system. All teams participated in a blind draw, with the winner getting the first overall choice. In exchange, the winner gave up its selection in the final round. The winner also was excluded from the next year's lottery, giving every team a chance to draft first over the 12-year period. Following are the NFL's 12 bonus choices:

YEAR	PLAYER	TEAM	COLLEGE
1947	Bob Fenimore	Chicago Bears	Oklahoma A&M
1948	Harry Gilmer	Washington	Alabama
1949	Chuck Bednarik	Philadelphia	Pennsylvania
1950	Leon Hart	Detroit	Notre Dame
1951	Kyle Rote	NY Giants	SMU
1952	Bill Wade	LA Rams	Vanderbilt
1953	Harry Babcock	San Francisco	Georgia
1954	Bobby Garrett	Cleveland	Stanford
1955	George Shaw	Baltimore	Oregon
1956	Gary Glick	Pittsburgh	Colorado A&M
1957	Paul Hornung	Green Bay	Notre Dame
1958	King Hill	Chicago Cardinals	Rice

Inspired choice: In 1993, Washington State University quarterback Drew Bledsoe was drafted first overall by New England. In 1994 he took the Patriots to the playoffs.

Unlucky pick: Indianapolis hoped tackle Steve Emtman would improve its defensive line when drafting him first overall in 1992, but injuries have marred his career.

THE QUARTERBACK CHASE

A top-flight quarterback always has been the most important piece to any team's puzzle and drafts often reflect that. The 1971 and 1983 selection meetings were especially memorable.

In 1971, quarterbacks were the top three picks with Stanford's Jim Plunkett going first to the Boston Patriots, Mississippi's Archie Manning second to New Orleans and Santa Clara's Dan Pastorini third to Houston. All went on to prosperous NFL careers.

The 1983 draft opened with Baltimore's selection of Stanford's John Elway and five more quarterbacks followed in the first round. Kansas City picked Penn State's Todd Blackledge No 7, Buffalo grabbed Miami's Jim Kelly No 14, New England picked Illinois' Tony Eason No 15, the New York Jets tabbed California-Davis' Ken O'Brien No 24 and the Miami Dolphins pulled off a coup by taking Pittsburgh's Dan Marino No 27. Elway was traded to Denver before signing with the Colts.

There have been exceptions to the quarterback rule. The 1988 draft was so devoid of quarterback talent that Washington's Chris Chandler was the first one selected—late in the third round, by Indianapolis, the 76th player overall.

ONWARD TO GREATNESS

Not all great players are selected in the first, second or third rounds. Some late-rounders defy logic and go on to NFL stardom.

The New York Giants had no idea they were getting a Hall of Fame offensive tackle when they took a flyer on Morgan State's Roosevelt Brown in the 27th round of the 1953 draft. Likewise,

nobody envisioned Alabama's Bart Starr as a championship quarterback and future Hall of Famer when Green Bay grabbed him with a 17th-round pick in 1956. Another Hall of Fame-bound quarterback, Louisville's Johnny Unitas, was Pittsburgh's ninth-round pick in 1955.

Other future Hall of Famers started their careers in more conventional fashion.

Running back Bill Dudley, selected by Pittsburgh in 1942, was the first No 1 overall pick to reach football's highest acclaim. Linebacker Dick Butkus and running back Gale Sayers, a pair of Chicago Bears first-rounders, were drafted back to back (third and fourth) in 1965. Three of the top six picks in the 1957 draft went on to legendary careers—Green Bay running back Paul Hornung (No 1), Pittsburgh' quarterback Len Dawson (No 5) and Cleveland' running back Jim Brown (No 6).

Four teams used their first-ever NFL draft picks on future Hall of Famers: The Bears took two-way tackle Joe Stydahar in 1936, NFL newcomer San Francisco grabbed two-way tackle Leo Nomellini in 1950, the expansion Cowboys took defensive tackle Bob Lilly in 1961, and the expansion Tampa Bay Buccaneers picked defensive tackle Lee Roy Selmon in 1976.

ODDS AND ENDS

Brotherly Love: Colorado offensive lineman Pete Brock was selected by New England with the 12th pick of the 1976 draft and brother Stan, also a Colorado offensive lineman, was selected by New Orleans with the 12th pick in 1980; Bubba Smith, a Michigan State defensive lineman, was selected No 1 overall by Baltimore in 1967 and brother Tody, a defensive lineman from USC, was selected 25th overall by Dallas four years later; brothers Gene and Marvin Upshaw were selected in the first round of successive drafts in 1967 and 1968. Gene, an offensive lineman out of Texas A&I, was picked by Oakland while Marvin, a defensive lineman out of Trinity, was nabbed by Cleveland.

Team Power: Nebraska wide receiver Irving Fryar (Patriots) and offensive lineman Dean Steinkuhler (Oilers) were the first and second picks in 1984; USC running back Ricky Bell (Buccaneers), offensive lineman Marvin Powell (Jets) and defensive lineman Gary Jeter (Giants) were the first, fourth and fifth selections in 1977; Miami quarterback Vinny Testaverde (Buccaneers) and running back Alonzo Highsmith (Oilers) were the first and third players chosen in 1987.

Where Did You Go? The Chicago Bears used their 1953 first-round pick on junior college back Billy Anderson, who starred at Compton Community College; the Phoenix Cardinals' first-round 1991 choice was defensive lineman Eric Swann, who had never played college football; Hall of Fame quarterback YA Tittle was a 1951 first-round selection of San Francisco—after he already had played three full professional seasons. Tittle became eligible for the draft when his Baltimore Colts team folded.

Wanna Play Some Football? National Basketball Association greats John Havlicek, KC Jones and Pat Riley all were NFL draft picks. Havlicek was selected on the seventh round in 1962 by Cleveland, Jones was a 30th-round pick in 1955 by the Rams and Riley, current coach of the Miami Heat, was Dallas' 11th-round pick in 1967; four first-round NFL draft picks played professional baseball: Harry Agganis (Browns 1952), Steve Filipowicz (Giants 1943), Don Lund (Bears 1945) and Bo Jackson (Buccaneers 1986).

The first picks in

Year	Player	Pos	Team	College
1936	Jay Berwanger	RB	Philadelphia	Chicago
1937	Sam Francis	FB	Philadelphia	Nebraska
1938	Corbett Davis	FB	Cleveland	Indiana
1939	Ki Aldrich	C	Chicago Cardinals	TCU
1940	George Cafego	RB	Chicago Cardinals	Tennessee
1941	Tom Harmon	RB	Chicago Bears	Michigan
1942	Bill Dudley	RB	Pittsburgh	Virginia
1943	Frank Sinkwich	RB	Detroit	Georgia
1944	Angelo Bertelli	QB	Boston	Notre Dame
1945	Charley Trippi	RB	Chicago Cardinals	Georgia
1946	Frank Dancewicz	QB	Boston	Notre Dame
1947	Bob Fenimore	RB	Chicago Bears	Oklahoma A&M
1948	Harry Gilmer	QB	Washington	Alabama
1949	Chuck Bednarik	C	Philadelphia	Pennsylvania
1950	Leon Hart	E	Detroit	Notre Dame
1951	Kyle Rote	RB	NY Giants	SMU
1952	Bill Wade	QB	Los Angeles	Vanderbilt
1953	Harry Babcock	E	San Francisco	Georgia
1954	Bobby Garrett	QB	Cleveland	Stanford
1955	George Shaw	QB	Baltimore	Oregon
1956	Gary Glick	DB	Pittsburgh	Colorado A&M
1957	Paul Hornung	RB	Green Bay	Notre Dame
1958	King Hill	QB	Chicago Cardinals	Rice
1959	Randy Duncan	QB	Green Bay	Iowa
1960	Billy Cannon	RB	Los Angeles	Louisiana State
1961	Tommy Mason	RB	Minnesota	Tulane
1962	Ernie Davis	RB	Washington	Syracuse
1963	Terry Baker	QB	Los Angeles	Oregon State
1964	Dave Parks	E	San Francisco	Texas Tech
1965	Tucker Frederickson	RB	NY Giants	Auburn
1966	Tommy Nobis	LB	Atlanta	Texas
1967	Bubba Smith	DT	Baltimore	Michigan State
1968	Ron Yary	T	Minnesota	USC
1969	OJ Simpson	RB	Buffalo	USC
1970	Terry Bradshaw	QB	Pittsburgh	Louisiana Tech
1971	Jim Plunkett	QB	New England	Stanford
1972	Walt Patulski	DE	Buffalo	Notre Dame
1973	John Matuszak	DE	Houston	Tampa
1974	Ed Jones	DE	Dallas	Tennessee State
1975	Steve Bartkowski	QB	Atlanta	California
1976	Lee Roy Selmon	DE	Tampa Bay	Oklahoma
1977	Ricky Bell	RB	Tampa Bay	USC

the NFL Draft

1978	Earl Campbell	RB	Houston	Texas
1979	Tom Cousineau	LB	Buffalo	Ohio State
1980	Billy Sims	RB	Detroit	Oklahoma
1981	George Rogers	RB	New Orleans	South Carolina
1982	Kenneth Sims	DT	New England	Texas
1983	John Elway	QB	Baltimore	Stanford
1984	Irving Fryar	WR	New England	Nebraska
1985	Bruce Smith	DE	Buffalo	Virginia Tech
1986	Bo Jackson	RB	Tampa Bay	Auburn
1987	Vinny Testaverde	QB	Tampa Bay	Miami
1988	Aundray Bruce	LB	Atlanta	Auburn
1989	Troy Aikman	QB	Dallas	UCLA
1990	Jeff George	QB	Indianapolis	Illinois
1991	Russell Maryland	DT	Dallas	Miami
1992	Steve Emtman	DT	Indianapolis	Washington
1993	Drew Bledsoe	QB	New England	Washington State
1994	Dan Wilkinson	DT	Cincinnati	Ohio State
1995	Ki-Jana Carter	RB	Cincinnati	Penn State
1996	Keyshawn Johnson	WR	NY Jets	USC
1997	Orlando Pace	OT	St. Louis	Ohio State

Pick of the crop: NFL Commissioner Paul Tagliabue (extreme right) stands with some of the first round picks of the 1997 NFL Draft. (From left) James Farrior, Dwayne Rudd, Michael Booker, Shawn Springs, Darrell Russell, Bryant Westbrook, Orlando Pace and Antowain Smith.

Where the legends live forever

★★★★★★★★★★★★★★★★★★★★★

PRO FOOTBALL HALL OF FAME

It's like crossing a time line into a different world, an ancient era of helmetless players, unsophisticated equipment and evolving playing styles. Every visitor to the Pro Football Hall of Fame in Canton, Ohio, is greeted, fittingly, by a 7-foot bronze statue of Jim Thorpe, which guards the ramp leading to a rendezvous with yesteryear.

It's a journey that begins in 1892 with the first chronicled professional football game and ends more than a century later amid the glitz and glitter of Super Bowl XXXI. The trip covers five buildings and is enhanced by television monitors, tape recordings, slide machines and a new theater presentation that offers the sights and sounds of modern pro football.

Today's five-building, juiced-up Hall of Fame, which entertains hundreds of thousands of yearly visitors, is the offshoot of a two-building, no-frills Hall of Fame that opened its doors to the public as part of a September 7, 1963, dedication ceremony. One of those original buildings was topped by a 52-foot, football-shaped dome that remains today as the Hall's signature feature.

Enshrinement: A huge crowd listens to the annual enshrinement ceremony outside the Pro Football Hall of Fame in Canton, Ohio. An NFL preseason exhibition game concludes the festivities.

There never was much debate about the Hall's logical site after Canton city officials began lobbying for the honor in the early 1960s. Canton offered historical significance (it was the site where the National Football League was born in 1920), a rugged football tradition (the Canton Bulldogs won two of the first four NFL championships) and a central location that allowed access from many large U.S. cities.

The NFL designated Canton as the official Pro Football Hall of Fame site on April 27, 1961, and groundbreaking began 16 months later on a wooded parkland site donated by the city. When the Hall of Fame was dedicated in 1963, 17 charter members were enshrined and the occasion was punctuated by a Hall of Fame preseason game at Fawcett Stadium, which is located directly across the street from the Hall's main facility. That game, a 16-7 Pittsburgh victory over Cleveland, was the second in a series that continues today as part of every enshrinement weekend.

The Hall of Fame membership has grown from its original 17-man cast to 189, including the four-member class of 1996. The election procedure is different from that used by any other sport.

Tourist attraction: Since its opening in 1963, the Hall of Fame has drawn more than 6 million fans to the birthplace of the NFL.

Fans nominate players for induction by writing to the Pro Football Hall of Fame and election is determined by a National Board of Selectors made up of writers from each NFL city, five at-large voters and a representative of the Pro Football Writers Association of America. Players must be retired for five years before they can be considered, coaches can be considered the year after retirement and other contributors can be elected at any time. The committee meets every year on the day before the Super Bowl and nominees must receive 80 percent of their votes for election. Four to seven members are added each year.

Hall of Fame weekend has become a late-summer event, featuring fashion shows, a civic banquet honoring the enshrinees, a parade that draws 200,000-plus viewers, the enshrinement ceremonies and the AFC-NFC football game that features rotating teams and draws a 23,000-plus crowd. And, of course, there's the museum itself, which has entertained more than 6 million fans since 1963.

Among the highlights of the tour are an exhibition rotunda that recounts the game's history, an art gallery featuring award-winning football photographs, a research library, the twin enshrinement halls, a mementos room, the Super Bowl room and an area that electronically chronicles the evolution of the football-television relationship.

It's safe to say that the growth of the Hall of Fame has mirrored the growth of the sport it represents. When that 17-member charter class was inducted in 1963, the original two-building complex contained 19,000 square feet of interior display space. Three subsequent expansions have more than quadrupled that figure to 83,600 square feet.

The following biographies detail the careers of 50 of professional football's Hall of Fame players and founding fathers:

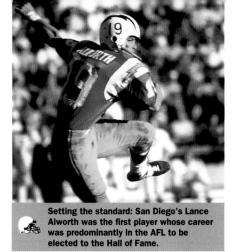

Setting the standard: San Diego's Lance Alworth was the first player whose career was predominantly in the AFL to be elected to the Hall of Fame.

LANCE ALWORTH: 6-0, 184-pound wide receiver. Born August 3, 1940, at Houston, Tex. Attended Arkansas. Alworth, known as "Bambi" because of his deer-like stride and graceful style, set virtually every AFL pass-catching record while playing for the San Diego Chargers in the 1960s. He finished his 11-year career with the Dallas Cowboys and played in Super Bowl VI, catching a touchdown pass. He was the first receiver to string together seven consecutive 1,000-yard seasons.

SAMMY BAUGH: 6-2, 180-pound quarterback/ defensive back/punter. Born March 17, 1914, at Temple, Tex. Attended Texas Christian University. One of football's first true passing quarterbacks, Baugh led the Washington Redskins to five Eastern Division titles and two NFL championships in the 1930s and 40s. Known as "Slingin' Sammy," Baugh led the league in passing six times. He also was an outstanding defensive back and his 51.4-yard punting average of 1940 and 45.1-yard career average still stand as NFL records. A charter member of the Hall of Fame.

BERT BELL: Team owner, commissioner. Born February 25, 1895, at Philadelphia. One of the visionaries who helped shape the NFL, Bell founded the Philadelphia Eagles in 1933. He later became co-owner of the Pittsburgh Steelers with Art Rooney. Bell, who came up with the idea for a draft of college players that was introduced in 1936, was named commissioner in 1946 and served with distinction until his death in 1959. A Hall of Fame charter member.

GEORGE BLANDA: 6-2, 215-pound quarterback/ placekicker. Born September 17, 1927, at Youngwood, Pa. Attended Kentucky. Blanda was a 12th-round draft pick (1949) who forged a 26-year career that covered 340 games with four teams and touched four decades. Before retiring in 1975, he played in seven championship games (AFL and NFL), threw 236 touchdown passes and amassed an NFL-record 2,002 career points. Late in his career with the Raiders, Blanda was known for his

ability to come off the bench and produce dramatic victories.

TERRY BRADSHAW: 6-3, 210-pound quarterback. Born September 2, 1948, at Shreveport, La. Attended Louisiana Tech. A strong-armed, steady performer who directed the Pittsburgh Steelers to four Super Bowl championships in a six-year period in the 1970s. Bradshaw, a two-time Super Bowl MVP, passed for 27,989 yards and 212 touchdowns over a 14-year career that ended in 1983.

JIM BROWN: 6-2, 232-pound fullback. Born February 17, 1936, at St Simons, Ga. Attended Syracuse. Many consider Brown the greatest running back of all time. A combination of power and speed, he led the NFL in rushing eight times from 1957-65 and recorded single-season yardage totals of 1,527 (1958) and 1,863 (1963). Brown finished his Cleveland Browns career with a then-record 12,312 yards, a figure that still ranks fourth all time, and 126 touchdowns (second). Brown retired at age 30 to pursue an acting career.

PAUL BROWN: Coach, general manager. Born September 7, 1908, at Norwalk, Ohio. Guided Ohio State to the 1942 national college championship. Brown was the architect of a Cleveland Browns machine that won four consecutive AAFC championships in the late 1940s and three NFL titles in the 1950s. His Browns competed in ten consecutive championship games (AAFC and NFL) from 1946-55. Brown coached the expansion Cincinnati Bengals (AFL/NFL) from 1968-75 and later became general manager. He retired with a 222-112-9 professional coaching record.

DICK BUTKUS: 6-3, 245-pound linebacker. Born December 9, 1942, at Chicago. Attended Illinois. Butkus is considered by many the greatest middle linebacker of all time. He was

On and on: George Blanda's storied career ended after 26 seasons and 340 games. A modern player would need 22 injury-free seasons to catch him.

a snarling, vicious competitor who neither gave nor asked for mercy. Butkus intercepted 22 passes and recovered 25 fumbles over his nine-year career (1965-73) with the Chicago Bears. The award that annually honors college football's outstanding linebacker was named in his honor.

AL DAVIS: Coach, general manager, owner, commissioner. Born July 4, 1929, at Brockton, Mass. Davis is the architect of an Oakland/Los Angeles Raiders team that has won three Super Bowls and ranks among the most successful franchises in football history. Always controversial, he helped force the AFL-NFL merger agreement in 1966 as AFL commissioner. Davis moved his Raiders from Oakland to Los Angeles in 1982 after winning a court battle against the NFL.

WILLIE DAVIS: 6-3, 245-pound defensive end. Born July 24, 1934, at Lisbon, La. Attended Grambling. After an early career trade from Cleveland to Green Bay, Davis became a dominant defensive figure on the 1960s Packers teams that won five NFL championships and the first two Super Bowls. A ferocious pass rusher and sure tackler, Davis' contribution to the Packers' dynasty often was lost in the shadows of Bart Starr, Paul Hornung and Vince Lombardi.

Monster of the Midway: Dick Butkus was perhaps the most feared linebacker in NFL history. His all-out, uncompromising intensity has never been surpassed.

OTTO GRAHAM: 6-1, 195-pound quarterback. Born December 6, 1921, at Waukegan, Ill. Attended Northwestern. Graham was a six-time passing champion in the NFL and AAFC, but his greatest legacy could not be measured in yards. He directed the Cleveland Browns to ten championship games in his ten-year career—four in the AAFC and six in the NFL. The Browns won seven of them and were 58-13-1 behind Graham in NFL play. Graham passed for 23,584 yards (AAFC and NFL combined) and 174 touchdowns.

HAROLD (RED) GRANGE: 6-0, 185-pound halfback/defensive back. Born June 13, 1903, at Forksville, Pa. Attended Illinois. The incredible fame Grange enjoyed as Illinois' Galloping Ghost carried over to the professional game and made the Bears football's top gate attraction in 1925. He became the NFL's first real superstar, drawing sellout crowds everywhere he played. He bolted the NFL in 1926 to form the rival AFL but returned to Chicago in 1929 and played through 1934.

JOE GREENE: 6-4, 260-pound defensive tackle. Born September 24, 1946, at Temple, Tex. Attended North Texas State. "Mean Joe" was the anchor of Pittsburgh's "Steel Curtain" defense that terrorized the NFL in the late 1970s and helped the Steelers win four Super Bowls in six years. Greene was a ferocious pass rusher and devastating run-stuffer in a 13-year career that produced nine Pro Bowl invitations.

LOU (THE TOE) GROZA: 6-3, 250-pound offensive tackle/placekicker. Born January 25, 1924, at Martin's Ferry, Ohio. Attended Ohio State. Groza was an unusual football combination—an outstanding blocker and a point producer. Groza joined the AAFC's Browns in 1946 and played in 13 championship games over his 21-year career, eight on the winning side. He scored 1,349 NFL points and kicked the winning field goal in the 1950 title game.

GEORGE (PAPA BEAR) HALAS: End, coach, team owner. Born February 2, 1895, at Chicago. One of the NFL's founding fathers and a moving force for more than 60 years as player, coach and owner of the Chicago Bears. The innovative Halas popularized the split-T formation and coached the Bears to a 324-151-31 record and seven NFL championships over 40 seasons. He retired after the 1967 season as the winningest coach of all time, a record that stood until 1993. A Hall of Fame charter member.

MEL HEIN: 6-2, 225-pound center/linebacker. Born August 22, 1909, at Redding, Calif. Attended Washington State. Hein, who played 15 seasons for the New York Giants, is considered the best center in NFL history. He was a 60-minute player who never missed a game as a professional. Hein, who helped the Giants capture two NFL titles in the 1930s, introduced many of the line-play techniques that still are used today. He was a charter member of the Hall of Fame.

PAUL HORNUNG: 6-2, 220-pound halfback/placekicker. Born December 23, 1935, at Louisville, Ky. Attended Notre Dame. Hornung, a 1956 Heisman Trophy winner, was a star for Vince Lombardi's powerful Green Bay Packers. A No 1 overall

draft choice, Hornung went on to win three consecutive scoring titles, including an NFL-record 176-point effort in 1960 (15 touchdowns, 15 field goals, 41 extra points). He played on four Packers NFL championship teams, including their Super Bowl I winner.

SAM HUFF: 6-1, 230-pound linebacker. Born October 4, 1934, at Morgantown, W Va. Attended West Virginia. Huff was one of the most tenacious and glamorized middle linebackers ever to play the game. He was the centerpiece of a ferocious defense that led the Giants to six conference titles and one NFL championship from 1956-63. The hard-hitting, run-stuffing Huff, noted for his head-on battles with running greats Jim Brown and Jim Taylor, finished his career with Washington in 1969.

LAMAR HUNT: Founder AFL, team owner. Born August 2, 1932, at El Dorado, Ark. Hunt founded the American Football League in 1960 and helped it persevere until a merger with the NFL was worked out in 1966. He opened the first AFL season as owner of the Dallas Texans but moved the team to Kansas City in 1963 and renamed it the Chiefs. Hunt's Chiefs won three AFL championships, lost to Green Bay in Super Bowl I and defeated Minnesota in Super Bowl IV.

DON HUTSON: 6-1, 180-pound end/defensive back. Born January 31, 1913, at Pine Bluff, Ark. Attended Alabama. Hutson is considered one of the greatest receivers in NFL history. He led the league in receptions eight times, receiving yardage seven times and scoring five times as a 1935-45 member of the Green Bay Packers. Hutson, a 9.7 sprinter, was impossible to cover and caught 99 career touchdown passes in an era of power football. He helped the Packers win three NFL championships.

DEACON JONES: 6-5, 260-pound defensive end. Born December 9, 1938, at Eatonville, Fla.

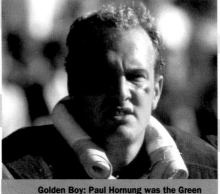

Golden Boy: Paul Hornung was the Green Bay Packers' bonus draft pick in 1957. His 176 points in 1960 remains the NFL single season record.

Attended South Carolina State and Mississippi Vocational. Jones was among the first of the new-breed defensive ends who combined quickness, size and agility. He came to the Rams in 1961 as a 14th-round draft choice and combined with Merlin Olsen, Lamar Lundy and Rosey Grier to form a legendary defensive front dubbed "The Fearsome Foursome." Jones played 14 seasons, the final three for San Diego and Washington.

CURLY LAMBEAU: Coach. Born April 9, 1898, at Green Bay, Wis. Lambeau was one of the early powers of the NFL. Working on behalf of the meatpacking firm where he was employed, Lambeau formed the Green Bay Packers in 1919, played halfback for the team until 1929, and coached it from 1919-1949. A fine judge of talent and a proponent of the passing game, Lambeau guided the Packers to six NFL championships and a 212-106-21 overall record. He also coached the Chicago Cardinals (1950-51) and Washington Redskins (1952-53). He was a charter member of the Hall of Fame.

JACK LAMBERT: 6-4, 220-pound linebacker. Born July 8, 1952, at Mantua, Ohio. Attended Kent State. Lambert combined with Jack Ham to form one of the greatest linebacking duos in pro football history. They were the heart of a "Steel Curtain" defense that keyed Pittsburgh's four Super Bowl championships in the 1970s. A fearsome hitter and intense competitor, Lambert was selected for the Pro Bowl nine times before retiring in 1984.

TOM LANDRY: Coach. Born September 11, 1924, at Mission, Tex. Landry was the first and only coach in Dallas Cowboys history through 1988, when he was replaced by Jimmy Johnson. A former defensive back for the New York Giants, the stone-faced Landry, who took the reins in 1960, guided "America's Team" to 13 division titles, seven conference championship games and five Super Bowls, winning two. His career record, 270-178-6, places him third on the all-time coaching victory list.

BOBBY LAYNE: 6-2, 190-pound quarterback. Born December 19, 1926, at Santa Anna, Tex. Attended Texas. Layne was a do-everything quarterback who struggled through two seasons with Chicago and the New York Bulldogs before directing Detroit to great success in the 1950s. He led the Lions to four conference titles and three NFL championships. Layne was so versatile that in 1956 he led the NFL in scoring: five touchdowns, 12 field goals and 33 extra points. He also passed for 1,909 yards that season.

BOB LILLY: 6-5, 260-pound defensive tackle. Born July 26, 1939, at Olney, Tex. Attended Texas Christian University. Lilly was an immovable object, one of the strongest players in NFL history. He was the first draft choice in Cowboys history (1961), their first Pro Bowl player (1962), first All-Pro selection (1964) and first Hall of Famer (1980). He helped lead the Cowboys to four NFL/NFC title games and two Super Bowls, including a 1972 victory over Miami. Lilly was the dominant player at his position for 14 NFL seasons.

VINCE LOMBARDI: Coach, general manager. Born June 11, 1913, at Brooklyn. Lombardi was the fiery, no-nonsense architect of Green Bay's 1960s dynasty. Playing the power football Lombardi relished, the Packers won five NFL titles and the first two Super Bowls during the decade. In nine seasons as Packers coach, Lombardi carved out a 98-30-4 record before retiring. He returned to coach the Redskins to a 7-5-2 record in 1969 and died a year later. The Super Bowl Trophy was renamed in his honor.

SID LUCKMAN: 6-0, 195-pound quarterback. Born November 21, 1916, at Brooklyn. Attended Columbia. Luckman, drafted by the Bears in 1939, was the perfect quarterback for George Halas' innovative T-formation. A slick ballhandler with a strong arm, Luckman quickly paid dividends by directing the Bears to NFL titles in 1940, 41, 43 and 46. Luckman, who would throw 137 touchdown passes in 12 seasons, fired an NFL-record seven in one game against the Giants—a mark that has been matched, but never broken.

TIM MARA: Team owner. Born July 29, 1887, at New York. Mara became a force in the early NFL when he paid $2,500 for a franchise and brought professional football to New York. Mara's Giants were not immediate hits, but he toughed out the hard times and brought the city four NFL championships as well as ten division or conference titles before his death in 1959. The franchise is still co-owned by his son, Wellington. Mara is a charter member of the Hall of Fame.

LENNY MOORE: 6-1, 198-pound flanker/running back. Born November 25, 1933, at Reading, Pa. Attended Penn State. Moore was a multi-gifted athlete who could line up in either the backfield or at wide receiver. Quick, fast and unpredictable, he was dangerous at either position. Moore, who helped Baltimore win consecutive NFL championships in 1958 and 1959, finished his career with 113 touchdowns, second at the time only to Jim Brown. He once scored TDs in an NFL-record 18 consecutive games.

MARION MOTLEY: 6-1, 238-pound fullback/linebacker. Born June 5, 1920, at Leesburg, Ga. Attended South Carolina State. Motley, as a fullback, was a human bulldozer who simply ran over anybody who got in his way. He was the power source for a Cleveland franchise that won five championships and finished second three times (AAFC and NFL) from 1946-53. Motley, one of the early black players in the post-war NFL, averaged 5 yards per carry in the NFL and still holds the single-game mark of 17.09 (188 yards, 11 carries).

BRONKO NAGURSKI: 6-2, 225-pound fullback/linebacker. Born November 3, 1908, at Ontario, Canada. Attended Minnesota. There was no finesse in Nagurski's game. When he got the ball, he ran over or through anybody in his path, including teammates. As a blocker, he was ferocious. With Nagurski leading the charge, the Bears won NFL titles in 1932 and 33. He retired after the 1937 season, but returned after a five-year layoff and helped the Bears win again in 1943. He was a charter member of the Hall of Fame.

JOE NAMATH: 6-2, 200-pound quarterback. Born May 31, 1943, at Beaver Falls, Pa. Attended Alabama. Broadway Joe took New York by storm when he signed with the AFL's Jets in 1965. He would go on to pass for 27,663 yards and 173 touchdowns. Namath's biggest moment came in 1969 when he led the Jets to an upset of Baltimore in Super Bowl III, fulfilling his brash prediction. Plagued throughout his career by knee problems, Namath played 13 seasons, ending his career in 1977 with the Rams.

ERNIE NEVERS: 6-1, 205-pound fullback/defensive. Born June 11, 1903, at Willow River, Minn. Attended Stanford. Nevers made the most of a short career that spanned five seasons (1926-27, 1929-1931) with the Duluth Eskimos and Chicago Cardinals, playing virtually every minute of every game. His endurance and ability to play with pain were legendary. One of pro football's first superstars, Nevers set a still-standing record in 1929 by scoring 40 points in a single game. He was a Hall of Fame charter member.

RAY NITSCHKE: 6-3, 235-pound linebacker. Born December 29, 1936, at Elmwood Park, Ill. Attended Illinois. Nitschke, a wild-eyed, maniacal presence at his middle linebacker position for 15 seasons, was the centerpiece for the Green Bay defense that dominated the NFL in the 1960s. Surprisingly quick for a big man, Nitschke could stuff the run, terrorize quarterbacks or defend against the pass. He helped the Packers win five NFL

championships and the first two Super Bowls before retiring after the 1972 season.

MERLIN OLSEN: 6-5, 270-pound defensive tackle. Born September 15, 1940, at Logan, Utah. Attended Utah State. Olsen was the centerpiece for the Los Angeles Rams' "Fearsome Foursome" defensive line, which terrorized offensive linemen through the 1960s and early 70s. Olsen was strong, talented and disciplined, a product of his intense work ethic. He played 15 outstanding seasons—earning 14 Pro Bowl berths—before retiring after the 1976 campaign to start an acting career.

ART ROONEY: Team owner. Born January 27, 1901, at Coulterville, Pa. Rooney began his NFL association in 1933 when he purchased the Pittsburgh Pirates (later renamed the Steelers), but it took 39 years for his team to win even a divisional championship. He was understandably overjoyed when the Steelers made up for lost time by winning four Super Bowls in six years, beginning in 1974. Through his travails, Rooney was a benevolent owner, loved by both players and fans. He remained active with the team until his death in 1988.

Double trouble: Defensive tackle Merlin Olsen was talented on and off the field. He was a Phi Beta Kappa student at Utah State.

PETE ROZELLE: Commissioner. Born March 1, 1926, at South Gate, Calif. Rozelle, a compromise candidate, was elected as NFL commissioner in 1960. He proceeded to lead the game to great prosperity in an outstanding 30-year tenure that ended with retirement in 1989. Under Rozelle, the league expanded from 12 to 28 teams, the AFL and NFL were merged, the Super Bowl became the showcase of all sporting events and lucrative television contracts turned football into a multi-billion-dollar industry.

GALE SAYERS: 6-0, 200-pound running back. Born May 30, 1943, at Wichita, Kan. Attended Kansas. Sayers ranks among the greatest running backs of all time, even though his career was cut short by a series of knee injuries. He was a stylish, almost poetic, runner who thrilled Chicago Bears fans with a 1965 rookie season that produced 22 touchdowns, an NFL-record-tying six coming in one game. Sayers would win two NFL rushing titles and score 56 touchdowns before retiring after seven sensational seasons. He still holds the NFL record for highest career kickoff-return average (30.56).

DON SHULA: Defensive back, coach. Born January 4, 1930, at Painesville, Ohio. Attended John Carroll. Shula was a competent defender for Cleveland, Baltimore and Washington for seven pro seasons, but his lasting fame was achieved during a 33-year coaching career with the Colts and Dolphins. Shula guided the 1968 Colts into Super Bowl IV, where they were upset by the Chiefs. He became coach of the Dolphins in 1970 and led the 1972 team to the first perfect season (17–0) in NFL history and the first of consecutive Super Bowl victories. He coached Miami for 26 seasons, leading the team to 11 AFC East Division titles and five Super Bowl berths. Shula retired in 1995 with a career-record 347 victories and a final coaching mark of 347–156–6.

OJ SIMPSON: 6-1, 212-pound running back. Born July 9, 1947, at San Francisco. Attended USC. After winning the 1968 Heisman Trophy, Simpson burst upon the NFL scene with the Buffalo Bills. A stylish, spectacular performer, Simpson topped 1,000 yards rushing five consecutive times, including a then-NFL-record 2,003 in 1973. He won four NFL rushing titles and finished his career in 1979 with 11,236 yards, seventh on the all-time list. Simpson holds the NFL record with six 200-yard games.

BART STARR: 6-1, 200-pound quarterback. Born January 9, 1934, at Montgomery, Ala. Attended Alabama. Starr, a 17th-round Green Bay draft choice in 1956, blossomed into a winning machine. Although not as gifted physically as some quarterbacks, he guided the Packers to six conference titles, five NFL championships and two Super Bowl victories in the 1960s with precision passing and heady leadership. Starr, always calm, cool and collected, once threw 294 passes without an interception. He was named MVP in Super Bowls I and II.

ROGER STAUBACH: 6-3, 202-pound quarterback. Born February 5, 1942, at Cincinnati. Attended Navy. Staubach, the 1963 Heisman Trophy winner at Navy, had to fulfill a four-year military obligation before turning pro. But he led the Cowboys to five NFC championships and two Super Bowl titles in an 11-year career that also produced five NFC passing titles. Staubach was a heady competitor who combined a powerful arm and excellent scrambling ability. He was especially adept with the game on the line.

FRAN TARKENTON: 6-0, 185-pound quarterback. Born February 3, 1940, at Richmond, Va. Attended Georgia. Tark may have been the greatest scrambling quarterback of all time. He wasn't bad when he actually threw the ball, either, setting NFL career records for pass

Two-team player: Fran Tarkenton (10) started and ended his career with the Minnesota Vikings. He spent five seasons with the New York Giants

attempts (6,467), completions (3,686), yards (47,003) and touchdowns (342). Tarkenton's secret was longevity—he played 18 seasons, 13 in two stints with Minnesota and five with the New York Giants.

JIM THORPE: 6-1, 190-pound halfback/defensive back. Born May 28, 1888, at Prague, Okla. Attended Carlisle. Thorpe, a former college football star, two-time Olympic gold medalist and professional baseball player, didn't make his pro football debut until age 27. But he still was the dominant player of pro football's early years. He was a frightful combination of strength, power, speed and quickness. Thorpe also was a big gate attraction as well as the NFL's first president.

YA TITTLE: 6-0, 200-pound quarterback. Born October 24, 1926, at Marshall, Tex. Attended Louisiana State. Tittle, dubbed the "Bald Eagle" after he lost most of his hair, was one of the game's best pure passers. A flick of the wrist could deliver a perfect spiral and he amassed 33,070 passing yards and 242 touchdowns over a 17-year career that started with Baltimore in the AAFC. In 1963, at age 37, Tittle threw a then-NFL-record 36 TD passes for the Giants. He led New York to three successive NFL Championship Games (1961-63).

JOHNNY UNITAS: 6-1, 195-pound quarterback. Born May 7, 1933, at Pittsburgh. Attended Louisville. Unitas' name is entrenched among the great passers in NFL history. He played 17 of his 18 seasons for the Baltimore Colts and amassed 40,239 career passing yards (fourth all time) and 290 TD passes (third). Unitas, always cool under pressure, led the Colts to three NFL championships, including Super Bowl V. From 1956 to 1960, he threw at least one touchdown pass in an NFL-record 47 straight games.

STEVE VAN BUREN: 6-1, 200-pound halfback. Born December 28, 1920, at La Ceiba, Honduras. Attended Louisiana State. Van Buren was a straight-ahead runner who powered his way to four NFL rushing titles and helped Philadelphia win consecutive NFL championships. In 1948, Van Buren scored the only touchdown in a 7-0 title-game victory over the Cardinals. In 1949, he ran through the mud for 196 yards in a 14-0 title-game victory over the Rams. Van Buren topped 1,000 yards twice in the days when that was considered a major feat.

PAUL WARFIELD: 6-0, 188-pound wide receiver. Born November 28, 1942, at Warren, Ohio. Attended Ohio State. Warfield was a smooth pass-catcher who built a winning legacy. In his first six seasons with Cleveland (1964-69), the Browns won five conference titles and one NFL championship. In his next five seasons with Miami, the Dolphins won three AFC titles and two Super Bowls. Warfield finished his 13-year career with 85 TDs and an average of 20.1 yards per catch.

BOB WATERFIELD: 6-2, 200-pound quarterback/safety/punter/placekicker. Born July 26, 1920, at Elmira, NY. Attended UCLA. Waterfield was a versatile performer who intercepted 20 passes, kicked 60 field goals and averaged 42.4 yards a punt during his career besides starring at quarterback. Extremely cool under pressure and able to play through injuries, Waterfield led the Rams to two NFL championships (one in Cleveland, another in Los Angeles) and captured two NFL passing titles. He retired unexpectedly in 1952 at age 32.

Membership roster

HERB ADDERLEY: Defensive back Green Bay Packers (1961-69), Dallas Cowboys (1970-72). Attended Michigan State. Inducted 1980.

LANCE ALWORTH: Wide receiver San Diego Chargers (1962-70), Dallas Cowboys (1971-72). Attended Arkansas. Inducted 1978.

DOUG ATKINS: Defensive end Cleveland Browns (1953-54), Chicago Bears (1955-66), New Orleans Saints (1967-69). Attended Tennessee. Inducted 1982.

MORRIS (RED) BADGRO: End/defensive back New York Yankees (1927), New York Giants (1930-35), Brooklyn Dodgers (1936). Attended USC. Inducted 1981.

LEM BARNEY: Cornerback Detroit Lions (1967-77). Attended Jackson State. Inducted 1992.

CLIFF BATTLES: Halfback Boston Braves (1932), Boston/Washington Redskins (1933-37). Attended West Virginia Wesleyan. Inducted 1968.

SAMMY BAUGH: Quarterback/defensive back/punter Washington Redskins (1937-52). Attended Texas Christian. Inducted 1963.

CHUCK BEDNARIK: Center/linebacker Philadelphia Eagles (1949-62). Attended Pennsylvania. Inducted 1967.

BERT BELL: Team owner Philadelphia Eagles (1933-40), co-owner Pittsburgh Steelers (1941-42, 1944-46), Phil-Pitt (1943). NFL Commissioner (1946-59). Inducted 1963.

BOBBY BELL: Linebacker Kansas City Chiefs (1963-74). Attended Minnesota. Inducted 1983.

RAYMOND BERRY: End Baltimore Colts (1955-67). Attended Southern Methodist. Inducted 1973.

CHARLES W BIDWILL SR: Team owner Chicago Cardinals (1933-43, 1945-47), Card-Pitt (1944). Inducted 1967.

FRED BILETNIKOFF: Wide receiver Oakland Raiders (1965-78). Attended Florida State. Inducted 1988.

GEORGE BLANDA: Quarterback/placekicker Chicago Bears (1949, 1950-58), Baltimore Colts (1950), Houston Oilers (1960-66), Oakland Raiders (1967-75). Attended Kentucky. Inducted 1981.

MEL BLOUNT: Cornerback Pittsburgh Steelers (1970-83). Attended Southern University. Inducted 1989.

TERRY BRADSHAW: Quarterback Pittsburgh Steelers (1970-83). Attended Louisiana Tech. Inducted 1989.

JIM BROWN: Fullback Cleveland Browns (1957-65). Attended Syracuse. Inducted 1971.

PAUL BROWN: Coach/General Manager Cleveland Browns (1946-62), Cincinnati Bengals (1968-75). Inducted 1967.

ROOSEVELT BROWN: Offensive tackle New York Giants (1953-65). Attended Morgan State. Inducted 1975.

WILLIE BROWN: Cornerback Denver Broncos (1963-66), Oakland Raiders (1967-78). Attended Grambling. Inducted 1984.

BUCK BUCHANAN: Defensive tackle Kansas City Chiefs (1963-75). Attended Grambling. Inducted 1990.

DICK BUTKUS: Linebacker Chicago Bears (1965-73). Attended Illinois. Inducted 1979.

EARL CAMPBELL: Running back Houston Oilers (1978-84), New Orleans Saints (1984-85). Attended Texas. Inducted 1991.

TONY CANADEO: Halfback Green Bay Packers (1941-44, 1946-52). Attended Gonzaga. Inducted 1974.

JOE CARR: President NFL 1921-39. Inducted 1963.

GUY CHAMBERLIN: End Decatur/Chicago Staleys (1920-21). Player/coach Canton Bulldogs (1922-23), Cleveland Bulldogs (1924), Frankford Yellow Jackets (1925-26), Chicago Cardinals (1927). Attended Nebraska. Inducted 1965.

JACK CHRISTIANSEN: Defensive back Detroit Lions (1951-58). Attended Colorado State. Inducted 1970.

EARL (DUTCH) CLARK: Quarterback Portsmouth Spartans (1931-32), Detroit Lions (1934-38). Attended Colorado College. Inducted 1963.

GEORGE CONNOR: Offensive tackle/linebacker Chicago Bears (1948-55). Attended Holy Cross, Notre Dame. Inducted 1975.

JIMMY CONZELMAN: Quarterback Decatur Staleys (1920), Rock Island Independents (1921-22), Milwaukee Badgers (1923-24), owner/coach/player Detroit Panthers (1925-26), player/coach Providence Steam Roller (1927-29), coach Providence Steam Roller 1930, coach Chicago Cardinals (1940-42, 1946-48). Attended Washington University (Missouri). Inducted 1964.

LOU CREEKMUR: Offensive guard/tackle Detroit Lions (1950-59). Attended William & Mary. Inducted 1996.

LARRY CSONKA: Fullback Miami Dolphins (1968-74, 1979), New York Giants (1976-78). Attended Syracuse. Inducted 1987.

AL DAVIS: Coach and general manager Oakland Raiders (1963-65), AFL commissioner (1966), team owner Oaklands/Los Angeles Raiders (1966-present). Inducted 1992.

WILLIE DAVIS: Defensive end Cleveland Browns (1958-59), Green Bay Packers (1960-69). Attended Grambling. Inducted 1981.

LEN DAWSON: Quarterback Pittsburgh Steelers (1957-59), Cleveland Browns (1960-61), Dallas Texans (1962), Kansas City Chiefs (1963-75). Attended Purdue. Inducted 1987.

DAN DIERDORF: Offensive tackle/center St. Louis Cardinals (1971-83). Attended Michigan. Inducted 1996.

MIKE DITKA: Tight end Chicago Bears (1961-66), Philadelphia Eagles (1967-68), Dallas Cowboys (1969-72). Attended Pittsburgh. Inducted 1988.

ART DONOVAN: Defensive tackle Baltimore Colts (1950, 1953-61), New York Yanks (1951), Dallas Texans (1952). Attended Boston College. Inducted 1968.

TONY DORSETT: Running back Dallas Cowboys (1977-87), Denver Broncos (1988). Attended Pittsburgh. Inducted 1994.

JOHN (PADDY) DRISCOLL: Quarterback Decatur Staleys (1920), Chicago Cardinals (1920-25), Chicago Bears (1926-29). Attended Northwestern. Inducted 1965.

BILL DUDLEY: Halfback Pittsburgh Steelers (1942, 1945-46), Detroit Lions (1947-49), Washington Redskins (1950-51, 1953). Attended Virginia. Inducted 1966.

GLEN (TURK) EDWARDS: Offensive tackle/defensive tackle Boston Braves/Redskins (1932-36), Washington Redskins (1937-40). Attended Washington State. Inducted 1969.

WEEB EWBANK: Coach Baltimore Colts (1954-62), New York Jets (1963-73). Inducted 1978.

TOM FEARS: End Los Angeles Rams (1948-56). Attended Santa Clara, UCLA. Inducted 1970.

JIM FINKS: General Manager Minnesota Vikings (1964-73), Chicago Bears (1974-1983), President and GM New Orleans Saints (1986-94). Inducted 1995.

RAY FLAHERTY: End AFL's Los Angeles Wildcats (1926), New York Yankees (1927-28), New York Giants (1928-29, 1931-35). Coach Boston/Washington Redskins (1936-42), AAFC's New York Yankees (1946-48), AAFC's Chicago Hornets (1949). Attended Gonzaga. Inducted 1976.

LEN FORD: Defensive end AAFC's Los Angeles Dons (1948-49), Cleveland Browns (1950-57), Green Bay Packers (1958). Attended Morgan State, Michigan. Inducted 1976.

DAN FORTMANN: Offensive guard Chicago Bears (1936-43). Attended Colgate. Inducted 1965.

DAN FOUTS: Quarterback San Diego Chargers (1973-87). Attended Oregon. Inducted 1993.

FRANK GATSKI: Center Cleveland Browns (1946-56), Detroit Lions (1957). Attended Marshall, Auburn. Inducted 1985.

BILL GEORGE: Linebacker Chicago Bears (1952-65), Los Angeles Rams (1966). Attended Wake Forest. Inducted 1974.

JOE GIBBS: Coach Washington Redskins (1981-92). Inducted 1996.

FRANK GIFFORD: Halfback/flanker New York Giants (1952-60, 1962-64). Attended Southern California. Inducted 1977.

SID GILLMAN: Coach Los Angeles Rams (1955-59), AFL's Los Angeles/San Diego Chargers (1960-69, 1971), Houston Oilers (1973-74). Inducted 1983.

OTTO GRAHAM: Quarterback Cleveland Browns (1946-55). Attended Northwestern. Inducted 1965.

HAROLD (RED) GRANGE: Halfback/defensive back Chicago Bears (1925, 1929-34), AFL's New York Yankees (1926), NFL's New York Yankees (1927). Attended Illinois. Inducted 1963.

BUD GRANT: Coach Minnesota Vikings (1967-83, 1985). Inducted 1994.

JOE GREENE: Defensive tackle Pittsburgh Steelers (1969-81). Attended North Texas State. Inducted 1987.

FORREST GREGG: Offensive tackle Green Bay Packers (1956, 1958-70), Dallas Cowboys (1971). Attended Southern Methodist. Inducted 1977.

BOB GRIESE: Quarterback Miami Dolphins (1967-80). Attended Purdue. Inducted 1990.

LOU GROZA: Offensive tackle/placekicker Cleveland Browns (1946-59, 1961-67). Attended Ohio State. Inducted 1974.

JOE GUYON: Halfback/defensive back Canton Bulldogs (1920), Cleveland Indians (1921), Oorang Indians (1922-23), Rock Island Independents (1924), Kansas City Cowboys (1924-25), New York Giants (1927). Attended Carlisle, Georgia Tech. Inducted 1966.

GEORGE HALAS: End, coach, team owner Decatur/Chicago Staleys (1920-21), Chicago Bears (1922-29). Owner Chicago Bears (1930-83). Coach Chicago Bears (1933-42, 1946-55, 1958-67). Attended Illinois. Inducted 1963.

JACK HAM: Linebacker Pittsburgh Steelers (1971-82). Attended Penn State. Inducted 1988.

JOHN HANNAH: Offensive guard New England Patriots (1973-85). Attended Alabama. Inducted 1991.

FRANCO HARRIS: Running back Pittsburgh Steelers (1972-83), Seattle Seahawks (1984). Attended Penn State. Inducted 1990.

MIKE HAYNES: Cornerback New England Patriots (1976-82), Los Angeles Raiders (1983-89). Attended Arizona State. Inducted 1997.

ED HEALEY: Offensive tackle/defensive tackle Rock Island Independents (1920-22), Chicago Bears (1922-27). Attended Dartmouth. Inducted 1964.

MEL HEIN: Center/linebacker New York Giants (1931-45). Attended Washington State. Inducted 1963.

TED HENDRICKS: Linebacker Baltimore Colts (1969-73), Green Bay Packers (1974), Oakland/Los Angeles Raiders (1975-83). Attended Miami (Fla). Inducted 1990.

WILBUR (PETE) HENRY: Offensive tackle/defensive tackle Canton Bulldogs (1920-23, 1925-26), New York Giants (1927), Pottsville Maroons (1927-28). Attended Washington & Jefferson. Inducted 1963.

ARNIE HERBER: Quarterback Green Bay Packers (1930-40), New York Giants (1944-45). Attended Wisconsin, Regis College. Inducted 1966.

BILL HEWITT: End/defensive back Chicago Bears (1932-36), Philadelphia Eagles (1937-39), Phil-Pitt (1943). Attended Michigan. Inducted 1971.

CLARKE HINKLE: Fullback/linebacker Green Bay Packers (1932-41). Attended Bucknell. Inducted 1964.

ELROY (CRAZYLEGS) HIRSCH: Halfback/end AAFC's Chicago Rockets (1946-48), Los Angeles Rams (1949-57). Attended Wisconsin, Michigan. Inducted 1968.

PAUL HORNUNG: Halfback/placekicker Green Bay Packers (1957-62, 1964-66). Attended Notre Dame. Inducted 1986.

KEN HOUSTON: Safety Houston Oilers (1967-72), Washington Redskins (1973-80). Attended Prairie View A&M. Inducted 1986.

CAL HUBBARD: Offensive tackle/defensive tackle New York Giants (1927-28, 1936), Green Bay Packers (1929-33, 1935), Pittsburgh Pirates (1936). Attended Centenary, Geneva. Inducted 1963.

SAM HUFF: Linebacker New York Giants (1956-63), Washington Redskins (1964-67, 1969). Attended West Virginia. Inducted 1982.

LAMAR HUNT: Founder AFL, team owner Dallas Texans/Kansas City Chiefs (1960-present). Inducted 1972.

DON HUTSON: End /defensive back Green Bay Packers (1935-45). Attended Alabama. Inducted 1963.

JIMMY JOHNSON: Cornerback San Francisco 49ers (1961-76). Attended UCLA. Inducted 1994.

JOHN HENRY JOHNSON: Fullback San Francisco 49ers (1954-56), Detroit Lions (1957-59), Pittsburgh Steelers (1960-65), Houston Oilers (1966). Attended St Mary's, Arizona State. Inducted 1987.

CHARLIE JOINER: Wide receiver Houston Oilers (1969-72), Cincinnati Bengals (1972-75), San Diego Chargers (1976-86). Attended Grambling State. Inducted 1996.

DEACON JONES: Defensive end Los Angeles Rams (1961-71), San Diego Chargers (1972-73), Washington Redskins (1974). Attended South Carolina State, Mississippi Vocational. Inducted 1980.

STAN JONES: Offensive guard/defensive tackle Chicago Bears (1954-65), Washington Redskins (1966). Attended Maryland. Inducted 1991.

HENRY JORDAN: Defensive tackle Cleveland Browns (1957-58), Green Bay Packers (1959-69). Attended Virginia. Inducted 1995.

SONNY JURGENSEN: Quarterback Philadelphia Eagles (1957-63), Washington Redskins (1964-74). Attended Duke. Inducted 1983.

LEROY KELLY: Running back Cleveland Browns (1964-73). Attended Morgan State. Inducted 1994.

WALT KIESLING: Offensive guard/defensive tackle Duluth Eskimos (1926-27), Pottsville Maroons (1928), Chicago Cardinals (1929-33), Chicago Bears (1934), Green Bay Packers (1935-36), Pittsburgh Pirates (1937-38). Attended St Thomas (Minnesota). Inducted 1966.

FRANK (BRUISER) KINARD: Offensive tackle/defensive tackle Brooklyn Dodgers (1938-44), AAFC's New York Yankees (1946-47). Attended Mississippi. Inducted 1971.

EARL (CURLY) LAMBEAU: Halfback Green Bay Packers (1919-29). Coach Green Bay Packers (1919-49), Chicago Cardinals (1950-51), Washington Redskins (1952-53). Attended Notre Dame. Inducted 1963.

JACK LAMBERT: Linebacker Pittsburgh Steelers (1974-84). Attended Kent State. Inducted 1990.

TOM LANDRY: Coach Dallas Cowboys (1960-88). Inducted 1990.

DICK (NIGHT TRAIN) LANE: Cornerback Los Angeles Rams (1952-53), Chicago Cardinals (1954-59), Detroit Lions (1960-65). Attended Scottsbluff Junior College. Inducted 1974.

JIM LANGER: Center Miami Dolphins (1970-79), Minnesota Vikings (1980-81). Attended South Dakota State. Inducted 1987.

WILLIE LANIER: Linebacker Kansas City Chiefs (1967-77). Attended Morgan State. Inducted 1986.

STEVE LARGENT: Wide receiver Seattle Seahawks (1976-89). Attended Tulsa. Inducted 1995.

YALE LARY: Safety/punter Detroit Lions (1952-53, 1956-64). Attended Texas A&M. Inducted 1979.

DANTE LAVELLI: End Cleveland Browns (1946-56). Attended Ohio State. Inducted 1975.

BOBBY LAYNE: Quarterback Chicago Bears (1948), New York Bulldogs (1949), Detroit Lions (1950-58), Pittsburgh Steelers (1958-62). Attended Texas. Inducted 1967.

ALPHONSE (TUFFY) LEEMANS: Running back New York Giants (1936-43). Attended George Washington. Inducted 1978.

BOB LILLY: Defensive tackle Dallas Cowboys (1961-74). Attended Texas Christian. Inducted 1980.

LARRY LITTLE: Offensive guard San Diego Chargers (1967-68), Miami Dolphins (1969-80). Attended Bethune-Cookman. Inducted 1993.

VINCE LOMBARDI: Coach, General Manager Green Bay Packers (1959-67), Washington Redskins (1969). Inducted 1971.

SID LUCKMAN: Quarterback Chicago Bears (1939-50). Attended Columbia. Inducted 1965.

ROY (LINK) LYMAN: Offensive tackle/defensive tackle Canton Bulldogs (1922-23, 1925), Cleveland Bulldogs (1924), Frankford Yellow Jackets (1925), Chicago Bears (1926-28, 1930-31, 1933-34). Attended Nebraska. Inducted 1964.

JOHN MACKEY: Tight end Baltimore Colts (1963-71), San Diego Chargers (1972). Attended Syracuse. Inducted 1992.

TIM MARA: Team owner New York Giants (1925-59). Inducted 1963.

WELLINGTON MARA: Team owner New York Giants (1937-present). Attended Fordham. Inducted 1997.

GINO MARCHETTI: Defensive end Dallas Texans (1952), Baltimore Colts (1953-64, 1966). Attended San Francisco. Inducted 1972.

GEORGE PRESTON MARSHALL: Team owner Boston Braves (1932), Boston/Washington Redskins (1933-69). Inducted 1963.

OLLIE MATSON: Halfback Chicago Cardinals (1952, 1954-58), Los Angeles Rams (1959-62), Detroit Lions (1963), Philadelphia Eagles (1964-66). Attended San Francisco. Inducted 1972.

DON MAYNARD: Wide receiver New York Giants (1958), New York Titans/Jets (1960-72), St Louis Cardinals (1973). Attended Texas Western. Inducted 1987.

GEORGE MCAFEE: Halfback/defensive back Chicago Bears (1940-41, 1945-50). Attended Duke. Inducted 1966.

MIKE MCCORMACK: Offensive tackle New York Yanks (1951), Cleveland Browns (1954-62). Attended Kansas. Inducted 1984.

HUGH MCELHENNY: Halfback San Francisco 49ers (1952-60), Minnesota Vikings (1961-62), New York Giants (1963), Detroit Lions (1964). Attended Washington. Inducted 1970.

JOHNNY (BLOOD) MCNALLY: Halfback Milwaukee Badgers (1925-26), Duluth Eskimos (1926-27), Pottsville Maroons (1928), Green Bay Packers (1929-33, 1935-36), Pittsburgh Pirates (1934), player/coach Pittsburgh Pirates (1937-39). Attended St John's (Minnesota). Inducted 1963.

MIKE MICHALSKE: Offensive guard/linebacker AFL's New York Yankees (1926), NFL's New York Yankees (1927-28), Green Bay Packers (1929-35, 1937). Attended Penn State. Inducted 1964.

WAYNE MILLNER: End/defensive back Boston/Washington Redskins (1936-41, 1945). Attended Notre Dame. Inducted 1968.

BOBBY MITCHELL: Wide receiver/running back Cleveland Browns (1958-61), Washington Redskins (1962-68). Attended Illinois. Inducted 1983.

RON MIX: Offensive tackle Los Angeles/San Diego Chargers (1960-69), Oakland Raiders (1971). Attended Southern California. Inducted 1979.

LENNY MOORE: Flanker/running back Baltimore Colts (1956-67). Attended Penn State. Inducted 1975.

MARION MOTLEY: Fullback/linebacker Cleveland Browns (1946-53), Pittsburgh Steelers (1955). Attended South Carolina State, Nevada. Inducted 1968.

GEORGE MUSSO: Offensive guard/defensive tackle Chicago Bears (1933-44). Attended Millikin. Inducted 1982.

BRONKO NAGURSKI: Fullback/linebacker Chicago Bears (1930-37, 1943). Attended Minnesota. Inducted 1963.

JOE NAMATH: Quarterback New York Jets (1965-76), Los Angeles Rams (1977). Attended Alabama. Inducted 1985.

EARLE (GREASY) NEALE: Coach Philadelphia Eagles (1941-42, 1944-50), co-coach Phil-Pitt (1943). Inducted 1969.

ERNIE NEVERS: Fullback/defensive back Duluth Eskimos (1926-27), Chicago Cardinals (1929-31). Attended Stanford. Inducted 1963.

RAY NITSCHKE: Linebacker Green Bay Packers (1958-72). Attended Illinois. Inducted 1978.

CHUCK NOLL: Coach Pittsburgh Steelers (1969-91). Inducted 1993.

LEO NOMELLINI: Defensive tackle San Francisco 49ers (1950-63). Attended Minnesota. Inducted 1969.

MERLIN OLSEN: Defensive tackle Los Angeles Rams (1962-76). Attended Utah State. Inducted 1982.

JIM OTTO: Center Oakland Raiders (1960-74). Attended Miami (Fla). Inducted 1980.

STEVE OWEN: Offensive tackle/defensive tackle Kansas City Cowboys (1924-25), New York Giants (1926-36). Coach New York Giants (1931-53). Attended Phillips. Inducted 1966.

ALAN PAGE: Defensive tackle Minnesota Vikings (1967-78), Chicago Bears (1978-81). Attended Notre Dame. Inducted 1988.

CLARENCE (ACE) PARKER: Quarterback Brooklyn Dodgers (1937-41), Boston Yanks (1945), AAFC's New York Yankees (1946). Attended Duke. Inducted 1972.

JIM PARKER: Offensive guard, tackle Baltimore Colts (1957-67). Attended Ohio State. Inducted 1973.

WALTER PAYTON: Running back Chicago Bears (1975-87). Attended Jackson State. Inducted 1993.

JOE PERRY: Fullback San Francisco 49ers (1948-60, 1963), Baltimore Colts (1961-62). Attended Compton Junior College. Inducted 1969.

PETE PIHOS: End Philadelphia Eagles (1947-55). Attended Indiana. Inducted 1970.

HUGH (SHORTY) RAY: Supervisor of Officials (1938-56). Inducted 1966.

MEL RENFRO: Cornerback/safety Dallas Cowboys (1964-77). Attended Oregon. Inducted 1996.

DAN REEVES: Team owner Cleveland/Los Angeles Rams (1941-71). Inducted 1967.

JOHN RIGGINS: Running back New York Jets (1971-75), Washington Redskins (1976-79, 1981-85). Attended Kansas. Inducted 1992.

JIM RINGO: Center Green Bay Packers (1953-63), Philadelphia Eagles (1964-67). Attended Syracuse. Inducted 1981.

ANDY ROBUSTELLI: Defensive end Los Angeles Rams (1951-55), New York Giants (1956-64). Attended Arnold College. Inducted 1971.

ART ROONEY: Team owner Pittsburgh Pirates/Steelers (1933-42, 1945-88), Phil-Pitt (1943), Card-Pitt (1944). Inducted 1964.

PETE ROZELLE: Commissioner NFL (1960-89). Inducted 1985.

BOB ST CLAIR: Offensive tackle San Francisco 49ers (1953-63). Attended San Francisco, Tulsa. Inducted 1990.

GALE SAYERS: Running back Chicago Bears (1965-71). Attended Kansas. Inducted 1977.

JOE SCHMIDT: Linebacker Detroit Lions (1953-65). Attended Pittsburgh. Inducted 1973.

TEX SCHRAMM: Assistant to president/general manager Los Angeles Rams (1947-56), team president/general manager Dallas Cowboys (1960-88). Inducted 1991.

LEE ROY SELMON: Defensive tackle Tampa Bay Buccaneers (1976-84). Attended Oklahoma. Inducted 1995.

ART SHELL: Offensive tackle Oakland/Los Angeles Raiders (1968-82). Attended Maryland-Eastern Shore. Inducted 1989.

DON SHULA: Defensive back Cleveland Browns (1951-52), Baltimore Colts (1953-56), Washington Redskins (1957). Coach Baltimore Colts (1963-69), Miami Dolphins (1970-95). Attended John Carroll. Inducted 1997.

OJ SIMPSON: Running back Buffalo Bills (1969-77), San Francisco 49ers (1978-79). Attended Southern California. Inducted 1985.

JACKIE SMITH: Tight end St Louis Cardinals (1963-77), Dallas Cowboys (1978). Attended Northwestern Louisiana. Inducted 1994.

BART STARR: Quarterback Green Bay Packers (1956-71). Attended Alabama. Inducted 1977.

ROGER STAUBACH: Quarterback Dallas Cowboys (1969-79). Attended Navy. Inducted 1985.

ERNIE STAUTNER: Defensive tackle Pittsburgh Steelers (1950-63). Attended Boston College. Inducted 1969.

JAN STENERUD: Placekicker Kansas City Chiefs (1967-79), Green Bay Packers (1980-83), Minnesota Vikings (1984-85). Attended Montana State. Inducted 1991.

KEN STRONG: Halfback/defensive back Staten Island Stapletons (1929-32), New York Giants (1933-35, 1939, 1944-47), AFL's New York Yanks (1936-37). Attended New York University. Inducted 1967.

JOE STYDAHAR: Offensive tackle/defensive tackle Chicago Bears (1936-42, 1945-46). Attended West Virginia. Inducted 1967.

FRAN TARKENTON: Quarterback Minnesota Vikings (1961-66, 1972-78), New York Giants (1967-71). Attended Georgia. Inducted 1986.

CHARLEY TAYLOR: Wide receiver/running back Washington Redskins (1964-75, 1977). Attended Arizona State. Inducted 1984.

JIM TAYLOR: Fullback Green Bay Packers (1958-66), New Orleans Saints (1967). Attended Louisiana State. Inducted 1976.

JIM THORPE: Halfback/defensive back Canton Bulldogs (1915-17, 1919-20, 1926), Cleveland Indians (1921), Oorang Indians (1922-23), Toledo Maroons (1923), Rock Island Independents (1924), New York Giants (1925), Chicago Cardinals (1928). President NFL (1920). Attended Carlisle. Inducted 1963.

YA TITTLE: Quarterback Baltimore Colts (1948-50), San Francisco 49ers (1951-60), New York Giants (1961-64). Attended Louisiana State. Inducted 1971.

GEORGE TRAFTON: Center/defensive tackle Decatur/Chicago Staleys (1920-21), Chicago Bears (1922-32). Attended Notre Dame. Inducted 1964.

CHARLEY TRIPPI: Halfback/quarterback Chicago Cardinals (1947-55). Attended Georgia. Inducted 1968.

EMLEN TUNNELL: Defensive back New York Giants (1948-58), Green Bay Packers (1959-61). Attended Toledo, Iowa. Inducted 1967.

CLYDE (BULLDOG) TURNER: Center/linebacker Chicago Bears (1940-52). Attended Hardin-Simmons. Inducted 1966.

JOHNNY UNITAS: Quarterback Baltimore Colts (1956-72), San Diego Chargers (1973). Attended Louisville. Inducted 1979.

GENE UPSHAW: Offensive guard Oakland Raiders (1967-81). Attended Texas A&I. Inducted 1987.

NORM VAN BROCKLIN: Quarterback/punter Los Angeles Rams (1949-57), Philadelphia Eagles (1958-60). Attended Oregon. Inducted 1971.

STEVE VAN BUREN: Halfback/defensive back Philadelphia Eagles (1944-51). Attended Louisiana State. Inducted 1965.

DOAK WALKER: Halfback/placekicker Detroit Lions (1950-55). Attended Southern Methodist. Inducted 1986.

BILL WALSH: Coach/general manager San Francisco 49ers (1979-88). Inducted 1993.

PAUL WARFIELD: Wide receiver Cleveland Browns (1964-69, 1976-77), Miami Dolphins (1970-74). Attended Ohio State. Inducted 1983.

BOB WATERFIELD: Quarterback/safety/punter/placekicker Cleveland/Los Angeles Rams (1945-52). Attended UCLA. Inducted 1965.

MIKE WEBSTER: Center/offensive guard Pittsburgh Steelers (1974-88), Kansas City Chiefs (1989-90). Attended Wisconsin. Inducted 1997.

ARNIE WEINMEISTER: Defensive tackle AAFC's New York Yankees (1948-49), New York Giants (1950-53). Attended Washington. Inducted 1984.

RANDY WHITE: Defensive tackle Dallas Cowboys (1975-88). Attended Maryland. Inducted 1994.

BILL WILLIS: Offensive guard/defensive guard Cleveland Browns (1946-53). Attended Ohio State. Inducted 1977.

LARRY WILSON: Safety St Louis Cardinals (1960-72). Attended Utah. Inducted 1978.

KELLEN WINSLOW: Tight end San Diego Chargers (1979-87). Attended Missouri. Inducted 1995.

ALEX WOJCIECHOWICZ: Center/linebacker Detroit Lions (1938-46), Philadelphia Eagles (1946-50). Attended Fordham. Inducted 1968.

WILLIE WOOD: Safety Green Bay Packers (1960-71). Attended Southern California. Inducted 1989.

Glossary of football terms

Audible: The quarterback shouting or signaling a change of play at the line of scrimmage.

Backfield: The area behind the lines of scrimmage on both offense and defense. Also the term for the quarterback and running backs.

Blitz: A pass rush by one or more defensive players from the backfield.

Block: The act (by the offense) of knocking defensive players out of the way to allow either the quarterback to pass or the ball carrier to gain yards.

Bomb: A long pass.

Chain crew: Two officials who hold the ten-yard chain markers. A third man holds the down marker.

Clipping: An illegal block on an opponent from behind and below the waist.

Complete pass: A pass which is caught by an offensive player.

Conversion: After a touchdown a team can elect to kick the ball over the crossbar for one point, or get it into the end zone by passing or running, for two points.

Cornerback: A defensive back.

Coverage: When the kicking team goes downfield after a kickoff or punt. Also refers to the playing of pass defense.

Crossbar: The bar which joins the two uprights over which a kick must go to score.

Dead ball: A ball not in play.

Defense: The team without the ball.

Defensive backs: Defenders who cover receivers. There are normally four, two cornerbacks and two safetys, but occasionally a fifth (nickel) or sixth (dime) defensive back comes into the game in certain pass situations.

Double team: When offensive players gang up on one opponent to block him.

Down: One of four plays required for the offense to move the ball 10 yards. Also when the ball carrier's knee touches the ground.

Drop back: The movement of either the quarterback retreating to pass, or a defensive player covering a receiver.

End: Defensive lineman who lines up outside the defensive tackle.

End lines: The lines on the field over which the crossbar stands, 10 yards beyond the goal line.

End zone: The 10-yard area in which a touchdown is scored.

Fair catch: A player on the punt—or kickoff—receiving team may signal a fair catch. He must not be tackled and may not advance the ball.

False start: A penalty against the offense when a player moves before the snap after getting set.

Field goal: A scoring kick (worth three points) when the ball goes over the crossbar and between the posts. It usually occurs on fourth down.

Flag: A yellow flag is thrown by an official to signal a penalty.

Formation: The alignment of the offense and defense before a play.

Free ball: A live ball not in possession of any player.

Fumble: When a player loses control of the ball. A player cannot fumble when a play is dead and the ground cannot cause a fumble.

Game clock: The clock which counts down from 15:00 in one second increments in each quarter.

Game plan: The offensive and defensive strategies utilized by the coaches to win a game.

Goal line: The line separating the field and the end zone. At each end of the goal line, there is small plastic pylon, but it is off the field of play.

Goal post: The two vertical posts joined by the crossbar, between which a kick must pass to be good.

Hail Mary: A long, desperate, pass downfield.

Half: The 30 minutes of the first and second quarters and the 30 minutes of the third and fourth quarters.

Halftime: The period between the second and third quarters.

Handoff: The quarterback giving the ball to a running back.

Hang time: The time a punter's kick is in the air.

Hashmarks: The short lines that are used for spotting the ball, running the length of the field and lined up with uprights of both goal posts.

Holding: A penalty when a player grabs an opponent to restrict his movement.

Huddle: When the quarterback meets with his team to describe the next play.

Incomplete Pass: A pass which is either dropped or falls to the ground.

Inside: The area between the offensive tackles in the middle of the field.

Interception: A pass caught by a defensive player.

Interference: A penalty called against a player who unfairly stops an opponent from catching a pass.

Lateral: A backward or sideways pass or underhanded toss, usually by the quarterback. If a lateral pass goes incomplete it is a fumble.

Linebackers: Defensive players (either three or four) who line up behind the linemen, or on the line, outside the ends.

Linemen: The men who play on the line on either side of the ball. Offensive linemen are the center, two guards two tackles and the tight end. On the defensive side, there are two ends and either one of two tackles depending on the alignment.

Line of scrimmage: The point from where the ball is snapped for each play.

Man-to-man: Defensive pass coverage where a defender is responsible for a particular man.

Misdirection: An offensive ploy when blockers go in one direction, and the play in another.

Motion: A single player who runs behind the line of scrimmage (parallel to the line or backward) before the snap is the man in motion.

Neutral zone: The gap between the offensive and defensive lines before the snap.

Offense: The team in possession of the ball.

Officials: The seven onfield people responsible for making all decisions in the game. They are: the referee, umpire, head linesman, line judge, side judge, field judge and back judge.

Offside: A player is offside when any part of his body is beyond his scrimmage line when the ball is snapped.

Onside kick: A short kickoff, which must go ten yards for the kicking team to recover, but if successful guarantees great field position.

Overtime: If the score is tied at the end of the game, one extra period of 15 minutes will be played. The first team to score wins. In the playoffs, the two teams continue playing until one of them scores, even if it takes more than one extra period.

Pass: A ball thrown forward.

Pass pattern: The route taken by an offensive receiver on a pass play.

Pass rush: The defense's attempt to sack the quarterback.

Penalty: Any infraction by a player is signaled by an official throwing a flag. Penalties vary from five yards to 15 and can include loss of down or ejection of a player. For some penalties, the offensive team can be awarded an automatic first down. Penalties do not have to be accepted.

Penalty marker: see Flag.

Pitchout: An underhand toss from the quarterback to a running back in the backfield.

Plane of the goal: The imaginary area above the goal line across which the ball (in a player's possession) must go for a touchdown to be scored.

Play action: A pass play which first looks like a running play.

Play clock: The time allowed between plays, either 25 or 40 seconds, depending on the previous play.

Pocket: The space, created by good blocking, that the quarterback retreats into before passing.

Possession: When a player controls the ball throughout the act of clearly touching both feet, or any other part of his body (except for his hands) to the ground in bounds.

Pulling: When an offensive lineman, normally a guard, runs in front of the ball carrier to block.

Punt: A kick downfield to the other team when the offense has failed to get a first down.

Quarter: A period of 15 minutes. There are four quarters in a game.

Quarterback: The signal caller and player who initiates each offensive play.

Receiver: An offensive player who catches a pass (a wide receiver, a tight end or a running back).

Receiving team: The team which reveives a kickoff or a punt.

Red zone: The area inside the 20-yard line.

Roll out: The act of a quarterback running to either side to pass.

Running backs: The offense's ball carrier.

Sack: When a quarterback is tackled behind the line of scrimmage, while attempting to pass.

Safety: A two-point play when the ball carrier is tackled inside his own end zone. Also a defensive backfield position.

Scramble: When a quarterback tries to elude the defense while trying to pass.

Screen pass: A delayed pass to a receiver, who has blockers in front of him, behind the line of scrimmage

Secondary: See Defensive backs

Set: The stationary position all lineman must take before the snap. Also the name for a formation.

Shotgun: An offensive formation where the quarterback lines up several yards behind the line of scrimmage. It is usually a pass play.

Sideline: The side boundaries of the field.

Signals: By the referee, the description of the penalty just called; by the offense, letters and numbers in code to describe the play.

Snap: The start of a play. The center hands or passes the ball back to the quarterback.

Snap count: The signal at on which the ball will be snapped.

Special teams: The groups of players who come in on all kicking plays.

Spot: The point where a play ends.

Strongside: The offensive side of the field where the tight end lines up.

Stunt: A planned rush involving two or more defensive players who loop around each other instead of charging straight ahead.

Tackle: Offensive and defensive linemen. Also the act of stopping the ball carrier.

Tight end: Blocking receiver who lines up on the line of scrimmage.

Time out: A chance for the teams to discuss tactics. Each team has three time outs per half.

Touchback: An interception, defensive fumble recovery, kickoff or punt which is downed inside the end zone. The defensive or receiving team starts play from its own 20-yard-line.

Touchdown: The offensive six-point play when the ball is carried or thrown into the end zone and caught. Touchdowns also can be scored on punt returns, kickoff returns, fumble returns, and interceptions. A conversion follows a touchdown.

Two-minute warning: A signal to both teams that two minutes remain in a half. A time out is called.

Upright: see Goal post

Weakside: The offensive side of the field opposite to where the tight end lines up.

Zone: A defensive formation where players cover areas of the field, instead of single opponents.